DR. ROBERT M. ANDRYSCO

TRICKS I TAUGHT MY MASTER

TECHNIQUES FOR TRAINING YOUR DOG

PUBLISHED BY RADIO SYSTEMS CORPORATION, KNOXVILLE, TENNESSEE

Radio Systems®
CORPORATION

Published by Radio Systems Corporation
10427 Electric Avenue, Knoxville, Tennessee 37932
Telephone: (423) 777-5404   Fax: (423) 777-5415
Toll-Free: (800) 732-2677
World Wide Web: http://www.radiosys.com
E-Mail: info@radiosys.com

Printed in the United States of America

Dedication

Tricks I Taught My Master is dedicated to all of the people and pets that have been a significant part of my life. Especially...

The two people who sacrificed so I could get to this point in my life, my parents, Bob and Bea.

The one person who has helped me more than he will ever know, my son, Nathan.

And, of course, my dog, Happy.

The characters in this book are real and the stories are true. However all of the names, of owners and pets, have been changed to protect the mischievous.

Table Of Contents

Why There's No Such Thing As Pet Psychology And Why There's Such A Crying Need For A Book By A Pet Behaviorist

PET PSYCHOLOGY DOESN'T EXIST

This is a book about pet behavior, and the techniques that you can use to correct those that you may consider inappropriate. It is written from my 14 years of experience in the animal behavior field. I believe it is the first book of its kind, prepared by a true practicing *Pet Behavior Specialist* here in the United States.

Please note that this is in stark contrast to what some people call "pet psychology." Simply stated, <u>there is no such thing.</u> In fact, no one really knows the origin of this misnomer, or how it came about. Perhaps a reporter somewhere just thought the two words sounded good together!

But the distinction is important. Although you may occasionally hear of a practicing "pet psychologist" these days, most real experts in the field prefer the term *Pet Behavior Specialist.* It more accurately describes what we do as professionals.

But let's take a closer look at so-called "pet psychology."

When a person visits a human psychologist, the purpose of his sessions is to guide the patient to his own understanding of the problem for which he seeks help. In so doing, patients come to know themselves better. They come to learn about their own psyches.

This is something that a dog cannot do. Psychologically speaking, they just can't learn to understand themselves. Or to change themselves inside.

That is not the purpose of the *Pet Behavior Specialist,* nor is it the purpose of the pet owner. You don't want to change your dog's personality. You only want to change particular behavior characteristics.

And just as a psychologist works to change the behavior of a hyperactive child, rather than her personality, a *Pet Behavior Specialist* trains a dog to alter only its behavior. This is **Behavior Management,** <u>not</u> pet psychology.

Unfortunately, since the term "pet psychology" has been used so pervasively, it will take some time before it disappears from our vocabulary.

In the meantime, what many people visualize is a disturbed doggie laying on a loveseat spilling its guts to the "psychologist." Or a catatonic cat crouched on a couch, with the "psychologist" sitting patiently on a chair next to it, pen poised and ready to take notes.

Relax! It doesn't happen! No respectable *Pet Behavior Specialist* puts a pet on a couch, talks with it, or "analyzes" it.

The *Pet Behavior Specialist* works to modify pet behavior. To do so, he or she must also be a specialist in modifying the **pet owner's** behavior. That's the tricky part. Because working with human beings is the most difficult task of all. Old habits are truly hard to break for us bipeds. Sometimes it can take a psychologist, but certainly ***not*** a so-called "Pet Psychologist."

Actually, taken together, the words "Pet Psychology" defy definition. *Psychology* is the study of the mind and of a being's behavioral characteristics as they relate to a specific area of knowledge or activity. The key word root is "psyche," which comes from the Greek word meaning "soul or self."

The psyche pertains to understanding oneself, a characteristic that pets just can't fulfill because they aren't truly self-aware. So no one can really get inside the mind of a dog; nobody knows how they think – although some "Pet Psychologists" ***say*** they do.

I thought that perhaps it would be fun to beat these pseudo-professionals at their own game, and present my behavioral observations from the dog's perspective. That is, not as determined by what *I* think goes on inside a dog's mind, but rather by relying on my years of experience with how pets ***actually react*** to different techniques in their domestic environments...and then personifying those reactions. Or, more accurately, "caninifying" them.

The result is this book, **Tricks I Taught My Master.** I've projected my cumulative experience onto my own dog, Happy. We both started in this field at the same time, as relative pups. He's been with me every step – and mis-step – of the way, as we set out to discover the definitive set of **Pet Behavior Management** methodologies.

Happy is as experienced as they come in this field. I think you'll enjoy his unique, tail-wagging perspective. You'll know it's Happy "talking" when you see that the anecdotes are printed in italics. And each of these Happy stories starts with a cartoon illustration of my long-time canine companion, consulting away from his "training-made-easy" chair.

You'll certainly benefit from Happy's first-hand accounts of the various training techniques, and his opinions on which work best for real-world pets, and most particularly, for their owners.

Dr. Robert Andrysco
July 1, 1995

1

How To Use This Book

Owning a dog is a lot like owning a car. You like a certain model, a certain color, a certain combination of fun and functionality. You might want something compact, or practical, or sporty. You have a thousand options to choose from. And that's the fun of it: to pick a pet that's uniquely you.

Once you get your dog off the lot, you have to break it in. You have to find the right fuel. You have to keep its fluids up, and get it out on the road regularly to keep it running smoothly. You have to wash it every week, and keep the bugs from building up. And you have to see the mechanic when it's time for routine maintenance.

Like most owners these days, you probably won't actually know much about your dog's engine, computerized control, or emission system. But, with proper upkeep, it will run just fine.

The only time you worry about your dog is if it starts acting funny. You know, if it stalls or backfires; if a leak appears beneath its chassis; if its engine starts smoking; or if it blows a gasket in heavy traffic. That's when you pray that it's still under warranty, and you take it to see the veterinarian – or, for behavioral problems, a *Pet Behavior Specialist*.

This book is like an owner's manual for your dog. Inside, you'll find many common-sense solutions for changing your dog's behavioral characteristics when they get a bit out of whack.

Now understand that there are no secret or sure-fire tricks to correct pet misbehaviors. But all the techniques that you'll find between the covers of this book are tried, tested and true. All have been used successfully.

If you try one method and it doesn't work out for you, you'll always find a number of alternatives. And although you may not have heard them before, the procedures on these pages follow a carefully considered path to a logical conclusion.

So how do you track that path? How do you use this book to tell you what your dog already knows about its own behavior? And how do you modify it accordingly?

Well, first of all, **Tricks I Taught My Master** was written for you to read from cover to cover. Its unique perspective, humorous anecdotes, real world situations, and easy-to-follow suggestions make it a real page-turner.

But it's also designed to be your comprehensive reference manual for dog training techniques. It starts with a description of the field of *Pet Behavior Management.* Then it goes on to shatter some of the myths popular with dog owners today, be they old wives' tales or state-of-the-scam "Pet Psychologist" psycho-babble.

Next comes perhaps the most important premise in the book: ***that pets are not human.***

This simple statement may seem obvious – overly so – but the implications are not. They're subtle...yet pervasive. So the prose goes on to deal with the ramifications of this "natural law" on the dog owners of the world. And to describe the changes...and training...that these owners may need to undergo to achieve the relationship that they want with their dog.

From there, the book describes why dogs develop undesirable behaviors. Some of the reasons may prove to be quite illuminating for those holding the leashes.

At that point, the book goes on to present many of the problems common to dog owners...with suggestions for how to solve them. Actionable suggestions. And a lot of them.

Most major subjects are covered in separate chapters. So you should find it easy to locate whatever you're looking for. *The Table Of Contents,* located on *page v,* should help you find these major topics of discussion.

Finally, there's a chapter on how to deal with occasional relapses from your dog's learned training.

Finally, if you need a micro-view of the information in this book, you can look up a subject in the *Index* found on *page 378.* It provides an excellent cross-reference for beleaguered owners who need information quickly in order to handle a specific situation.

2

A New Field Of Pet Behavior Management

I have some very good friends who found themselves in a bad situation a number of years ago. As a result, they felt forced to put their lovable Basset Hound to sleep. Mandy was an integral and loved part of a household that also included two children and three cats. But over the last of her twelve years she had acquired the habit of urinating on the carpet of her stately Chicago home.

Over the years, I had found Mandy's owner to be a caring person, whose deep concern for pets manifested itself years ago in the co-founding of a local Animal Welfare Society. To this day, this organization operates with volunteers and private funds to rescue unwanted cats and dogs, keeping them until suitable, well-scrutinized homes are found.

Although she was willing to spend hundreds of hours of her time to benefit pets – and educate the public as to their plight – years of trying to cope with her own dog's problem left her with what she thought was the only humane solution.

Hundreds of thousands of animals are destroyed each year by this country's humane societies. Countless others are cruelly abandoned on the roadside to fend for themselves. Few can do so. Ninety percent of these animals are destroyed or abandoned because their owners are unable to cope with such common misbehaviors as improper elimination habits, aggression, excessive noise or destructive chewing.

This need not happen to your dog. Solutions are available, and most are easy to execute if you only have the patience, the persistence, and this book.

The field of **Pet Behavior Management** is relatively new. But it can provide you with up-to-date knowledge and solutions to the problems of dog ownership. Over the last several decades, the professional *Pet Behavior Specialist* has emerged to assist you in correcting specific pet misbehaviors.

The field may be young, by traditional standards, but there are hundreds of people out there, all across the country, who are real, practicing *Pet Behavior Specialists*. Many work at it part-time, but more and more are making a full-time practice of this specialization. I am one of the latter.

Unfortunately, the field is growing slowly, primarily because no specific collegiate program is available for the education of potential *Pet Behavior Specialists*. There aren't any state certification or training programs. There is no government-regulated licensing available anywhere in the world.

As for myself, I had to create my own programs all the way through my formal education. My Ph.D. combines Veterinary Medicine, Animal Behavior and Human Behavior, and my Masters degree is in Veterinary Physiology and Pharmacology.

But I'm the exception to the rule.

The reason for this void in available education, and its probable continuance, is that few knowledgeable educators are qualified to teach the subject.

For now, most other *Pet Behavior Specialists* must educate themselves. Yet each brings a new perspective to the field, because they come from so many different walks of life.

Most of these people come from a related field, usually one peripherally involved with animals. Many are veterinarians, psychologists or social workers. So they are, for the most part, highly-educated professionals, usually with doctorates. This allows them easier lateral movement into the developing field.

These *Specialists* help to define the principles that form the foundation of the discipline. They are developing techniques and experiencing first-hand how pets react to these methodologies.

Although you need to be careful to check credentials and references closely, when you do find a *Pet Behavior Specialist* who is genuinely qualified, you'll usually find that he has a solution for your dog's problem.

As the field of **Pet Behavior Management** grows, we hope to reduce the staggering number of pets that are put to sleep every year. Great strides have been made in veterinary medicine since the turn-of-the-century. But the fact is that comparatively few pets are destroyed for birth defects, or even because they are too old or sick.

Statistics indicate that nearly ninety percent of all animals are destroyed because they *do not behave properly.* They bite, they chew furniture, they bark too loudly, or they urinate on the rug. They are young, healthy animals with absolutely no physical ailments.

Most concerned owners do take their dogs to the logical starting point: the veterinarian. Vets truly care about their patients. They're certainly not in the field for the money! So they'll give your animal the appropriate physical examination, run the necessary tests, and check all the possibilities in determining its condition. And if your dog has a physical problem, they're likely to find it. But oftentimes the problems aren't physical, they're behavioral. So no matter how diligent the doctor is, he's not likely to find the problem – because it isn't physically there.

And as they exhaust every possibility, they're forced to charge you the fees that mount with every office visit, test and procedure. Because as much as they love their work, they have to stay in business in order to enjoy it...so they have to cover their costs. And if no problems are found, they are left to offer the limited number of solutions they've been taught are at their disposal.

Their answer for some misbehaviors might be spaying or neutering. If that doesn't work, they might recommend a variety of medications that will help modify a dog's behavior. And, as a last resort, they may even suggest euthanasia.

Unfortunately, in my experience, none of these "solutions" actually changes pet behavior. The vet is doing what she knows to be best. But there is knowledge that she may not have...knowledge that complements her field: the knowledge of the *Behaviorist*. The fact that most veterinarians do not know these solutions is hardly surprising. It was never a part of their already extensive educational curriculum. So they may not know what else to tell their troubled clients.

This is an area which colleges and universities have sadly neglected.

Some years ago, a professor at a highly respected midwest veterinary school tried to convince those who set the curriculum to teach their students something – anything – about pet behavior. The response, however, was an unmovable, "No, we don't do that. We teach pet medicine, not pet behavior." As if the two are somehow unrelated!

Veterinary medicine in the United States is the best in the world. But invasive procedures are rarely the solution to behavioral problems. Why? I've explored this question for more than 14 years now, and from what information I have been able to gather, I find that it is because:

1. Owners choose to have the surgery done to their dogs when those dogs are very young – usually about six months old. They may never even have exhibited specific misbehaviors. Therefore, their owners cannot judge whether or not the surgery has actually altered their dog's behavior.

2. Owners wait too long to have the neutering or spaying performed. Although the surgery does eliminate hormone-directed behavior, by the time the dog has committed a misbehavior repeatedly, it is no longer hormone-directed. ***It's a habit.*** And surgical processes do not affect memory, learning or habits.

When a dog goes to the vet for neutering, the owner expects it to return a dramatically different animal.

And at first it may appear that is just what has happened. The dog arrives home in a nice, mellow condition. Wouldn't you after such an ordeal? However, this condition lasts only a few days.

Once the dog has recovered from the anesthetic and regained its strength after the surgery, its misbehaviors return.

This is when many owners give up. And can you blame them? They've already consulted with the highest earthly authority they can think of on such matters. And even their vet can't tell them what to do next.

Most veterinarians are aware they need assistance when it comes to pet misbehavior. They are hungry for solutions. Most – once all other avenues have been explored – will happily refer a client to a *Pet Behavior Specialist.*

But for animals who are merely misbehaving, the *Pet Behavior Specialist* should be the **first** resort. If vets would be willing to refer immediately, owners could save themselves so much frustration...and perhaps a small fortune.

Misbehaving dogs cost their owners a lot of money. Before you finally decide to consult a *Pet Behavior Specialist,* your dog may have caused thousands of dollars in damage over several years. In that time, you may have purchased hundreds of dollars worth of books, cleaning agents and other repair and replacement materials in your search for solutions to the problem.

Compare these expenses with the cost of a *Specialist.* A visit to your home, with 60 days of follow-up via telephone, will probably cost you less than $150. And in most cases, the rate of probable cure exceeds 85%. All this makes the going rate quite reasonable!

Nonetheless, it remains your own responsibility to change your dog's behavior. It is the responsibility of the *Pet Behavior Specialist* to educate you about the best way to do so.

Changing a specific behavior is, of course, impossible to accomplish without involving the owner directly. Because for each misbehavior a dog exhibits, there is a corresponding behavior in the owner. So you must be willing to cooperate completely.

You can't simply pull your dog aside and say, "Hey, look, you have to change what you're doing." Teaching you how to change your behavior will, in turn, result in your animal's behavioral change.

At first, this approach may sound radical. "Me change **my** behavior? But I'm not the one who tinkles on the rug!" But if you take a step back and look at your situation objectively, you'll see that yes, indeed, the problem is yours. After all, it's your rug! So you're the only one who can solve the problem.

DOG OWNERSHIP REQUIRES COMMON SENSE

Fortunately, the solutions offered by the *Pet Behavior Specialist* are founded in common sense. So they're easy to grasp, even if your dog is causing you to "lose your grip."

In fact, they may be too easy to grasp. Most owners react to the common sense approaches of the *Pet Behavior Specialist* with an incredulous, "That's it? Why didn't I think of that?"

But then again, hindsight truly is 20-20. Especially if you have the keen senses of a dog. In fact, my dog Happy presents the case for the pet's perspective better than any biped ever could in this example of a situation that canines commonly come up against.

One day I got a call from Baron, a large, well-groomed Doberman Pinscher. The problem, he explained, was that his humans didn't know how to control him properly. And, as a result, things around Baron's house were somewhat out-of-control.

He told me that they allowed him to chase the female human around the house, from the living room through the hallway into the dining room, and then back down the hall in an endless circle. And just for good measure, he would take a few nips at her haunches.

The male would just laugh, Baron told me. He was rather large, even for a human; perhaps 280 pounds. And he insisted that they didn't have a problem with the courtly canine.

The female was pretty small, as humans go. Baron thought she might not even weigh 100 pounds. But she stood right up to her mate. And she swore she was ready to kill Baron.

I brought The Master out with me to see if we could help the poor dog – Dr. Andrysco has a way with humans. Most dogs believe the old axiom that you can't teach an old human a new trick. But The Master has a trick or two of his own up his sleeve.

When we got there, the male insisted that Baron was trained. Baron himself protested, suggesting that he thought he'd remember boot camp if it had ever happened, but nobody paid him any attention. Baron just shook his head.

The Master asked who had trained Baron, and the male answered, "Of course he's trained – he came with pedigree papers."

The male believed that a dog born with a pedigree came pre-trained!

We discussed the matter further, and then The Master asked Baron to show us how the male got him to sit.

But the male butted in. "No problem," he said, and he promptly sat on Baron's behind!

In the end, Baron's humans were easy to train, once they saw that the training would be useful. The Master had the female put a training collar and leash on Baron. Then he instructed her about how to tell Baron what she wanted him to do. She was told to grab the leash, tell him to sit, and quickly yank the leash. By the third try, Baron showed them that he understood, by sitting quietly.

Everything was going smoothly. But then, for some reason, she started jerking the collar again and again. Baron and I were extremely upset. But The Master calmed down the female, and explained to us that this was the result of frustration caused by the communication gap.

Once she had been properly trained, her behavior fell right into line. Today, Baron is well-handled, and a model canine citizen.

This story had a happy ending. But sometimes getting there can be a battle. Why? Usually because of the very simplicity of a *Specialist's* solution.

Unfortunately, the simplest instructions are often too difficult for human beings to follow. Here's Happy to show you how intellect can get in the way.

I once knew a Schnauzer named Napolean with a true need to chew – and a house full of things to chew on while his human was away.

For some reason, the human saw this as a problem. In my experience humans collect all kinds of chewables for that rainy day that never comes.

So I trotted The Master out to see this human. He sent her out to a pet store to buy a rawhide chewable. And she was given strict instructions to give it to Napolean only when she had to leave him alone during the next two weeks.

This was good advice. The Master knows that nine out of ten veterinarians recommend rawhide for their patients who chew. And in taste test after taste test, canines prefer the taste of a rawhide chewable to just about any household object, most of which, frankly, do not meet our exacting culinary standards.

But do you know what? That human didn't follow The Master's advice. It's hard to imagine what she was thinking. Maybe she was worried that Napolean would choke on the rawhide chew while she was away. Never mind that Napolean had, over ten years, chewed on dozens of plants, purses, pants and other preferred items around the house with no problems whatsoever.

But what really got my fur up was her second excuse. She figured she'd give Napolean the rawhide chew while she was home, to keep him occupied. What she really wanted to do was read the newspaper or watch television undisturbed.

I didn't say anything. But fortunately, Napolean knew that when you own a human, you're responsible for their well-being. He wanted to get his human out from in front of that television and into the fresh air.

After all, if that female wanted him to chew only the rawhide chewable, he was perfectly content to do so. But if he had to chew on a couch potato to liven things up around there, Napolean was willing to do that, too.

As Happy witnessed, getting people to believe that a suggested solution will work, and convincing them to carry through with it, are two totally different problems. And follow-through is by far the more difficult of the two.

Even the most intelligent owner may have such difficulties. Many are unable to follow simple directions, like: "Command your dog to 'Sit' just one time, then approximately two seconds later give a short, one-half second jerk on the dog's training collar."

This sounds simple but, again, old habits are not easy to break, especially for human beings. The techniques for training or retraining a pet to eliminate a misbehavior may be basic and easy-to-follow, but they are not necessarily common sense to a human!

When people get a dog for the first time, they do with it what they know. And they only know how to treat another human. So they attempt to educate it like they would a human. But this doesn't work because dogs **aren't** human. They don't think like humans think, and they don't learn like humans learn.

The solutions to curing pet misbehaviors lie in perfect dog sense, but dog sense must be taught to people. People like Tom and Mary, whom Happy knows well. They had a very different kind of pet behavior problem:

Another growler I heard concerned an old Poodle named Andre. He lived with a male and a female human, and their adolescent from a litter of one.

This adolescent, who was 13 in human years, gave Andre a unique problem. Every time this kid came upon Andre while he was lying down, she gave him a kick.

Of course, Andre did the only thing he could think of under the circumstances – he would leap out and bite her on the foot. Perhaps this was a bit of an overreaction, but Andre was a small dog, not obedience-schooled in the ways of the world.

This male and female sat in Andre's living room and told The Master about what they apparently perceived as Andre's aggressiveness. Believe it or not, they were afraid he had turned mean. Or that he was retarded. Or, perhaps, that he had developed a brain tumor.

Andre was incensed. He had been thinking the same thing about their girl. But I calmed him down.

Further questioning revealed that Andre bit only the adolescent, and that he had never attacked another human pack member or stray that passed through his house. That's when The Master cracked the case. He discovered that for nearly two years, the girl had been kicking the little dog out of her way.

The Master revealed that Andre was biting the adolescent's foot in anticipation of her kick! The male and female were amazed. "You're right, that's it!" they exclaimed. They had never made the connection.

As I see it, by this time the girl was probably kicking Andre mostly out of fear that he would bite her again. It was a vicious circle.

But Andre wasn't a vicious dog. Just a smart one.

What some humans don't understand, I guess, is that canines can't afford to differentiate between a human kick given out of boredom, impatience, malice, or fear. To us, a kick is a kick. Lucky for us we have our canine teeth to keep everyone honest.

Andre's reaction was, "This girl kicks me. And whatever the reason, I don't like it. So every time she walks by I'm going to get her first!"

The answer to this problem was rather simple once The Master translated it for the humans. It wasn't difficult to train the adolescent not to kick Andre.

In truth, she'd been so frightened and annoyed with Andre's bite that she was ready to avoid him completely, as The Master instructed.

This is consistent with Pavlov's famous experiments which proved that when a dog salivates, eventually a human will supply a food reward.

A *Specialist's* simple solutions almost always have the owners walk a mile on their own pet's paws. This gives them more perspective on the behavioral problem – and, perhaps, a little more patience.

One common problem, however, that really tries the patience of a pet owner is the kitchen trash can.

Owners often complain when their dog dallies in the daily developments. Yet oftentimes, the solutions to these problems don't even involve any training at all. Happy can cite many such examples:

I know of many such dogs. We're attracted to all those wonderful aromas. To us, the kitchen floor can be a delectable smorgasboard with a wonderful spread of garbage.

If, for whatever implausible reason, our humans choose to withhold these delicacies from us – perhaps in lieu of a Slimfast diet – we'd recommend a covered trash can. Or even a relocation of our repast to the cabinet next to the sink. You see, out-of-sight, out-of-mind doesn't work well with us pooches. Not with our nose for news. You have to erect real barriers.

Still, many humans play dumb. (Under laboratory conditions many actually prove quite intelligent.) They might say, "Well, it wouldn't work because I don't have a trash can with a lid."

The Master says that Behavior Specialists should sell trash cans with lids. If they did, they could make millions of those little green papers they like to collect and trade!

Unlike situations where no real training is necessary – as in Happy's last example – there are certain situations where training is an absolute necessity. Yet the circumstances are, for some reason, outside the bounds of human consideration.

Automobiles are a perfect example. An owner once told me: "I have a dog that acts like a maniac every time I put him in a car. He's going to get us both killed."

When I asked him, "When do you teach him to behave in a car?" he sheepishly replied, "While I'm driving."

Happy doesn't want your dog to end up as a statistic. Here's what he has to say about dogs and cars:

Most humans I know have a large toy they call a car. They get inside these toys, and chase each other around at very high speeds. But remember, for dogs this is a different game altogether. We don't know the rules. And 55-miles-per-hour is much faster in dog time. I guess the only horsepower we're really comfortable with is the kind that helps us chase squirrels and rabbits.

But we're an adaptable species. Heck, we were in space before humans were!

So if you have to drag us into your game, at least show us what is expected of us.

At first, don't even start the engine. Put us in the back seat – no smoochin' – and get us used to the feel of that corinthian leather. Or that nifty naugahyde.

We can control ourselves just fine inside a car once we know the proper etiquette. Of course, we'd rather be chasing you down the road.

Is all this just common sense? Perhaps. But as I suggested earlier, hindsight is twenty-twenty. And when it comes to dog owners, it's the role of the *Pet Behavior Specialist* to turn that hindsight into foresight.

3

Shattering The Myths

There is no greater mythology in human history than that created for, and dedicated to, the dog and its various behaviors. Literally thousands of books have been written which perpetuate these myths. And, although no one seems to know their origins, the same set of apocryphal stories are told and re-told – so that now these ideas are so strongly ingrained into our thinking that they are accepted by most as fact.

I do not accept them – nor do the animals themselves in their ultimate application. Yet many dog owners do accept these myths. In fact, many take them as gospel. And who can blame them, when they have read these same fallacies time and again? No one has seriously challenged their legitimacy before. So in this chapter I present the evidence that shatters many of the myths in question.

MYTH 1: MY DOG IS GAY

Often, when I'm working with the male owner of a male dog, he'll pull me aside rather embarrassedly and tell me, "I think my dog is gay."

Sometimes they take a more direct approach to this taboo subject, saying, "I have this male dog that sexually mounts other male dogs. How do I deal with him?"

Or sometimes, a more fearful owner will ask me, "Do dogs get AIDS?"

These men relax a bit, often reddening, when they hear my chuckle in response.

Many men, particularly those who consider themselves very masculine – even macho – believe that if their male dog mounts another male dog, it is gay. But dogs cannot be homosexual. Being gay implies a conscious choice to have sex only with the same gender. Dogs are incapable of this thinking process...and of making this decision.

Pet Behavior Specialists, after extensive experience with the full range of canine behavior, have concluded that a male dog mounting another male dog is only its way of showing domination, of releasing excitement or frustration, or of playing.

Even with his steady temper, my dog, Happy, has exhibited such behavior. For example, in a park setting, he might be playing excitedly with two other dogs. Happy may take the sexual mounting position during rough play and have to be called off. When he assumes this position he is only exhibiting his excitement. It's his way of showing domination, gaining attention or declaring, "I'm tougher than you guys."

Again, dogs don't think like humans think. It's natural for them to act this way. But perhaps Happy can put the topic even more plainly:

The Master took me out to see a Beagle named Caleb, who was in training with a human female. I watched the regimen for 45 minutes. Then, during a break in the action, the female's mate summoned the courage to ask us, "Why is Caleb gay? I caught him mounting another male dog."

He didn't ask, "Is Caleb gay?" He didn't even ask if dogs could be gay, when we just don't think that way.

In fact, he dismissed The Master's explanation of how we dogs use this technique to show dominance, or over-excitement, with a wave of his hand.

He'd made up his mind that Caleb was gay, and that was that. And the poor human was so shaken by this revelation that he didn't even want Caleb's training to continue.

At first, I felt badly for poor Caleb, who never stood a chance to regain the man's respect. But eventually, I felt worse for this poor, insecure man, who measured his own masculinity by his former friend's actions – and so misinterpreted this very masculine show of physical dominance.

MYTH 2: CORRECTING YOUR DOG
<u>AFTER</u> THE FACT WORKS

One prevailing theory holds that correcting a dog after it misbehaves eliminates the misbehavior. Perhaps this line of reasoning caught on by word-of-mouth. You might say, "I trained my dog by disciplining him after the fact." A friend might agree that she trained her dog the same way.

Actually, it is unlikely that either of you used this method – at least not successfully – because correcting a dog after the fact just does **not** work. Ever. In fact, it's probable that both dogs are still misbehaving...but few people want to admit one of life's little failures to a friend or neighbor.

So let's examine this myth more closely. Think about the recent evolution in the relationship between pets and people. Even just fifty years ago, dogs did not live inside the home as frequently as they do today. At that time, instances of dogs urinating or defecating inside the home were rarely heard.

But as the years passed, the technology of the world progressed. And as it did so, dangers to a dog left outside, and to its own devices, increased. As a result, today pets are frequently left at home, inside and alone, to amuse themselves for eight or ten hours at a time. Under these circumstances, it is not difficult to understand how a dog can easily fall into bad habits.

When a dog owner, for instance, comes home from a hard day's work to discover that his best friend has left a "gift" for him in the middle of the living room rug, his first response is predictable. He'll find the dog, drag it over, point at the mess, yell, and stick the poor dog's nose in it. This, the myth suggests, is discipline after the fact.

It's funny though, the strength of the discipline seems to vary directly with the kind of day the owner has had, or how heavy the traffic congestion was on the drive home.

When the discipline is done, the dog hangs its head and looks undeniably guilty, and the owner thinks, "Great, this method works!"

But the next day, or a week later, the dog defecates in another undesirable spot inside the house. So the truth of the matter is that correcting after the fact did not work.

Often, coming home to such a problem – especially a second time – can set off a rampage. And a dog is the ideal victim, because an owner can severely discipline a dog, and ten minutes later it will return, rubbing up against her saying, "I love you."

Owners think they feel better because they taught their dog what it did wrong. Actually, that is not why they feel better at all. They feel better because they worked out their frustrations – but this was accomplished at the expense of their pet.

Instead, the owner should clean up the mess, and then get a tennis racket and beat the bed. Or go out in the back yard and yell to release the frustration. Owners who follow this advice not only feel better about themselves, but their dogs tend to behave better.

The big question is, does the owner want a dog who *appears* to look like it knows it did something wrong at the time of correction, but misbehaves again? Or does he want a dog who does not misbehave? Usually, the owner wants to totally eliminate the misbehavior.

Scientific studies have demonstrated time and again that dogs do not have long-term memories.

In experimental settings, it has been proven that a dog cannot retain an event or associate a reward or discipline to something that happened **1.8 seconds** after the behavior. Therefore, it cannot connect the misbehavior which took place hours ago with the owner coming home and correcting it for defecation, or destructive chewing, or any other misbehavior.

A dog's mind simply doesn't work that way. Dogs do not have the ability to plan or reason. That is why they cannot master the skills that a monkey can learn – the use of tools, for example. A dog cannot reason things out the way humans do.

Happy, can you shed any light on this myth?

I'd like to take exception to that crack about the monkey, but several seconds have already passed, so my opportunity's passed me by.

Face it, we live in the present — the here and now. It's how we were designed. So the facts are in on Correction After the Fact. In fact, a Corgi once called me to say that her human had been disciplining her after the fact for three years.

"It's not working," she related.

"Obviously," I responded. "But why is your human still doing it?"

"He doesn't know what else to do," the bemused Corgi said.

Quickly, I called The Master to suggest some different approaches for this situation. Three years is a long time for a dog to wait until a master comes around to the facts.

MYTH 3: DOGS LISTEN BETTER
TO HUSBANDS

Many women complain loudly to Happy and me that their dogs listen to their husbands while totally ignoring their own commands. Their husbands invariably agree that, yes, they are the best dog trainer in the world, and that they have absolutely no problems with their dog. Only the wife and children have a problem getting the dog to obey.

"All I have to do is yell at this dog, and he straightens up," these husbands confirm.

Women seem to think that this phenomenon occurs because their husbands are bigger, stronger, and have deeper, louder voices. "So Fido knows he will follow through with his threats."

Men are often more physical than women when disciplining pets...sometimes excessively so. Obviously, an animal will respond more promptly thereafter.

Husbands are often more physical with rewards, too. They get on the floor and wrestle with the dog. They play fetch with it and throw objects for it to return. They run two miles or jog with it. They take it hunting and fishing. Their relationship is much more physical.

But this is just a part of the reason for a pet's prompt response to masculine commands.

More of it has to do with the dog's own schedule, and how the family interacts with it. In many more traditional households the woman may be home during the day. This is when the dog is at its highest energy level. It's also when the woman may be at her highest distraction – or even frustration – level. She may be caring for small children, or an elderly parent. She may be cooking meals, or engaging in some philanthropic activity, or doing the laundry. Meanwhile, her Rottweiler is romping through her laundry piles...or charging the postal carrier...or chewing on her best Reebok.

When her husband returns at the end of the day, he finds a pet worn out from energetic daily activities. And a wife in the same condition. So he changes into his jogging shorts, and takes the

Rottweiler with him for a short run. When they return, he settles onto the couch to read the newspaper with a dog who lays contentedly at his feet for the evening.

So when his wife approaches him with the urgent request for Rottweiler training, his understandable response is "Training? But there's nothing wrong with this dog. He's great!"

So **schedule** is a critical element in many husband-wife-dog triads.

But when it comes to commands, the most important distinction of all is that in the dog world, not everyone is equal. Males are dominant. So dogs of both sexes view their male and female masters much differently. Males are always accorded more respect, whether that male is another dog or a human being.

The male dog is always, and has always been, the leader of the pack. So male and female dogs both view male dogs and humans with more respect than female dogs and humans. In fact, their respect depends more on the sex of the animal than on its size. Therefore, they respect small males more than large females.

And unlike in today's human environment, a female dog is not expected to challenge a male dog for the leadership role. And, should she ever do so, she will probably back down more easily than a male would. Similarly, a dog does not expect to be challenged by a female human being.

This is an unchallengeable law of nature. The way a dog views the sexes cannot be changed, because, unlike humans, they cannot reason. This is why any dog will respond with more respect and obedience to what it perceives as the "male" or "dominant" voice of authority.

This does not mean, however, that women cannot take control of a dog. Far from it. Happy has a wonderful story where a woman – in the face of intense pressure from her husband – found herself in complete control of a sensitive situation:

The Master had me along for some training sessions, but I needed a cat nap, so I stayed in the car. Well, I couldn't sleep a wink with all the commotion inside the house.

Apparently, there was a rambunctious young Golden Retriever named Jake in there. At two years old, he was a rebel without a cause, which isn't unusual for Golden Retrievers that age. He was frenzied and frenetic. And the human female of the house was frustrated. It was obvious that Jake had no respect for her at all. He never listened to her and he was always jumping about and playfully biting her.

She finally said enough was enough, and called in The Master. True, she was small by human standards, but she was determined to gain control of this seventy pound ball of flying fur.

So The Master had her put a training collar and leash on the young rebel, and they began working with him, praising him when he did well. The first session went very well. Session number two went even more smoothly. The woman began to see improvement. And she started feeling more comfortable with Jake, and gaining some measure of control.

"This is great," she said, "because Jake has always been wonderful for my husband. He'll snap his fingers and Jake will do anything for him. I'm the one who can't ever control him."

But that day was the infamous "Session 3." So while I tried to catch my 40 winks, The Master was working with the female's two teenage sons. Everything went well until the arrival of the female's mate. He walked in fresh from work, still in his three-piece suit. He stood silently in the foyer watching the session, not acknowledging it.

But his presence was acknowledged by his mate, who forgot everything she had learned during the previous sessions. She was sweating, yelling, screaming and getting very frustrated. That's when all heck broke loose. Naturally, Jake picked up on the changes in her approach, and he just went bananas.

Finally, her male interrupted the session, telling The Master: "Excuse me, maybe you don't realize it, but my wife can't control this dog. The reason she's acting so flustered is because I'm watching. So she doesn't want to make any mistakes."

With that, he made his exit. And so did the female, who left the room crying.

About this time I finally nodded off. The excitement was, for the moment, over. But while I slept, The Master held a conference alone in the basement with the female. How would he return the woman to her proper position of respect with the four males? She'd already started to gain Jake's respect. She'd been doing so well.

Well, The Master did his thing, He rebuilt her confidence, even when the three men would have none of it. She was too small. She was too weak. She was, needless to say, very angry. But The Master had a plan!

When Session 3 resumed, the female did all the right things with Jake...even in the presence of the three males. The teenagers then took turns practicing the new methods of control with the dog. But when it was the male's turn, he refused.

"I don't have to take a turn," he said. " Jake listens to me."

The Master then explained how helpful it would be to his mate and the two youngsters if Jake was controlled in a consistent manner. Still he was hesitant.

"Jake listens to me," he insisted. "He does anything I want."

"Anything?" asked The Master. "Will Jake sit and stay for you?"

"Yes, anything," the male replied.

"Jake will listen to you off-leash no matter what happens around him in this living room?" The Master continued.

"Yes," the male said, irritably.

"All right, put Jake on a 'sit and stay' command," said The Master, springing his trap. "I'm going out to the car to bring in my dog, Happy."

"Jake won't sit and stay for that!" he cried.

"But you just told me he would sit and stay for you off- leash, no matter what happens," said The Master quite courteously.

I was his trap. The female was enjoying the worried look on her mate's face.

Finally, after some negotiating wherein it was agreed that Jake would remain on a leash, The Master roused me. And I put on quite a show, if I do say so myself! It didn't take much. The undisciplined Jake immediately went berserk. He stood on his hind legs, barking and growling ferociously. Golden Retrievers are so immature! The male had no control whatsoever.

When he'd made his point, The Master snapped his fingers and pointed at me. This is our signal for me to quiet down and sit, at my leisure, in the corner. Good old unflappable Happy!

Well, everyone was impressed. They didn't realize that The Master and I had done this a thousand times before.

But the show was just beginning.

"Phyllis will now show you three men how to handle your dog when it is totally out of control," The Master announced.

The female looked as frantic as Jake did, but more determined. She picked up his leash and, using the correct techniques, controlled Jake within 10 seconds. He sat and stayed for her, panting and growling slightly, but under much better physical control.

From this point on, the female was in command. She had finally received the respect she so deserved!

MYTH 4: DOGS ARE UNTRAINABLE FOR THEIR FIRST SIX MONTHS

The idea that puppies are untrainable until they are six months old is totally illogical. It's a bit like saying you can't teach a child until it's two years old. The origin of this myth is much easier to pinpoint than most, however.

Where does a new puppy owner turn to find out about training his new best friend? Traditionally, there have been three main information sources: friends, veterinarians or a capable group obedience school.

But when you call a school, the first question they ask is "How old is your dog?" If you tell them, "Twelve weeks," they're sure to answer, "That's ridiculous. Dogs don't even begin to learn until they're six months old." Or, "If you train him before he's six months old, you'll ruin his personality. You'll train the 'puppy' out of him." Most obedience schools won't take dogs until they are six months old. They have, for them, some very good reasons for this standard rule.

By the time a puppy is six months old, most owners – with a bit of old-fashioned luck – eliminate the most obnoxious puppy behaviors, so the school doesn't have to. These include: excessive noise, play-biting at the leash, urinating and defecating in improper places, and a thousand other little things puppies do.

These schools also know that young puppies, if not most dogs, just cannot handle learning in a distracting environment. And 35 dogs in a single group is as distracting as it gets! Is it any wonder that dog obedience schools want the least disruptive dog possible in their classes?

These important considerations notwithstanding, there are many more reasons you should begin to teach your puppy how to behave properly early in life.

First, puppies **do** learn. They don't just sit around observing nothing for six months. They are obviously learning something. So why not teach them what to chew on, where to urinate and defecate, not to bite, and to sit and stay on command?

It is not wrong to "take some of the puppy out of the dog." During the period from two to six months, you might see a lot of behaviors that you'd classify as cute. But they won't look cute a year from now when your dog weighs 80 or more pounds.

Some puppy behaviors – biting your hands, chewing the furniture, yelping like a mad dog for no reason at all – can be extremely irritating. You need to take steps to eliminate these behaviors. They won't just go away on their own.

And remember that it is confusing for a puppy when you allow it to do anything it pleases for a period of time, and then you try to eliminate all misbehaviors at once.

During the first six months of life, some very significant things happen to a puppy. For example, puppies acquire their adult teeth somewhere from 18 to 22 weeks of age. And, if left unattended, they can do a great deal of destructive chewing damage. They just don't know any better. So you have to teach them. You must be able to redirect this behavior, teaching your puppy what is acceptable to chew on.

Many misbehaviors are easier to correct when the dog is very young. For instance, dealing with an aggressive puppy is much easier for the owner than dealing with an aggressive six-month-old that is bigger, stronger and smarter.

And young puppies learn very quickly. One proper correction with a training collar will teach an eight-week-old puppy what it might take a hundred corrections to teach a six-month-old.

Perhaps the most important reason to begin teaching a young puppy goes back to its dim and distant days in the wild, where dogs roamed in packs. When a young puppy wandered away from its mother, she would immediately go after the pup and bring it back.

Scientific studies have proven that it is **always** the 49th day on which the puppy is permitted to roam, and is not brought back by its mother. It's as if she is saying, "Go out little puppy. Now you are ready to learn about the world around you. I won't bring you back. Go learn on your own, and come back on your own."

Yet the mother, or another dog, will still discipline the puppy if it does something wrong.

If a puppy is capable of learning on its own in a field or woods, it can certainly learn in a contained human household. But now it's up to the human to teach it to behave.

The bottom line is that both you and your puppy need to be educated when the puppy is just eight weeks old, or as soon as the puppy first enters your household. And if a group obedience tells you, "We don't train you, we train your dog," find another one. Because you must learn together with your puppy from day one.

MYTH 5: DOGS WITH MANY CHEW TOYS WON'T CHEW YOUR BELONGINGS

Owners have been known to give their pets a bizarre range of things to chew on. Why? Because they believe that the more things that they give their dog to chew on, the less likely it is to chew on their personal possessions. Unhappily, nothing could be further from the truth.

The **only** things a dog should be given to chew on are 100% rawhide chewables, or a real, properly prepared, beef shank bone. When you give your pet anything else to chew on, you invite the risk that she'll learn to chew on the wrong thing. Classic examples are an old shoe, a sock or jeans tied in knots (with which to play tug of war).

Occasionally, people even give their dogs baskets of toys. Some dogs have their own toy box imprinted with their name. Yet others have baskets of squeaky toys, rubber toys, nylon toys and textile toys. Owners of small dogs and toy breeds in particular seem to feel the need to provide toys for their "babies," who "need" cute, little toys to make them happy.

These owners have two things in common. Their dogs **are** destructively chewing, and they all make the same comment: "I give him everything he needs. I don't understand why he has to chew on my stuff."

Scent is of foremost importance. The owner's smell is the primary scent on all objects he or she handles. Even if a sock or shoe is washed frequently, or an owner handles a squeaky toy only once a week, the scent remains primary on the object.

In advanced sessions, obedience trainers conduct scent discrimination tests. Owners are required to pick up one of 20 wood dumbbells, hold it for a few seconds, and put it down, all without their dogs watching. The pets are then required, sometimes as much as an hour later, to find the particular objects that their masters touched just once. Most well-trained dogs can do so.

What happens at home is that you unconsciously teach your dog that all chew toys have your scent. Eventually your dog will generalize that this scent is representative of a proper chewable. Then, when you're not home, your dog looks around for the most interesting, newest, desirable chew toy. And it picks something that has your scent on it. She could choose anything in the house, even something she's never chewed on before. It only qualifies if it is attractive and carries your scent.

To pre-empt this pattern, you should redirect your dog to one specific object which does not smell like anything else in its environment.

A rawhide chewable is the most preferable offering you can make. Even though you have to handle it to give it to your dog, once the chewing begins, the rawhide becomes the primary scent, overriding your own. This significantly reduces the risk of your dog generalizing to inappropriate objects.

Almost all breeds are prone to destructive chewing. Retrievers will chew on the objects that they retrieve. Lhasa Apsos are notorious for chewing on towels. But as Happy can tell you, the rehabilitation of one Black Labrador takes the prize for its originality in our experience:

Brandy was never too bright, I guess. He'd chewed up his humans' household since he was a pup. And as he got older, the problem grew worse.

By the time he was six, Brandy had chewed down a tree in his back yard that was 3" in diameter. He chewed and clawed through a solid oak hall door. He pulled woodwork off the walls. He decimated furniture. It seemed that every day his humans would return home to progressively greater destruction.

His humans tried everything they could think of to stop Brandy's problem. They gave him hundreds of his own toys to chew on. They squirted hot pepper sauce on furniture. They even brought him real bones! But nothing worked.

For months these humans didn't even run with their pack of friends, sacrificing their social lives to stay home and keep Brandy company. Curiously enough, he never chewed inappropriately while someone was home. This gave The Master an idea. A unique idea. A singularly batty, but human, idea!

To fool Brandy into believing that someone was always home, he and the other humans created a life-sized doll, dressing it in the male's clothing. Then they laid it on the sofa without the dog observing.

The male, who was an electronics buff, had rigged a tape recorder into the body of the doll. Then, whenever Brandy came within a few feet, a pre-set remote control on his collar turned on the recorder, which played the owner's voice.

Knowing that we dogs are bastions of sense, if not sensibility, these crazy humans sought to maintain the illusion by capitalizing on Brandy's nose – with the male's clothing; Brandy's eyes – with the life-sized doll; and Brandy's ears – with the tape recording of the male's voice.

Occasionally, the male would even wear the clothing worn by the doll and lie on the couch. When Brandy would approach, he would get up and move about, thus adding movement to the list.

The humans set up this scenario whenever they left Brandy home. Over time, the doll became a part of their family. And believe it or not, Brandy quit his destructive chewing. Eventually, the humans were able to slowly have the doll "move into a closet!"

Every ten times Brandy was left home alone, the doll would be missing. Then every nine times the doll would be gone, and so on.

Although all this was a rather elaborate and unorthodox way to break Brandy of a difficult habit, the program worked! And that's what counts.

The more classic case occurs when an owner tells me, in a rather hopeless tone, that his Golden Retriever chews on his shoes and socks. Then, while we're sitting on the sofa discussing the problem, the Retriever promenades by, sock in tow.

"Is this the problem child?" I ask.

"Oh yes," he tells me, "she knows the difference between her sock and my sock."

"If she knows the difference," I counter, "why is she chewing on your sock?"

"She does it because she's mad at me," he responds. Or, "She does it because she's spiteful." Or even, "She does it because she's stupid." The list of rationalizations goes on and on.

Owners, sadly enough, rarely make the connection. If you give your pet one sock, he will assume it is acceptable to chew on *any* sock. Or, if you offer a puppy a shoe to chew on, she will forever think it proper to chew on whatever shoe she might find.

Oddly, there are many owners with this problem who also tell me, "I'd really like to teach Peaches to get on only one of my couches, but I know she can't differentiate between couches, so I assume I'll have to teach her to stay off of everything." Go figure!

Many dogs also love to chew on paper. People who have mail slots that permit the pieces of mail to fall directly onto the floor often have a special problem. Discerning dogs frequently go wild when they hear the approach of the postal carrier. They wait excitedly for the mail to slide into a neat pile at their paws.

Then they delve into the pile with gusto and, when you arrive home, you find a pile of shredded letters and bills. (No one ever complains about shredded advertising!)

It's strange how long some people will put up with this problem. They seem to think, regardless of its frequency, that it just won't happen again.

The solution is as simple as can be. Install an outside mailbox and find something else to worry about!

MYTH 6: ONE MUST HURT A DOG TO CONTROL IT

The cruelest myth of all is that stated above. It is **not** necessary to inflict pain on an animal in order to control it. Some people do dominate their animal with pain in the belief that their pet will obey to avoid further pain. So they beat it, step on its toes, knee it in the chest, whip it on the haunches, uppercut its chin – I have seen and heard it all. But for all their cruel and insensitive efforts, this theory is not sound.

The best way to control a dog is by using the methods that dogs use on one another. You never see one dog hitting another or stepping on another's toes. One dog does not gain the advantage over another dog by inflicting pain on it.

A dog gains control of his opponent in one simple motion, grabbing it by the back of its neck or by the throat. This temporarily (or partially) collapses his opponent's trachea, decreasing its air supply.

Dogs have used this method of control and discipline on each other for thousands and thousands of years.

It causes no pain, but provides a momentary, intimidated surrender. Dogs are accustomed to accept this type of correction. They are physically designed with a flexible trachea and a strong neck in order to tolerate such actions.

This, of course, is one reason that electronic training collars are an accepted and suitable method used in obedience training. The devices work using a harmless electronic stimulus to create a momentary simulation of the control situation described above as a means of correction. Properly used, at the appropriate time and with the warranted intensity, the training collar mimics the methods that dogs understand on an elemental level.

Have you ever seen a large shaggy dog straining and pulling its owner along on a brisk "walk?" Although the dog is obviously doing the pulling, it is coughing and gasping at the same time. But the pulling continues unabated.

What has happened is that the dog is pulling so hard that it has partially collapsed its own trachea. The coughing and gasping you hear are natural reflexes which re-expand the trachea. So, although physically built to accept a collapsed trachea, the dog also has built-in methods of re-expanding it.

Not surprisingly, this method of correction is the same as that used by the mother on her puppies.

Golden Retrievers are known for their predilection to jump up on people. The owner who attempts to curb her Retriever with the various violent methods described earlier rarely changes the dog's behavior. The pain does not deliver the message for the dog to stop jumping up on people.

The technique that has the best chance to succeed is the use of a training collar. Some people refer to this as a "choker" collar. I prefer the term training collar. The word "choker" implies the need to choke your dog in order to train it. This is neither true nor necessary.

Please see Chapter 6, *How Pets Learn,* under the heading "Training Methods and Equipment," for more details about using this common correction methodology.

When your dog jumps up, reach around behind its neck, grab its training collar and simply pull it down. The pull does not have to be painful, just hard enough to mimic the methods a dog already innately understands.

Owners who repeatedly use pain to force a dog down often claim that they have to continue hurting the dog because it continues to jump on people. Their assumption is that the dog likes pain. Nothing could be further from the truth. Their method just isn't getting their message across.

Violent techniques are an example of behavioral abuse of dogs, although many owners deny that this is what they're doing. They truly believe that physical abuse is the only prevailing abuse. But behavioral abuse is much more prevalent, as Happy sadly reports:

There was a human female who lived on a large wooded estate, owned by 11 Great Danes, in the center of a midwestern state.

Because she was having a great deal of difficulty handling this number of large, active dogs, she carried a cattle prod on her belt. *When three or four of these dogs began to act aggressively towards her or towards each other, she zapped them on the sides with the prod, which was a real shock to them. But this did nothing to change their behavior.*

After calling The Master for counsel, she agreed to try an electronic training collar instead. These collars electronically correct us in a harmless, but startling way that reminds us of how we were corrected as pups. Maybe that's why they seem to work so well. Anyway, these collars quickly solved the problem.

Dogs are not physically or mentally prepared to accept a beating by a human. It is outside their natural experience. Other dogs have never done this to them, whether for teaching or for domination and leadership. So rather than respond to pain, dogs often retreat into excessive or aggressive behavior.

If an owner beats a dog and it becomes submissive, the owner may believe he has trained it. Although it may be a trained animal, it will never be a trained *pet*, and that makes all the difference in the world.

MYTH 7: MY DOG IS BIGGER THAN ME

The single statement most heard by *Pet Behavior Specialists* and obedience trainers alike is, "My dog is bigger than me," or "My dog is stronger than me."

Usually, this address is made by a woman with a dog which, regardless of size or breed, she is unable to control. The dog invariably drags her down the street on their walks, greets visitors with loud barking and aggressiveness, and jumps on whatever furniture it wishes.

The inevitable questions of a *Pet Behavior Specialist* begin.

"Are you taller than your dog?" I'll ask.

"Yes," she'll reply.

"Do you weigh more than your dog?" I'll continue.

"Yes," she'll reply.

"How can he be bigger than you," I'll ask, "if you are taller and physically outweigh him by 60 pounds?"

"Well, perhaps he's not bigger than me. But he's stronger," she'll maintain, starting the process over.

I often wonder how an owner can look down at a 30-pound Cocker Spaniel and perceive that it's bigger than she is. It's amazing. They have truly convinced themselves that this is so, and use it as an excuse for not being able to handle their pet.

The smallest pet I've ever heard anyone ever make this claim about, believe it or not, was a tiny, very aggressive, white Miniature Poodle named Tonto. Happy was there:

Tonto's owner was a gentle human female in her 70s. When we arrived, this two-pound Mr. Macho was in total control. And to show it, he went around lifting his leg on everything.

The poor woman yelled at the dog for these delinquent acts, or disciplined him by smacking his haunches. But Tonto would not submit. Instead, he'd make quick, threatening movements at her. Then he'd curl his lip and bite at her hand.

Understandably, she was deathly afraid of him when he was at his most aggressive.

The Master's cure was elementary. He directed her to refrain from yelling or hitting. Instead, she was to approach Tonto, grab his collar or leash, and give it a small jerk. And she was cautioned to be careful with a two-pound animal, as it is easy to misjudge and yank too hard at first.

This took some convincing. The female cried and worried that if she did this, Tonto would rip her apart.

"He's bigger than me; he's stronger," she said.

The Master quickly applied a little logic to the situation.

*"Tonto is a tiny, two-pound animal. True, he **might** draw blood. You may see a little red dot on your finger after he bites you. But you **have to** reach in and grab the collar."*

Another similar situation involved a small but stubborn Lhasa Apso. Butterscotch traveled well in a car, but, upon returning home, utterly refused to budge from the back seat. Happy relates:

When they returned from a trip, Butterscotch would growl as ferociously as a tiny dog can.

"I'm not going anywhere," he'd say. "I'm comfortable right where I am."

"I can't get him out of the car no matter how hard I pull," his human pouted to The Master.

51

"How much does he weigh?" The Master asked.

"About 20 pounds," she said.

"How much do you weigh?" The Master pushed forward.

"Well, I'd rather not say," she stalled, "but over a hundred pounds."

"And you can't pull a 20-pound dog out of the car?" The Master smiled.

"Well, I pull him as hard as I can," she maintained.

The Master followed this with a brief demonstration. A quick tug on the leash, accompanied by an order for the dog to come out, quickly popped Butterscotch out of the car. Next it was the female's turn. After a bit of practice, the same technique worked for her as well.

Grumbling, but only slightly, Butterscotch ran off to find another comfortable spot that would also sit well with this persnickety human.

Like Butterscotch's owner, many are convinced they will harm their pet with this technique, or that the dog is too tough to handle even with it. These two extremes are usually just their justification for avoiding the eventual confrontation. And in fact, they may actually be convinced that their dog will hurt them in such a situation.

MYTH 8: DOGS ARE PEOPLE

How often have you heard an animal lover say, "My dog thinks he's human."

Have you ever asked them, "How do you know your dog thinks he's human?"

And did they give you an answer like, "Well, he has human qualities."

Remember, I know that Happy is a dog – I'm merely projecting my own actual experiences with animals onto him for presentation purposes.

But many people truly believe their dogs are human. They treat them like humans; they discipline them like they are human; they reward them like a human; they feed them human food; they dress them in clothes; they put jewelry on them; they believe they can spell; they think they understand English. All in all, they think their dog is human.

When I ask, "When you look at your dog, exactly what do you see?" I often experience a long drawn out process to obtain the answer I know to be true: "I see a dog."

My firm belief is that human beings prefer to be treated in the accepted ways of a human being. Further, if a human were treated like a dog, she would be quite unhappy. This alone makes a strong case for the opposite situation. A dog is most content being treated as a dog. It is unlikely that a dog is happiest when treated as a human.

Humans, however, love their pets so much, they handle them as they themselves prefer to be treated. Convincing people who have been treating their dog like a human for so many years to change their habits can be extremely difficult, as Happy will explain:

The most extreme case we've ever seen involved a well-dressed, perfumed Pomeranian named Cujo. (His owner obviously never saw the movie.)

No self-respecting dog would accept this situation. So Cujo took quite a rough ribbing from the rest of us. Of course, this wasn't fair — and it made the poor pup irritable.

Cujo lived in a wealthy household. He didn't eat dog food; the housekeeper cooked him lemon chicken with thick white, chicken breasts and served it on stoneware. Cujo didn't have dog dishes, dog food or dog shampoo. He had china. He had salon-tested wash and conditioner.

He climbed wherever he pleased. He wouldn't sleep on the floor; he slept on a bed. And he peed everywhere. Cujo was never disciplined, and he bit most houseguests.

You'd be irritable too if you had four legs and your humans forced you to wear the pants in the family!

Unfortunately, there's no convincing some people that dogs are not, never will be, and don't want to be people. We want to be ourselves.

MYTH 9: IF YOUR DOG ISN'T LOOKING AT YOU, IT'S DEAF

Most owners, when asked to demonstrate how they get their dog to sit, will look it in the eyes, point their finger and say "Sit." Hopefully, the dog sits.

If, for some reason, the dog is not in a position where they can look it in the eye, owners begin by calling the pet's name over and over.

When the dog finally looks at them, they tell it to sit. Almost all dog owners initially seeking training seem to go through this stage. They think that their dog cannot hear them unless it is looking directly at them.

When the dog is decidedly distracted, perhaps smelling something of interest, owners find themselves yelling "Come, come" at the top of their lungs when they are only ten feet away. They reason that the dog won't come because it can't hear them; that lost in the concentration of smelling, hearing stops! Do eyesight and smell affect an animal's hearing?

I don't think so! If those owners would say a more attractive word, such as "biscuit," the pet would hear them immediately! Almost any unique sound, such as whistling or snapping fingers, will attract the dog.

But for some unknown reason, people seem to expect a correlation between sight and hearing in a dog that exists in no other animal. On further discussion, most agree that their dog can hear them, but that she chooses not to respond.

In my experience, many dogs learn that they don't have to look at their owner until their owner's yells reach a certain pitch. Then it's, "Uh-oh, she's going to hit a thousand decibels. Now she really means business."

It's a bit like parents who feel the need to discipline a child in public. They threaten, "You had better straighten up before I count to three. One, two, three." And just when they hit "three," the child rethinks her position and obeys because she knows she's in real trouble if she doesn't.

Perhaps the doggie discipline should start at "One," for quicker response and action.

MYTH 10: NEUTERING/SPAYING IS A MIRACLE CURE

Many veterinarians and, as a result, much of the public, believe that neutering or spaying a dog will calm it, eliminate aggressive behavior, halt urination in inappropriate places, stop destructive chewing and halt pulling on a leash. This myth has been around for so long that it is deeply ingrained, and it will be extremely difficult to purge. Yet it must be.

Years ago, dogs had more freedoms than they do today. Most were kept outside. At the time, neutering was done to reduce roaming, and keep the animal closer to home. For that purpose, if done around the appropriate age of six months, neutering **may** have helped. In theory, this surgical procedure eliminates hormones before they produce behaviors.

However, this theory has never been proven to my satisfaction.

I once received a call from a woman with a Bernese Mountain Dog. She had been having difficulty with Charlie, who was one-and-a-half, whenever she attempted to correct him, take something from him, or, in fact, to challenge him in any way. In response, he acted aggressively towards her. She was concerned because she had just had him neutered six weeks ago, and she was still waiting for the "calming effect."

She chose to ignore the aggressive behavior in the hope that it would disappear of its own accord. Unfortunately, by walking away from it, she is reinforcing it. Charlie will assume that, because no correction has been made, the behavior is appropriate. Soon she will have a major problem on her hands with a 100-pound dog. When

Charlie is full-grown, he will be much more formidable to correct. Generally, as you'd expect, the larger the dog is, the more difficult the resolution.

And Charlie's owner will have to wait a long time for that "calming effect."

Neutering and spaying do not change behavior; they do not change memory; they do not change learning.

Perhaps most importantly, they do not change old habits. Situational-dependent behaviors are not caused by hormones.

Any change which may occur will be to hormone-directed behaviors only. And hormone-directed behaviors are remarkably few. They include urinating to mark territory, wandering after females in heat and sexual mounting. That's about it. They very rarely include over-excitability or aggressiveness.

One reason many veterinarians advocate neutering and spaying is that they've been taught that these procedures change many behaviors. This thinking is perpetuated because these vets are infrequently informed by their clients when the surgery does not work to alleviate the behavioral problem at hand. Owners just think that spaying or neutering is their last hope, and, if the behaviors remain, they are stuck with them.

The veterinarians themselves are so busy that they seldom have a system of follow-up for these types of situations. If they never hear from an owner again about the problem, they just assume that their solution has helped.

Humane societies, to their credit, advocate neutering and spaying to help eradicate unwanted litters.

Nonetheless, you must remember not to expect the surgery to eliminate those behaviors which are not hormone-directed.

4

Changing Owner Thinking

Tricks I Taught My Master *is as much about changing the behavior of* **humans** *as it is about changing ours.*

From our standpoint, most of what you'd call our misbehaviors can be attributed to your own actions, inactions and reactions. Does this apply to you? See for yourself. The Master will review the signs of owner "misbehavior" later in this chapter.

But for now, please understand, I'm not pointing any tails here. I just want to help you improve communication with your pet...to get through to her. That's the most challenging part of the process. So when you're ready to work with your dog, consider it an active challenge to change the way you think.

You may see some of these ideas as controversial, coming, as they are, from a canine.

"Training owners?" you may say. "Balderdash!"

But we pets know better. If you want to permanently change your dog's behavior, you have to put yourself on a short leash. Changing **your** *habits is the only way to do it.*

Look at the humans who pay a professional trainer to help them correct what they consider to be a canine misbehavior. What do they do? They let the trainer take their dog away and train him. When the training's complete, he returns home.

What's the result? Usually, a well-trained pet. But there's a catch! This approach only ensures that the dog will behave properly for the **trainer**.

61

*But that wasn't the purpose of the training, was it? What you want is for your pet to behave on a daily basis for **you** at home. So sending your dog somewhere else for training – no matter how good the trainer – will rarely work.*

If you don't participate in the training, it's only a matter of time before your dog begins misbehaving again. That's because you haven't learned how to interact with your dog. And that's the only way she'll retain her new habits.

It's tragic. It's a vicious circle. You know you're not doing something quite right, but you're too embarrassed to call the trainer again to get some help.

This is too bad. Because if the trainer never hears from you, she can only assume that your dog is working just as well for you as it did for her.

*Ultimately, the only one who knows better is the dog, who has regained control of the situation. And this situation clearly indicates that without a change in **human** behavior, your best friend will continue to walk all over you.*

WHY HUMANS MUST CHANGE

You need to communicate to your dog in the way that your dog has the highest chance of understanding. Therefore, to educate your pet, you must more or less mimic the way one dog responds to another.

For example, you never see one dog **yell** at another. You never see a dog **hit** another with her paw.

Yes, it's true that negative reinforcement is sometimes part of the training process. But what you and I consider to be negative may not be so to a dog. If you look at their natural environment, and their pack mentality, you'll realize that some of the actions they're confronted with in the human world may be entirely alien to them.

Take hitting, for example. Could hitting be meaningless to dogs? Probably. It's unlikely that they understand what this action means from a human standpoint (although the human probably doesn't have much ground to stand on if she has to resort to blows).

Sure, a dog will respond to pain. But his natural instinct is to find a way to stop it. Your pet may learn to avoid the punishment, but she will not eliminate the misbehavior which, of course, is your ultimate goal.

I would question any "correction" used by an owner that doesn't fit with the methodologies used by the species in its natural environment.

If you've been trying to change your dog's behavior, and you haven't had much success, ask yourself the following questions:

1. How have I tried to correct my pet's behavior?

> Usually, owners try one method for a short while, and then move on to another. When, in turn, this doesn't work, they move on to yet another method. And so on. What a pet needs is consistency, but in this instance it's totally lacking.

2. Are the methods I've been using working?

It's easy to see whether or not the misbehaviors are still intact. But many owners can't see beyond their pet's face. Dogs can look pretty sorry when they want to. And many owners think that if their pet *looks* sorry, it *understands* what it's done wrong. Somehow, this is supposed to enable them to change their behavior on their own. Actually, most dogs look pathetic not because they know what they've done wrong, but because they have *no idea* what is wrong...yet they can sense that their fur's about to fly.

3. Does disciplining after-the-fact work?

No, it does not. Chapter 3 gives a full explanation of why this is so.

4. What is my definition of success?

Success has many different meanings, all dependent on the needs of the individual owner. Do you want your dog to change its behavior to conform to your wishes? Or would you be satisfied if only she wouldn't misbehave while you're watching? Then again, if she's still misbehaving, have you met your goals?

5. Do I feel comfortable with the way I'm correcting my dog?

There's a difference between feeling good, and feeling good about yourself. Many conventional "correction" methods allow owners to release stress by taking their frustrations out on their dog. This may make them feel good momentarily, but in the end they may not feel so good about themselves.

These techniques don't do much for the well-being of the dog. They can harm a pet physically or emotionally. And even if they did produce results, the ends would simply not justify the means.

If you're unsatisfied with answers to any of these questions, then the methods you're using to correct your pet aren't working. More importantly, if you haven't seen any results – real changes in your pet's behavior – then you can be sure your present methods aren't working either.

THE SOLUTION: CHANGE OF OWNER METHOD AND RESPONSE

It becomes obvious when a change of teaching method and owner response is necessary. It's really no more than common sense.

But step number two, choosing the correct modification method, depends on the misbehavior. This book will help you to match the correct action to the inappropriate behavior.

The third step is the most difficult. It involves altering normal human behavior while you teach your pet with the new correction methods. This doesn't sound especially hard, but overcoming old habits is never easy. When you've taught your dog one way (or, more likely, several ways) for a year or two, even to no avail, **you're conditioned.** You have to break through that conditioning.

What you'll have to train yourself to do will be very new...and for good reason: Animals perceive things differently than people do. But to communicate you need a common frame of reference. And because no one can change a dog's perspective, you have to change yours.

You can't change the way your dog learns, but you can change the way you teach.

Why Change Is Difficult

You have to change the way you think and respond in relation to your dog.

This may sound like an easy answer. Nothing could be further from the truth. This is a very difficult principle to apply. Why?

For one thing, it's hard to convince some owners that their years of experience may not be enough. Many people have owned dogs all their lives, but this may total only three or four dogs. That's not a lot of experience in the field.

So when they get a new dog, and it doesn't respond to their techniques, they're stunned...but they remain certain that it will come around to their way of thinking.

They may even think they have a lemon on their hands; that their dog is weird, dumb or difficult. Yet they continue to use the same old techniques, hoping the dog will eventually figure it out.

It doesn't, of course. Because three lifetimes worth of owner experience – even in dog years – isn't likely to stack up to the knowledge of a *Pet Behavior Specialist.* We're out there doing it every day with dogs of every description. So we're more likely to have the right prescription.

Common sense solutions are easily executed. Changing a life-time of human habit is not.

For instance, there's a simple solution to most destructive chewing problems: Give your dog an appropriate size rawhide chew bone **only** when you're **away** from home.

But what happens when an owner is asked to execute this plan? Some say they don't want to take the rawhide away from their dog when they get back home because of the time and effort it takes. Or the slobber they have to withstand. Others are worried because the dog might choke in their absence. (Forget that their dog has been happily chewing the bones they've given her for years with no choking problems.) Still others note that without its rawhide, their dog aggravates them.

All these excuses amount to one thing: a dog that still has a destructive chewing problem.

Once you make a final decision that your dog's behavior **must change,** and you're determined to achieve this goal, you'll have to set aside all excuses. Retraining a pet is no more than applying common sense continuously, consistently and determinedly.

DOGS ARE NOT HUMAN

Oftentimes, owners think that their dogs misbehave "to get back at them." Some even believe that their pets "hate them." They reason that they've just coerced their dog into doing something it didn't want to do, so misbehaviors are pet retribution.

This is simply not true. Pets *can't* reason like humans do. They *can't* think logically like a person; they *don't* have the emotions of a person; they *can't* talk; they *can't* spell; and they *don't* earn a living.

Pets act the way they do because they're behaving in normal pet ways.

But still, incredibly, it's common for human beings to attribute human reasons for everything their pets do. In fact, it's critically important that pet owners understand that their dogs **aren't** human beings. ***They are animals!***

Yet I come across more owners who actually believe their pets can spell. Of course this is patently impossible. Pets may respond to how an owner pronounces a word, or to what their owner does afterward. But they most certainly can't spell. Here's Happy to spell it out for you with a story.

The Master and I were visiting friends on the West Coast, when the adult male of the human household boldly announced that Max could spell.

Right away I thought to myself, "Oh no, here we go again."

But The Master was even faster. He said, "The best way to find out if Max can spell is to give him a test."

"A test?" asked our host, ready to protest.

"A spelling bee," The Master continued.

"Okay," said Max's owner, "ask him to spell 'out.' He knows that word."

The Master looked right at Max, who met his gaze. "Max," he said, "I'm going to spell a word for you. I want you to tell me what it is."

Max looked forlornly over in my direction, then back.

"O U T," spelled The Master. Nothing happened.

"O U T," The Master repeated. Again nothing.

Max's human jumped in to save his puppy's reputation. "You're not doing it right," he offered. "You spelled it wrong!"

"What do you mean I spelled it wrong?" said The Master. "How can you spell a three-letter word wrong?"

"Very easily," said Max's human, scrambling. "Let me show you the right way."

He grabbed the dog's face and held it in place to ensure eye contact, and then he spelled it out for ol' Max in long drawn-out vowels and consonant: "O U T!"

All he had to do was ask. Max could've told him he couldn't spell...but he didn't want to break his human's heart, so he went along with the charade.

All this doesn't make Max any less of a dog. We dogs don't hear English language, or even words, like you humans do. We respond to sounds.

We may sit at the dinner table with humans, but we'll still eat like dogs. Sometimes we may even try to mimic human behavior, but we always revert to our own dog behaviors. We're very comfortable with them. And we're proud to be able to stand on our own four paws and pontificate on the subject.

Just don't ask us to spell it!

Normal human tendencies are never a good thing to rely on when training your dog. You can't treat a dog like a human; you need to handle it like a dog.

In fact, many dogs just can't adapt to being treated like people. These become problem pets. Or perhaps, more accurately, those pets have encountered some problem humans.

Further, when animals are confused, they become frustrated. They don't like being unable to predict what happens next, so they deal with it by taking an active stance. These manifest themselves in what are called "Fight or Flight" responses.

We see some of these same responses in humans. But we tend to deal with them logically. Sometimes, in the course of events, our children go through little blue periods. Often, we can talk them logically through their troubles. Sometimes, we need to give them some reassurance.

Such techniques work for people. They do not work for animals.

You can't reassure a frightened pet out of a Flight response. It is true that you can encourage a pet to come out from a hiding spot with soothing words, food rewards and petting. But by doing so, you may actually be reinforcing the negative behavior of being frightened and hiding. Positive reinforcement has a way of doing just that.

The correct response in this situation would be for you to ignore your dog until she comes out on her own. Then, lavish her with plenty of affection.

With people it's a reasoning process; with dogs it's a conditioning process. And there's a world of difference between the two.

No one truly knows what pets think, but their behaviors are quite obvious. So are the effects of their actions.

Sometimes, the behavior of people isn't as easy to comprehend. But the effects of our actions are just as easy to see. And, ultimately, these actions – and their effects – can be devastating to a dog if they're not carried out with his needs in mind.

Most of the time, what people have in mind is themselves. No, not in a selfish way. Almost the opposite. In fact, if anything, these owners are very selfless and caring, if a bit misguided.

They see how they're supposed to treat their dog, and they know they wouldn't want this done to themselves...or to their children.

They feel guilty, especially when using confinement techniques, or training collar methodology. They can't see themselves in the confined space of a kennel; they hate to diet, so even if it's absolutely essential, they're automatically against withholding food or water.

But they are people, not dogs. And dogs live by a different set of rules. Your dog appreciates being treated like a dog, just as humans appreciate being treated like people.

This brings us to the final proof that your dog is not human. Point to it and ask any family member what they see.

They may say the dog's name first, but when you press them, they will say, "I see a dog." **Never forget this.**

If you're **still** not convinced, ask yourself a simple question: When was the last time you saw a human drinking from the toilet?

BEHAVIOR MANAGEMENT PLANS FOR OWNERS

A *Behavior Management Plan* is a necessity because dogs are extremely clever at teaching their masters new tricks. Controlling humans is really what being a pet is all about! They think of their human as just another animal. And it's their conscious goal to control as much of your behavior as they possibly can!

Hence, the need for a plan. Think about it. *Behavior Management Plans* are not created for an animal to follow, they're written for you to follow!

First, you'll need to identify several things in order to prepare an effective plan for your specific needs:

1. your dog's specific misbehavior;

2. your own reactions to this misbehavior;

3. the changes you need to make to your own behavior, immediately, consistently and using only one method.

A **Behavior Management Plan** is the primary tool of the *Pet Behavior Specialist.* You – as the owner – must agree to it and understand it before implementation. The *Plan* is a working process which allows you to work directly and consistently with your dog on a continuing basis. The ultimate goal is to change your dog's behavior to one that's acceptable to you.

Plans are flexible in nature. Sometimes, the agreed-upon changes to your behavior need to be altered or refined to fit unique circumstances. Alternative processes are available for substitution. What matters is finding the correct process for each of your pet's particular misbehaviors.

An integral part of the **Behavior Management Plan** calls for you to set up situations in which your pet will misbehave. I have found this to be a much sounder approach than sitting by idly hoping to catch a pet in the act.

For example, you might pretend you're on the telephone if that is when your puppy always acts up. Or you might ask a friend to ring the doorbell if your dog tends to"over-greet" visitors to your home.

Purposely inducing the misbehavior allows you to prepare for the correction in advance of the event.

At the same time, the goal of a new *Plan* is to break you of any old, disruptive habits. **That's the central premise of this book.** And also one of the most difficult to accomplish.

Take the overused command, "No."

When applied to pet training, the use of this single word is probably the most difficult habit of all to break when your pet misbehaves.

How often do use use the word, "No!" during a year? Think about it. A thousand times? Two thousand? More?

Learning not to say, "No!" can be extremely challenging. Most people don't even realize they're saying it.

When you enter a room, and find your dog sitting on a couch – against house rules – you should grab your pet's training collar and pull it down to the floor.

Instead, an owner usually says, "No. Get down." Then she pulls the dog down off the couch.

Verbalization is such an instinctive response to people that we just don't realize we're doing it! But the first step in breaking a habit is recognizing that it exists!

Actually, I classify "No," "Bad Dog" and "Get Down" as warning signals. An illustration of the warning signal occurs when your dog jumps up to greet a person, or show affection.

"Get down," you say, and your dog obeys.

How do you respond to this situation? Most owners respond by saying, "Good dog."

But what does your dog actually learn from this exchange? She learns that it's fine to jump on you, until you tell her to get down. And then you'll reward her!

This is probably not what you intended to convey. But that's the message that got through to your dog, who has, in fact, obeyed you in every detail. On the whole, there's not a lot for you to be happy about in this situation. Yet, this is very common for misbehaviors that occur infrequently.

Owners often unknowingly use these verbal warning signals, which actually tip a dog to your next move. They tend to stop a behavior, in progress, that you don't mind seeing **on occasion**.

What you need are actions rather than words.

When you decide you're truly ready to eliminate the misbehavior, just grab your dog by the training collar and **say nothing**. Pull your dog off of you and down to the floor. This method teaches the dog to associate the corrective stimulus with the misbehavior. The dog learns, "When I jump on people, I get corrected."

Next, it learns that the best way to avoid the correction is not to jump on people. This will be addressed in detail in Chapter 13, *Other Dog Misbehaviors*.

At the same time, a **Behavior Management Plan** must be convenient for you. This is not a small factor. If the steps in the *Plan* aren't expedient, you're not likely to follow through with them. In order for the *Plan* to work, it must be something that you:

1. can be convinced to try;

2. are willing to do;

3. can execute easily;

4. have time to perform.

But if you're unwilling or unable to meet any one of these four criteria, your *Plan* isn't worth the paper it's printed on.

Any **Behavior Management Plan** needs to be developed to fit your specific needs and circumstances. After all, only you can transform your dog. Nonetheless, there are many self-described *"Pet Behavior Specialists"* or trainers out there who never address the owner's role, or your relationship with your pet. If you come across a practitioner with this philosophy, walk away at once.

But when you find a reputable *Pet Behavior Specialist*, and you follow your **Behavior Management Plan** diligently, you're likely to be successful with your training. The rate of successful behavioral change is astounding. (See "Successful Cure Statistics" in Chapter 14, entitled *Handling The Occasional Relapse*.)

TYPES OF OWNERS

Happy has some definite opinions about the owners we've encountered during our travels together. He's identified some patterns that may give us some insight into owner personality types, and how these traits may affect owner relationships with their dogs.

We dogs have studied the human race for thousands of years now. I myself have devoted 12 years to the study of canines and their humans. And what I've discovered is that it takes all kinds. There are humans of every shape and size for us to choose from. And that's good because it means we can match our humans to our needs.

Humans tend to respond instinctively towards their dogs. But humans think differently than we do. So sometimes it can be difficult to determine just how they'll respond in certain circumstances. Over the years I've identified a number of "personality patterns" and the factors that I've seen impact habitual human behaviors.

These may include a human's emotional make-up, present mood, financial status, what the neighbors may think...even, believe it or not, their current attire. It may also include the dog's physical size.

Some of these human traits may sound quaint, or even absurd, to the average dog, but we need to be cognizant of the factors that impact human decision-making so we can comfortably predict your behavior.

77

Let's examine each characteristic:

• *Emotional Make-Up*

  Certain types of humans have a tendency to puppy their dogs. These people are often very shy, or elderly. Others just don't have an aggressive bone in their bodies. Now don't get me wrong, every dog loves to be pampered, no matter how old he is. But babying can result in increased expectations on the part of the dog, a lack of discipline...and even prima donnas.

Other types of humans are more aggressive. This can be a good thing. It helps us to establish the ground rules of life in human society. But there can be problems with overly-aggressive humans. The "macho" type seems to feel he can kick anyone around, canine or human. He has a tendency to correct us more than he should.

Still others feel the need to correct us in public because it makes them feel tough. But in the eyes of their pack, they're often regarded in the opposite light, as too weak to treat their dog with love and respect.

*Obviously, these are very general sketches of people, and they are **not** the typical humans owned by dogs.*

• *Present Mood*

An owner's mood changes according to the many small things that happen to her in a given day. The human world is much more complicated than the canine world we've created for ourselves. So we have to watch out for quirks in the human continuum. Did they have a bad day at work? Did they get caught up in traffic on the way home?

Good moods mean good times. Humans act much more like canines when their spirits are high. But bad moods make overcorrection more likely. Fortunately for us, most humans are quite well-centered.

• *Financial Status*

It's funny, but money can be a big factor in the amount of time a human is willing to invest in his dog. As a rule, the larger the income, the less time they have for us. These humans are often more difficult to train because they run on extremely busy schedules. At the same time, they're usually willing – and able – to spend more on outside analysts and trainers for their pets.

Curiously, the more affluent may also be willing to endure a pet "misbehavior" longer, because they have the money to replace belongings damaged by dog destructiveness.

• *Nosy Neighbors*

We dogs are driven to chase bones. Humans are driven to keep up with the Jones. There's nothing wrong with either agenda. But both have an impact on how humans interact with their hounds.

When it comes to correction, what do the neighbors think? Well, inside the home a misbehavior is automatically met with the appropriate correction method. But outside the home, in full view of the neighborhood, the correction may not be as consistent.

The same is true with human children. Inside the home, children are corrected for their misbehaviors. But outside the home, something inside a human makes it hard for her to admit that her child has done anything wrong. And corrections in public? Not likely!

In a shopping mall, children frequently misbehave because they know their parents hate to cause a scene. Pets are often seen stealing this scenario.

• *Current Attire*

As silly as it sounds, what you're wearing has a big impact on how you interact with your pet. You're dressed for training success when you're wearing blue jeans. But a dog doesn't know by your clothes that you're raring to go for a walk; or that if she jumps on you, you'll give her a friendly pat.

Nor does she know that a tuxedo or evening gown means that she needs to keep down because you have plans for a special night on the town.

This can be very confusing for us. We can't tell cut-offs from a cummerbund. We don't wear clothes, remember?

• *Pet Dimensions*

All humans tend to treat large dogs differently than they do the miniatures. That's only common sense. After all, everyone knows an 80-pound German Shepherd can do a lot more damage than a two-pound Daschund pup.

But remember, any self-respecting dog is going to defend himself – or his domain - when challenged.

The Master and I were guests at an out-of-town party several years back. Hosting the event were a young human couple and their children.

Apparently, the couple had agonized over this party because their four-year-old Miniature Daschund, Tony, had been very aggressive lately with family and neighbors alike.

During the party, Tony came face-to-face with one of the other guests who was sitting on the floor. That's when the party games started. Tony bit down on this gentleman's index finger as hard as he could. What was worse, he wouldn't let go.

The guest shot up from his sitting position with Tony dangling precariously from the end of his finger. While he shook his hand back and forth in the air, Tony continued to raise a ruckus, growling fiercely. All the while the little dog hung on, determined to make his point with his tiny canine teeth.

The guest didn't know whether to laugh or cry!

Finally, one of his humans grabbed Tony, properly, by the back of his neck near the collar, correcting him. With that, the Daschund finally released his hostage finger.

But that didn't end the dispute. When his human put him down, Tony attacked again, lunging at the bewildered guest in classic German Shepherd form. He got a good grip on the guest's pant leg, clinging relentlessly.

Eventually, Tony tired. His humans were able to dislodge the deranged little dog, and to calm him down.

With the victim's needs attended to, and the other guests gathered around to survey the damage, a remorseful host asked The Master if the Daschund's behavior was correctable. (It was.)

"Why?" The Master responded dryly. "He's the life of the party!"

"Maybe," she answered. "But we don't want any lawsuits!"

I always thought this was a pretty funny story, but there's no great moral to it. Nobody's life was threatened; no stitches were necessary. Even under an attack that ferocious, the damage that a Miniature Daschund can do is minimal!

OWNER MISBEHAVIORS

Now that you know a little more about the quirks and circumstances that can affect the relationship between you and your dog, you'll be better prepared to carry out your **Behavior Management Plan**.

But there are also a number of common owner misbehaviors that can inhibit the training process. You'll need to address these before you'll have any success modifying your pet's behavior. They include, but are not limited to:

1. Over-Verbalization

Simply, over-verbalization is an owner talking too much during the training process; yelling; shouting; or saying, "No!" These sounds send confusing signals to your dog.

Usually, over-verbalization is the result of impatience or frustration. It is a bad training habit based on human emotion. Often, it is done unconsciously. In many cases, unknowing owners will even deny that they've used the word "No."

2. Physically Hitting The Pet

Hitting is the worst of the owner misbehaviors. It is a response built upon anger and ignorance.

3. Weak Resolve

Many owners don't offer a measured response to their pet's misbehaviors. A weak correction sends all the wrong signals to a wayward dog, and is typically based on the unfounded fear of injuring the pet.

4. Panic

Panic can lead to problems of inconsistency in the appropriate application of the proper correction.

Sometimes this emotion is understandable – as when a dog licks a very tiny baby's face. Although this action may be unanticipated, you must avoid the temptation to alter your pattern of correction.

Many owners, in a case like this, will lose control. Their response is an over-correction, either in duration or intensity. This type of response will confuse a dog.

5. Inconsistent Responses

If your Chocolate Lab jumps up on the couch and your son joyfully wrestles with it while you're trying to teach the dog to stay off of the furniture, you may have a problem.

This problem will be reinforced later if your husband allows the dog to climb up there with him while he watches the game.

Eventually, when you get home after a long, hard day at work, if you catch that dog up on the couch, you're going to correct her in accordance with your **Behavior Management Plan**.

Two out of three times on the couch, your dog has received a significantly positive response. She thinks she's doing something appropriate. But when you're on the scene, your Lab knows she's in big trouble on that same couch. This means utter confusion for the pet.

Try to make sure that everyone in your family is on the same page of your *Plan*. This is the only way to ensure the consistency you need for successful training.

The long and short of it is that most owners are willing to let their dogs have control in small, incremental instances each day. It's important for your dog to know when he may have control and when he may not.

Ultimately, it is the confusion over this distinction that causes most dog misbehaviors.

Be aware of your dog's attempts to control you. Canines try many different tactics to try to control their humans' behavior. Some are acceptable and some are not. Make sure that you can tell the difference. Make sure you respond to these tactics appropriately:

- If your dog bares her teeth to get you to back off, correct her. This is unacceptable behavior.

- If your puppy drags your new $100 running shoes into the living room, and tests them out with his teeth, correct him. This is an unacceptable enticement for you to play with him.

- If that same puppy comes into your living room, climbs up onto the sofa, snuggles close and nudges your hand for petting, allow it (if he's allowed up onto the sofa). This is acceptable affectionate behavior, even if it takes a dozen nudges.

- If your dog learns to sit and longingly watch you eat a sandwich, to receive a morsel of food, allow it. This is acceptable behavior, whether or not you relent.

It's your responsibility to teach your dog the difference between acceptable and unacceptable behaviors. Your pet must learn the rules for its own good, and for that of the household.

All family members must work together consistently to reinforce those rules. That way, you'll have a better chance to train your dog – and to maintain her good behavior.

5

Why Dogs Develop Undesirable Behaviors

One of the first questions I'm asked by owners is *why* their pets have developed these new, unwanted, undesirable traits. The answer is never an easy one. That's because, usually, it's the owner's fault.

Now please don't panic here, or strike a defensive stance. Think back to how we defined a pet misbehavior. If you'll remember, it is simply a behavior that you don't like. Further, 97 to 99% of what we'd classify as misbehaviors are *normal* dog behaviors that we just don't want to see in the human home, or outside it.

Things are different for dogs in their own environment. There, the word "misbehavior" is a misnomer. In the wild, dogs will do what comes naturally to them. To make a temporary sleeping den, they'll circle repeatedly, bunching up leaves and debris. Getting comfortable is an instinctive behavior.

But back home, humans may be uncomfortable with this tendency. "Debris" may be something entirely different to you or me. Like a sentimental souvenir, an expensive heirloom or your intimate apparel!

If your dog chews on an old sock, it's not a problem; but if she chews on an antique chair, it becomes a misbehavior. Immediately.

The point is that it takes an owner to step in and say, "Okay, now we have a problem. I don't like what's going on."

Owners often wonder precisely why their pets misbehave. But pinpointing the problem is almost always impossible. And counter-productive. That's because the purpose is usually to point fingers. But identifying the cause *can* be valuable if it will help you to effect change.

Unfortunately, the factors that will affect your pet's performance are infinite. It may be illness. It may be something physiological. Or you may be causing it yourself, unconsciously. Here are a few examples:

- Urination or defecation problems may be triggered by a temporary bladder infection or a brief illness, causing as little as a single loss of control.

- Watching out a window, your dog may be excited by something he sees, causing him to jump down and "go" in an inappropriate spot.

- A pet rescued from an industrial setting may have problems distinguishing your clean linoleum from a dirty factory floor.

- To a young puppy, chewing on a chair leg may seem no different than chewing on a stick outside in the yard.

- If you give your dog an old, dilapidated shoe to gnaw on when she first comes into your home, she won't be able to discern the difference between it and your new Nikes the next week.

- An assertive dog may hold a set of keys in his mouth and growl aggressively. When you trade those keys for a tasty milk bone, your dog might conclude, "Hmm, this is neat. I growl and get a treat."

In your mind, the problem has been solved. But actually, it's just been compounded. Interestingly, it's how the **person** perceives the situation that is usually incorrect.

A dog's perception is reality. They see things through eyes unclouded by human emotions. Everything is black-and-white. They do things instinctively, repeatedly. And they have their own set of rites and rituals. So it's easy for them to understand ours.

Like when you're preparing to leave the house. They pick up on the repetitive human behavior that suggests this may be so. This will excite your dog because there's a chance she might be allowed to accompany you.

Happy knows this situation very well. He lays down in the same place every time, on his stomach with his head between his front legs. He holds his tail very still, and looks up at me, plaintively asking to go along. Don't you Happy?

Sure I do. Most dogs prefer to travel with their humans. Going with you is always a positive; but staying behind is an even bigger negative. Why? Well, it all goes back to the pack. There, we ran together or we didn't run at all. So when you leave us at home, we can only see it as a punishment.

How do we respond? It depends on the situation. But when we're left behind, we're left wondering. We feel chastised. Frustrated. "Oh, what did we ever do to deserve this treatment?" And this can be a problem for you, if we're left to our own devices.

Now I've worked with The Master long enough to know that this isn't what you have in mind. But I also know what goes through the mind of a distraught dog who's left behind.

To distract themselves, they'll do just about anything: dig dirt out of a planter; chew on the new couch; pee in the middle of the dining room rug.

*Gee, that would even make a dog like me feel better! And I **know** better. It's what we dogs do to release our frustrations. Unless our humans learn to master the situation.*

PET PERCEPTIONS

Remember, a pet is not a human being. Your dog interacts with her world, and reacts to its stimuli, with the instincts of an animal.

How Pets Learn

In Chapter 6 I'll describe how animals learn through conditioning. For this reason you must recognize that you can't change the way your pet learns. To achieve your desired outcome, you have to change the way you teach.

Emotion is the complicating factor. When people teach their dogs to sit, for instance, they may say, "Sit," and then use the training collar when she doesn't. That's all well and good...until she repeatedly fails to perform on command. That's when owners can become frustrated, even angry. And it can be a vicious cycle as the dog recoils or retreats in fear and bewilderment. At this point, owners often show their impatience by physically pushing the dog's back end to the ground and yelling the command.

This only confuses the dog. And it often results in behavior best described as out-of-control. Dog and owner alike.

So how do you bring things back under control? Consistent behavior...on the part of the pet *owner*. This is, quite simply, the only way to get through to a dog – because dogs think differently.

How differently do dogs think? Think about it.

Consider how you drive your car. When you're confronted by a red light, you put your foot on the brake to slow your vehicle. And as time passes, this becomes a mindless task for you. You don't even think twice about it, let alone *how* to do it.

But for your dog, nothing ever becomes a mindless task. He always has to work through that initial thought process.

Yes, as an animal he thinks, but he does so differently than we do. Your pet doesn't plan ahead. He doesn't think, "Now if I'm driving a car and I come to a red light, this is what I'll do."

Instead, he would get into your car and drive until he came to the light. **Then** he'd start to think about it. And the thought process is always the same.

How Pets Perceive Their Environment

Dogs have all of the same senses that humans do. But compared to us, their senses are very different in relative strength and sensitivity. So you should know that dogs do *view* their environment much like we do...and they *hear* it, too. But most importantly, they *smell* it!

The sense of smell is a dog's most vital sense. It enables them to seek out toys, to find their food and toilet area, and to detect what type of animal they're encountering.

Simply stated, scent is how a dog figures everything out.

Dogs make determinations about everything in their environment through their sense of smell. Sure, sight may help them to recognize an object, but they can't tell what it is all about until they smell it.

Or they may first hear something. They may even bark at it or run to it. But when they arrive, they'll smell it thoroughly to evaluate what it is and how it will act.

Smell is also a dog's guide to moving through its environment. A kind of divining rod for daily life. For dogs, it's the scent that pays the rent. And an aroma is worth a thousand words. This is very different from people, who rely more on their vision.

For us, seeing is believing. And what we see is what we get. Take a simple walk through your neighborhood. You watch the neighbor kids grow up. You keep an eye out for strangers. New landscaping gives you a different perspective on that old house. But all in all, the scenery never changes much. Note the choice of verbs in this description. See what I mean? People know what will happen by sight; dogs know what will happen by smell.

Dogs have an even more impressive sense of smell than cats do, even though cats have been effectively using this sense for many more generations. A dog's sense of smell is more finely tuned, and they use it over a longer range.

That makes it ideal in the shorter-range setting of the human home. There, even hearing-impaired dogs have absolutely no problem getting along, because they don't need their sense of hearing to survive. None of us do. But without a sense of smell, that same dog would be defenseless...out of touch with her environment.

Happy has a pal named Sam, a cute little Corgi, who illustrates this point perfectly. If his owner puts Sam's food on the floor near him, he will sit and look in its general direction, not seeing it at all. Then his nose kicks in, and he gets a whiff of chicken and cheese. Yum! Obviously, aroma doesn't travel at the speed of light, but to Sam, it's worth the wait.

You feed and water your dog before leaving for work in the morning. So what does she do during business hours? First she eats. Then she drinks. And finally she falls asleep. After her snooze she'll sniff around the house looking for the proper area for elimination. That is, a site she's used before.

Along with finding nourishment, locating the proper toilet area is another very important use of a dog's sense of smell. Without it, dogs would never find their toilet area. Instead, they would go indiscriminately all around the house.

But dogs are definitely discriminating creatures. Although they don't understand human language, they do understand sound. They just don't perceive these human "sounds" the same way that people do.

For example, there is the human sound, "No!" Every family I know uses this word so often that it's almost impossible to break the habit.

To a human, the "No" sound means: "Stop doing that and don't ever do it again!"

To a dog, the same sound means: "I'm allowed to do whatever I'm doing until I hear this loud, distinctive sound, and then I have to stop."

So again, using the same sense – in this case the sense of hearing – dogs perceive their environment very differently than we do.

The sense of sight is equally different for dogs. They don't see things as clearly as people do. They see their surroundings in more shadowy terms. To a dog, "full color" means black-and-white with only the most vibrant hues coloring their world.

As we review specific misbehaviors throughout this book, you'll come to a better understanding of how your pet's senses influence their perspective. But most dogs exhibit normal dog behaviors in their adopted environment. It's very rare to see problems caused by **abnormal** dog behavior.

How Dogs Perceive Human Beings

These days, human beings are **the** significant stimulus in a domestic animal's environment. But that's not how your dog sees you. He sees your household the same way he sees any other group of animals: as a pack.

So when your pet looks at you, he doen't see a husband, a wife or a child. He sees a challenge to his position in the social order. He sees just another animal with which he must deal – and which he wants to dominate.

Unfortunately, in the canine clan, not everyone starts out on equal footing in the hierarchy. In fact, what we're talking about is purely patriarchy.

In pack studies, we've found that it's always the male dog that is in control. Male dogs lead. Male dogs enforce. As a rule, male dogs just aren't challenged by female dogs, which tend to back down more easily.

All in all, all dogs view male dogs with more respect. This view also extends to their relationship with the human pack, within which they respect male human beings more than female human beings.

This may sound like a very different kind of animal, often found running in human circles, what we used to call the Male Chauvinist Pig. Domination was his game, too.

But in canine circles, the chauvinism extends to the opposite sex, too. Even **female** dogs hold human females in lower regard. And fair or not, we can't do anything to change it. It's axiomatic. It's just the way animals are.

Actually, pets probably think about their people in animal terms, just like some people tend to think about their pets in human terms. Because that's what they know.

If dogs could talk, they'd probably say, "My owner learns like a dog. He gets down on the floor and plays with me like a dog. He must be a dog!" How human of them!

Dogs may even see canine characteristics in their owners. Perhaps Happy can shed a little light on this perception.

Sure, I've walked a mile in The Master's Hush Puppies (two pair) so I have a good idea about how he'll see certain things. But most dogs aren't as lucky as I am. Their view is all dog. And they see their humans' actions accordingly. Here are some examples of what I mean:

- *When you stand up and peer down at a dog, she can only see it as an aggressive stance...the same as if a strange dog were to approach, raise its hair, lift its shoulders and stare down at her.*

- *The way we see it, your hand serves the same function as our mouth — we both use them to grab hold of things, discipline, and move objects.*

- *In our world, if one dog wants another to back off, it will growl ferociously. When they do, the second dog will sometimes leave. Most dogs find that this works in the human world, too. When we want you to back off, we'll growl fiercely; and like that second dog, sometimes you'll turn away, too.*

- *You also play the same games. If a young puppy has a stick and another dog wants it, the dog chases the puppy and tries to take it away. If a puppy has a very expensive wallet (with a lot in it) and you want it, you chase the puppy and try to take it away, too! Just the same.*

- *When two of us play roughly, or get into a dogfight, the winner will be the one who grabs the other by the back of the neck, throws it onto its back, then grabs it by the throat.*

Perhaps this sounds primitive to a more "enlightened" species, but it works. (And I see worse on the tube all the time. Except in the dog shows, of course.)

So if you really want to discipline your dog, do it like we do. Mimic us. Start by grabbing your four-legged friend by the back of the neck. This will give you the upper paw!

Unfortunately, I've seen too many humans try other, more eccentric measures. Everything from kidney punches to professional wrestling maneuvers.

There's nothing in our world to compare with these techniques...or to prepare us for them. So when a human resorts to them, we don't know what to think. Except that maybe you're not a dog after all.

Return a moment to Happy's third example. Because **Tricks I Taught My Master** is concerned mostly with misbehaving pets, it is important for you to understand that *most pets perceive their human owners as very inconsistent, unpredictable animals.*

The reason for this is simple. If one dog steals another dog's bone, the bone owner approaches the thief and growls; and the other dog backs off. That's about the only response that the bone owner is going to receive.

But if you replace the bone in this example with a brand new sweater, and the owner is a human, the dog still sees the situation as the same. Unfortunately, we don't see it that way, do we? If your dog steals your favorite sweater, you might respond to him in any number of ways. You might:

- Discipline him correctly.

- Chase him.

- Decide that you're just too tired to deal with it that particular evening, and walk away.

- Ignore him.

- Divert him with food in an attempt to rescue your sweater.

As owners, we vary our responses because we have emotions. And beyond the love we have for our pets, anger, frustration and impatience can often affect how we respond to them.

For the dog this is a real dilemma. They just don't know how to deal with this phenomenon. Here's Happy to explain what may be happening inside your dog's head.

Let me start by saying that every dog on the planet thinks that humans should have their heads examined. We're just not cruel enough to subject anyone to a "cat" scan.

Besides, it doesn't take a brain surgeon to diagnose what's wrong with humans. You're the very model of inconsistency. We never know what your next move will be. And I doubt that you do either, with all those emotions running free.

But there's no prescription for unpredictability. And that's what we find so stressful. As dogs, our expectations are simple. We know precisely what response is appropriate in any given situation. Hey, we're social animals. So if you're inconsistent, it really complicates matters for us.

Stress is the number one complication. We don't deal well with stress. As a species we just don't take enough vacations. Instead, we look for something to chew on. Or worse. As a dog, I'll be the first to tell you that relieving yourself is excellent for frustration relief.

Another way we release stress is to attack the cause. Sometimes literally. Some dogs will act very aggressively to make a doggone inconsistent human go away.

Fortunately, you have to go pretty far before most dogs will resort to this approach. And if you use your noggin, you can avoid such confrontations altogether.

From a dog's-eye view people *are* unpredictable. And it's this disparity that's at the root of all problems between pets and owners.

Fortunately for us, dogs are different from other domestic animals. They're giving...and forgiving. And so persistent. They seek out their owners much more often than house cats do.

Happy follows me everywhere, even from room to room. Cats don't usually do this. It hasn't been expected of them for thousands of years.

So dogs interact with their owners hundreds of times more than their cat counterparts. This means that cats have to react to human unpredictability a lot less often than dogs do, even though they're more capable of controlling people.

Still, all dogs seem to know, instinctively, that in spite of the unpredictability of their owners, certain behaviors will control them. Happy may not be The Master of Control, but he's certainly got the techniques down pat.

What can you tell us, partner?

We dogs may not have the array of emotions that you humans have, but we sure do know how to play on them. Let me see if I can give you an example without giving away any trade secrets.

Certain scenarios seem to sucker you every single time. Try this one. No matter what kind of mood you're in, if the dog you live with sits there quietly, puts her ears back, and gives you those big, batty eyes, she's got you under her paw!

Another trick of the trade is the panhandle. You'll know you've been had if your dog lays his nose down, raises his paw in the air and gives a little whimper. It's hard to resist responding to measures like this.

Now you may not believe me, but I'll tell you that we don't consciously plan little play-actions like these. But somewhere in there is the knowledge that we can control you when we want to.

But we know to bring out the big ones only when we really need them. We'll save them for just the right circumstances. Like when you're having pizza. Or when we want our tummies rubbed.

I'm still surprised humans are so gullible. I guess it's those same emotions that get you in trouble in the first place.

I only wonder why you expect so much less out of those darned cats. They seem to get away with everything. So naturally they see humans in less complicated terms. When they see you at all.

I know a black cat named Harley, who put it quite simply for me one day:

"I don't need the humans in this house. They're such a bother. If they get too close, or they do something I don't like, I'll just hiss at them and they'll go away. If they want to play, I'll just ignore them. And if they insist, I'll resist. Nothing speaks louder for a cat than our claws do!"

"Humans? Humbug. They're almost too easy to control. I've got it made!"

This may sound cocky to you, but if you look around you won't find many cats who would disagree. That is, if you can find one!

Both cats and dogs can fend for themselves for awhile in the wild – or in what passes for the wilderness these days – finding enough food and water to survive. But today, even cats have been provided for by humans for so long, that they rarely must make it on their own...let alone protect themselves.

Back on the domestic front, cats tend to look on the human being more like a servant, while dogs look at us more like masters.

How our pets perceive us is one thing. How they perceive our visitors is quite another. Often, the owners that I see claim that their dogs are only aggressive towards specific protagonists: like women wearing hats, or men with beards, or anyone in uniform.

Again, this is a misperception on the owner's part. Usually, what happens is that the owner tries to identify something that they feel is unique about a particular situation.

This deduction, however brilliant, is usually not the cause. Why? Well, to dispel any such theories, you have only to refer back to a pet's level of perception within its environment.

If you'll remember, a pet sees form, rather than precise figures, in basic black-and-white. So hats or beards or uniforms aren't likely suspects to trigger an unusual reaction.

Yet a hat or beard may hide a person's facial expression, presenting a new type of shadowy look to a dog. The forensics will probably be out forever on this case, because we just can't get inside the canine mind.

It could be that dogs classify humans in groups. If some *move* totally differently than all the others they know, they may give a different, and unexpected, reaction.

How Dogs View Other Animals

Dogs do perceive cats, squirrels, raccoons and other animals as different from themselves. Their exact perception depends on a number of variables, including: the location of the meeting, its suddenness, the movements the animal makes and what it smells like.

From there, a lot depends on how the dog has been taught to react to the animal in question. If he doesn't know how to react, he'll strike a classically confrontational posture. First, he'll check things out from a distance, his stance neutral. He won't retreat or move forward until the other animal makes a move, or picks up a scent.

Other animals present a more reliable, predictable picture to your pet than do most people.

Happy has three basic approaches when meeting a new dog, and he's met more pets than most dogs could ever hope to encounter.

In Approach One, he will trot fearlessly up to a new arrival, sniff it and immediately begin serious play activity. This is his: "You're consistent; you're not threatening" modus operandi.

Approach Two is Happy's "Run for Fun" response. In it, he'll instantly chase the other animal. This is definitely a species-specific scenario. He's never chased a bird, regardless of its type. He'll trot right by as if nothing is there.

A squirrel, on the other hand, offers an excellent opportunity for the obligatory chase scene. For Happy this means good exercise and a release of any pent-up frustrations. It's a fun game and no one's any worse for wear when it's over, because Happy hasn't ever caught up with his quarry.

Even cats aren't out of the question for this kind of confrontation...except for those occasional cats whom Happy senses will hold their ground on him, or worse yet, become the aggressor.

Happy, always on the lookout for a fun frolic, has even made a beeline for a big work glove, anticipating the chase all the way. I'd left the glove bunched up and sticking out of the grass, and he obviously mistook its small, shadowy shape for a savory squirrel or rabbit.

He chased the glove for a split second, then halted, confused because it didn't move. So he reverted to Approach One, sneaking-up on it instead. Still it didn't move. Finally, he did a little trot toward it. But it remained immobile. Eventually he walked right up to it, sniffed it and left, deeming it unworthy of his attention.

Approach Three is Happy's "Big Bertha" technique. In it, he gives the other animal a big, wide berth. It's always interesting to watch this approach in action. Happy only uses it when he's left alone with an unknown animal he doesn't want any part of.

Don't mistake the trappings of this approach. Happy never acts afraid of this potential threat, or even aggressive. Rather, he'll observe the stranger from the corner of his eye, pretending not to pay it any attention. All the while he'll watch it very carefully.

Happy keeps his distance from a dog when he's unsure if or when it will lash out at him.

In less structured situations, these distinct behaviors often blur. If Happy comes across a new dog while wandering in the yard, he'll watch it carefully out of the corner of his eye, while coming closer and closer to it. He'll take his time smelling and listening. Finally, he'll initiate play.

This hesitancy is understandable. Neither dog is quite sure of the other. So each will strike a neutral posture. But neither dog wants the other to think it too submissive or too aggressive. So the natural laws of the pack ultimately promote play.

To a dog, all animals are something to run to, or to run from. And each dog must decide what that animal's intentions are before making its choice on the proper approach to take.

Cats react to other animals very differently from the way that dogs do. They play differently, too. They're not stimulated to play as often, as easily, or for as long as dogs. Yet they may be drawn into play by a new, unique object...or by another cat.

In most cases, though, when one cat is approached by another cat for the first time, both cats will act tough and standoffish, rather than immediately entering into play, as dogs do.

Do dogs and cats ever play together? Of course they do. They're not natural enemies, no matter how they're portrayed in books and cartoons. They can live quite happily together.

But why, then, do dogs chase cats? Because chasing cats – or squirrels, or rabbits, or joggers – is a fun thing to do! And most animals will keep running, reinforcing the game for the dog. That is, until the cat turns around and claws it across the nose! Or until the squirrel climbs a tree. Or the rabbit ducks into its hole.

In households with both dogs and cats, it's usually the cats who rule the roost simply because they refuse to take any nonsense. If a dog bothers them, they run away or hide. When they're tired of being chased, they stand their ground, bat the dog in the nose, and hiss or spit at it.

It never takes long for a dog to decide that she values her life much more than a quick game of Cat and Mouse.

When you introduce a new pet of a different species into your household, allow the two to work out their living patterns on their own. For two weeks, let the dog chase. Let the cat run. Let the dog jump playfully on the cat. Let the cat spit.

In that time, they'll establish their own boundaries, if left to their own devices. Your cat will either escape his persecutor, or make a stand. Your dog will either continue the chase, or take some spit in the face.

Either way, the situation will work itself out. Because your cat and dog understand each other much more clearly than pets understand people!

In fact, rarely will a dog purposefully try to harm a cat, although it may not look that way to you. After all, you love them both. But if a real problem does develop, there's an easy solution. Make your dog sit, stay and be calm in the presence of your cat. And praise her lavishly when she does.

And one final word of caution on the relationship between cats and dogs. Size has nothing to do with it. So regardless of the size of your cat or kitten, be careful that your dog isn't hurt. Cats may be smaller, but they have a bigger selection of weapons at their disposal – one mouth and four sets of sharp claws!

THE COMMUNICATION GAP

There's a communication gap. It's been around for generations. But the one I'm talking about isn't the one you're used to hearing about.

Yes, that one still exists, too. It's the age-old rift between a 15-year-old and her 35-year-old parents. This child can't possibly understand everything with the same level of comprehension as her parents. Her thinking is limited by her relative lack of experience.

But this situation does provide us with a useful analogy. Because a similar gap exists between the way a pet thinks and the way a person thinks. And again, the difference is in the experience. It just isn't the same.

In Chapter 4, we compared normal behavior for dogs and for humans. And we found that there was no comparison. For pets and for people, the match is truly a bad one. But we can still make the relationship a good one.

We just have to remember that we can't use normal human behaviors to change normal pet behaviors. We need to adapt our actions to how our pets think, and what they will understand.

MISBEHAVIOR IS AN OWNER DECISION

It's your decision. That's what it comes down to. In my experience, 97 to 99% of all designated "misbehaviors" are actually **normal** behaviors for a dog. What does this mean?

It means that they only become misbehaviors when you decide you can't tolerate them.

There's nothing wrong with this decision on your part. But it's important to make the distinction if you want to solve your problem, because these normal dog behaviors include: eliminating where and when they choose to; chewing on the objects they choose to; being aggressive when they choose to; eating what they want, when they want to; and rising when they want to.

None of these actions is abnormal. And contrary to what many would like to believe, they don't indicate a retarded, schizophrenic, or depressed dog. They don't portend psychological problems of any kind.

So let's take a look a what is "normal." A classic example of a pet "misbehavior" concerns the family couch, and the dog's propensity for climbing onto it.

Of 100 families, only 50 may deem this couch-climbing a misbehavior. And of these 50, each will have its own definition of the proper – and improper – behavior:

- "I only want my dog on the couch sometimes."

- "I don't want my dog on the couch when people visit."

- "I want her on the couch only when I invite her up."

- "I want him on my old couch, but not on the new one."

Such minute discrepancies in the definition are difficult for a dog to digest. For most, there really isn't any difference in the distinction. They're either on or they're off.

"Either let me snuggle up in the corner of the couch with you, or teach me to stay off of it!"

Some dogs can, with a great deal of assistance, and persistence on your part, learn these subtle differences; others never do. More often than not, in the midst of this dilemma, a dog will learn to get onto the couch only when you're not at home.

And as adamant as some people are about couch-climbing, under any circumstances, many seem to find this situation humorous.

They tell me, "When I come home, I always hear a little thump from the vicinity of the couch. I feel it and sure enough, it's all warmed up for me. Sparky was on the couch the whole time I was gone!"

It seems that what these owners are really after is a dog that knows not to enjoy the couch in their presence. It's only a misbehavior if they're caught in the act!

But sometimes it's the humans who get "caught in the act." One day, Happy and I happened upon a most unusual situation; a love triangle between a Basset Hound, a young woman in her early thirties, and her newlywed husband. But there was something amiss amidst all this bliss.

Apparently, all it took was a wedding license to turn a longstanding dog-owner relationship upside down, and a welcomed pet behavior into an unwelcome misbehavior.

Happy and I tried to serve in the dual roles of *Pet Behavior Specialists* and Marriage Counselors. Here's the consummate counselor, Happy, with the details.

*One day, we got a call from a four-year-old Basset Hound named Bart, who'd been living with a human female for a number of years. Their relationship, he assured us, was a good one. That is, until **he** entered the picture.*

"He" was the female's new mate. They'd been married recently in a public ceremony. Bart had been too uncomfortable with the new arrangement to attend.

The problem started when the newlyweds returned from their honeymoon. Where did the problem start? In the master bedroom, of course. It was the stuff of TV dramas.

You see, this female had always allowed Bart to share her bed. He saw this as a warm gesture on the woman's part, accepting the courtesy. It was kind of a pre-nuptial agreement.

But three's a crowd, even on a king-sized mattress. And it wasn't long before the new husband was fit-to-be-tied with the situation. As far as he was concerned, Bart had no place in the bedroom.

"He takes up too much space," the husband complained of her canine companion. "And he snores, too."

Well, that was the last straw for the estranged dog. A minor dispute over the sleeping arrangements was one thing. Poor sportsdogship was quite another. That's when Bart asked us if we wouldn't mind coming over to train the human couple.

But by the time we arrived for our first session, things had gone from bad to worse. The male and the female weren't speaking to each other, and Bart was feeling responsible (but not sorry) for the situation.

The husband was beside himself. He felt that Bart stood in the way of the couple's, well, "interaction." Apparently, Bart had caught them "in action" the previous week. It was an open and shut case of "caninus interruptus." In the man's eyes, poor Bart was more than a distraction, he was a private nuisance.

Poor Bart had been so embarrassed, he'd blushed right through his fur. But this unfortunate incident only strengthened his resolve. He decided to take matters into his own paws. He wasn't about to give in to the newcomer, whom he saw as pushy and manipulative; and a blanket-hog, besides.

So Bart tried to reclaim his lost territory...by marking it. The night before we made the scene for our second session, he'd made a scene of his own by urinating on his rival's side of the bed. Even he now admits that, although his aim may have been noble, his methodology was somewhat off the mark.

The determined dog did register a direct hit. But all he "menaged" to do was to break up the shaky "trois."

The husband – realizing by now that he was a marked man – shot straight up into the air out of deep sleep, kicking, screaming and sputtering. Bart's mistress reacted just as quickly...and even more decisively. She banished Bart from her boudoir; retired him permanently, as a matter of fact, to his own dog bed.

By the time we arrived the following afternoon, it was all over but the shouting. There was still plenty of that going on, believe me. But the triangle was broken. And the affair was over.

This turned out to be a situation with a simple solution. And the couple figured it out for themselves. All they had to do was close the door on the ol' dog.

But occasionally, someone does call for assistance with a problem that isn't fixable. Some normal dog behaviors that turn into "misbehaviors" in the human home just can't be changed.

THE DEFINITION OF SUCCESS

Just as pet misbehavior is defined by the owner, so is the successful retraining of a pet. This is different from definitions of success in just about any other endeavor, where success usually implies 100% achievement.

But when applied to pet training, **success is defined as behavior that satisfies the owner.** When you're happy with the final outcome, the correction has been successful. Frequently, this even means that your pet will still show traces of the misbehavior, but reduced to a level with which you can comfortably live.

To the owners of a dog who's been urinating in the house three or four times a day, mistakes just once a week may be Utopia!

A good example is the story of Babe, a year-and-a-half old Bichon. Unfortunately, to her family, Babe was better known by her "pet" name: Public Enemy Number Two. Or "Number Two" for short.

Here's Happy to tell you why!

Babe's humans had a problem. She was a wonderful dog; friendly and even-tempered. But the young Bichon was defecating at will all over her house. Not a single room was safe. That's why the "Number 2" name stuck.

By the way, Bichons are notorious for their housebreaking problems. They just don't want to let go of the old canine ways. I've spoken to several about it, and they're quite adamant.

But in Babe's case, she was at least willing to compromise. The Master and I served as mediators. And after a lot of work, we arrived at an understanding.

The Master taught Number Two to "go" in just one place – the corner of the basement. Everyone agreed that they could live with this arrangement. In fact, her humans were ecstatic! And now Babe's back to Number One in their hearts again.

In the beginning, you may be willing to accept a less-than-perfect solution. Most owners seem to be happy with a pet that makes only a mistake or two per month.

Pet behavior can almost always be improved, though your pet will never be totally perfect. But there are points of diminishing return, after which the time commitment is too great for the likely results. In such cases, I'd recommend standard maintenance of your dog's training regimen, nothing more, nothing less.

Change never happens overnight...but it does happen. If you take the time and expend the effort.

6

How Dogs Learn

To train or retrain your dog, you need to understand how he learns. All animals learn through the conditioning process. But every species is different. The distinct learning patterns that distinguish dogs are determined by temperament, social conditioning and genetics.

Like all animals, dogs are blessed with a well-balanced arsenal of "in-born" behaviors, a kind of genetic guide book for any situation. Actions come to them instinctively, the same actions and reactions that their forefathers and foremothers relied on before them.

But instinct accounts for only a part of the canine parcel. Social conditioning completes the package.

The dog is a social animal. So if you want to track learning, you have to start with the pack. And if you want answers, you have to go right to the leader, which – in this case – is my partner, Happy.

HAPPY HELPS US WITH PACK BEHAVIOR

My four-legged forerunners ran in packs. Even contemporary canines will do so if left to their own devices. In fact, domestic dogs do, too – but the surprise is on you, because you're a part of it! So my question is, who domesticated whom?

Just so you know what you've gotten yourself into, let me review the pack system for you. The social dynamics are simple. There's one leader, and everyone else is a follower.

Human researchers who have studied the pack, like John Paul Scott in the 1970s, have determined that male dogs dominate the system. Now I have a lot of respect for John Paul. He worked like a dog...and, as a result, he found out how to think like one.

But let's hope Congress didn't spend millions in PAC-money on a social program like that! All they had to do was ask one well-adjusted dog, and he could've spelled it out for them.

Of course male dogs run the show in our society. We can't help it. We're not as enlightened as you humans are. In fact we're quite chauvinistic. Not that we're proud of it. It's just a part of us. And whether you're male or female, it will help you in your training if you remember this.

Perhaps it will help you to understand us if I tell you a little bit about how disputes are settled in a pack environment.

All disputes arise with a challenge to the leadership of the pack. Matters are settled the old-fashioned way: in a one-on-one, no-holds-barred, knock-down, drag-out dog fight.

The rules of the confrontation are few. You're the winner when you put yourself in a position to collapse your combatant's trachea.

Now humans always have the same reaction to this description. "Oooh, how primitive," or "How cruel." But really, it's no big deal. We've been settling arguments that way for millions of years. And our bodies are built to take the "punishment." Heck, our Moms use it on us when we're just pups!

It's only temporary, and certainly doesn't hurt. What it does do is get the message across loud and clear. The holder is telling the holdee, "I'm the one. I've proved my domination over you."

The bottom line is that this is how we dogs prove our superiority to each other...and this determines the leadership role for the pack. But you better be able to "make the mark" before you "bark the bark."

Female dogs just don't participate in this macho stuff. They never have. I've never actually seen one go for the throat when it comes to pack leadership without backing down readily.

But if they don't show much interest in pack politics, you should see the challenge a female dog puts up when it comes to her pups. And even in the human world, you've got to agree that her priorities are in the right place there.

So anyway, once you know the hierarchy, the next thing you need to know is how a dog projects the pack's social structure onto your household.

The scent of a woman immediately sends the wrong signal to dogs of either sex, who know innately that males are dominant. So training can be more difficult for women, because, in our culture, females aren't supposed to challenge the male leadership domain.

This position is often reinforced by the physical traits of the human sexes. Men tend to be larger and more commanding. (Clumsier and louder, many human females contend.) Either way, we dogs respect this kind of control.

To garner the same kind of respect, it's important for human females to exhibit a strong, persistent and consistent persona when training a dog. This is really the only way to guarantee that you'll get results.

The other thing that amuses us is when humans balk at some of the techniques and equipment used to train us. It's actually almost the same reaction they have to a pack challenge. Perhaps that's because the training collars are designed to mimic this quick, temporary and harmless tracheal collapse.

If you just try to remember that we're comfortable with this approach from the very beginning, perhaps you'll be better prepared for the whole training experience.

CONDITIONING TECHNIQUES

People are essentially logical beings. But because animals – and specifically dogs – do not act according to logic, the process used to train them is not one based on logic, but on conditioning. **This is important to remember. You can't expect a dog to react to human logic because it ISN'T human.**

One "logical" human reaction to a poor training session is the concept of canine reassurance. During training, when a misbehavior continues, an owner often seeks to reassure their pet with kind words and caresses. But dogs don't make this connection. They're "illogical." So they come away from this experience with exactly the opposite message. All that petting gives them positive reinforcement for their bad behavior.

Only when a pet performs the correct behavior is it proper to reinforce it positively.

But logic is not the tool that will cause this to occur. The right equipment and the techniques outlined in the remainder of this chapter will help you to condition your dog to respond as you wish.

Much of what you'll read is based on Pavlovian Theory. Ivan Petrovich Pavlov was a Russian physiologist who lived from 1849 to 1936. His best-known work demonstrated conditioned and unconditioned reflexes in dogs.

Happy has a few theories of his own on Mr. Pavlov and his work. And he's just salivating for the opportunity to tell you about them.

HAPPY HELPS US WITH PAVLOVIAN THEORY

Around the turn of the century a human named Ivan Pavlov pioneered work in the field of psychology that was destined to bring our two species closer together. Much too close, if you ask me. But maybe that's just my reflex reaction to his scientific method.

Ultimately, Pavlov's Theory greatly influenced the development of today's behaviorists in many fields. His work, I'm told, is studied in all modern psychology courses. It also has its place in the field of Pet Behavior. So let's take a closer look.

Pavlov suspended a canine partner (who has received none of the credit for this breakthrough work) in a harness. A small electrode was then attached to the hind leg of his accomplice. This fiendish contraption was rigged to send a small shock to the sensibilities of the suspended scientist.

With everything in place, Pavlov proceeded. He allowed his assistant to hear a tone. This tone was consistent from one to the next at a set decibel level. Then, exactly 1.8 seconds after each tone, the harnessed hound received a shock.

As history tells it, this was an enlightening experience for everyone involved. Especially after three or four tries, when it finally dawned on the dog that the tone meant he was going to be shocked. Remember, we dogs live for the moment, so it takes us some time to put two-and-two together.

About this time, the Pup On The Way Up was ready to opt out of the experiment. In fact, he started thrashing about pretty well...even before the shock arrived. He was anticipating the moment, so to speak, just as Pavlov had conditioned him.

Well, during one of these episodes, this daring dog just happened to touch two metal plates together somewhere above his head. That sneaky Pavlov had positioned these there to inhibit the shock. So when his assistant made the connection, all he got was a tone.

Well, it didn't take long for the dog to figure this out. He may have said to himself, "There's that danged tone again. I wish I could high-tail it out of here before the shock."

But then, in an instant, he remembered his conditioning, "But if I push these two metal plates together with my head, I won't get shocked at all."

Sooner than later, when the dog heard the tone, he remained calm, simply lifting his head after every tone, and heading off the shock.

What does all this mean? It means that what Pavlov lacked in bedside manner, he made up for with brains. He and his forgotten partner proved that dogs learn through conditioning.

Pavlov's conditioning theory applies directly to you when you're training your dog:

- Pavlov's tone is replaced by your command: "Sit."

- Pavlov's shock is replaced by your jerk on the training collar.

- Pavlov's partner lifting his head to inhibit the shock is replaced by your dog touching her rear to the ground.

When you're teaching your dog to sit, make sure you jerk her training collar within two seconds after saying the command one time. After three or four tries, she will learn that "Sit" means: "I'm about to have my collar jerked."

To avoid the jerk of the training collar, your dog will learn to avoid this correction by sitting.

But consistency is the key to this training pattern. As Pavlov continued to experiment he discovered that:

- If the tone was always different, the dog wouldn't learn;

- If the shock was always different, the dog wouldn't learn;

- If the dog had to do something different each time to avoid the shock, it wouldn't learn.

So if you yell "Sit," and then whisper it five times immediately afterwards, your dog won't have any idea what you want it to do.

Only after your pet learns what "Sit" **means** can you gradually change what the command sounds like, raising or lowering your tone. Many owners are just lucky when teaching their pets, because, on occasion, a dog will pick up on unconscious changes of word or tone by their owner.

TRAINING YOUR DOG

The process of training a dog is one of conditioning, using Pavlov's Theory and accepted pack practices. ***Tricks I Taught My Master*** teaches you to make use of these basic concepts when you teach your pet the five basic commands that every family dog should know. These are the commands that are important even for dogs who won't be shown or participate in obedience trials.

In order of importance, they are:

1. **Sit:** The dog must touch her buttocks to the ground for a few seconds. This does not mean that she must stay in that position.

2. **Stay:** The dog must remain in his current position and hold it until the commander says to do otherwise.

3. **Come:** The dog must move to the person who spoke the command, and sit in front of – or next to – him.

4. **Heel:** The dog must move next to the side of the commander, and do what she does. If she moves fast, the dog must move fast; if she slows down, the dog must slow down; if she turns left, the dog must turn left.

5. **Lie down** or **down:** The dog must lie in the prone position, head up, for a few seconds.

The sixth command is **Break** or **Free**, which allows the pet to do whatever it wishes...except to misbehave!

Beyond the Big 5, and the command that releases them, there are a number of other, lesser commands. These include:

- **Off:** The dog must get off the furniture.

- **Stand:** The dog must stay in a standing position. The dog must not move. (This command is primarily for dogs in a show ring, but it's also helpful when a dog is on the examination table in the veterinarian's office.)

- **Up:** This is an invitation for the dog to come up to the commander...even permission to climb on furniture.

- **Fetch:** The dog must go and pick up an object and bring it back to the commander. Some owners teach their pets to seek a specific item: "Go get your green squeaky frog. Go get froggy." Or, "Go get your ball."

- **Kennel** or **Load Up:** The dog must move into a cage, kennel or car.

Then there are the trick commands. These are commands reserved for special occasions, often to show off a dog's obedience skills in informal situations. These may include any of the following:

- **Roll Over:** The dog must lie down and turn with tummy up.

- **Play Dead:** The pet must lie down on her side, motionless. Sometimes owners form a gun outline using their thumb and forefinger and say, "Bang" to tell the dog to play dead.

A friend of Happy's asks his black Labrador Retriever, Teal, "Would you rather be married or dead?" Teal plays dead!

- **Speak:** The dog must bark.

- **Shake:** The dog is required to sit up on his hind quarters and offer a paw to shake. Happy can give five!

- **Hold:** The dog must retain an object in her mouth, or balance it on her nose. A friend of mine has a female Mixed Spaniel named Obie. She takes a lit cigarette and puts the unlit end into Obie's mouth for her to hold. Talk about second-hand smoke!

- **Sit Up** or **Sit Pretty:** The dog is required to sit, and lean back, with forepaws up in the air.

- **Jump:** The dog must leap up and grab an object, perhaps a dog biscuit. Happy's "Up" command requires him to go up a slide ladder and come running down; the kids love it!

In all, there are three different types of correction techniques used to teach the five major commands that are available to the owner. All have their different application. They are:

1. The proper use of the training collar,

2. The proper use of the *electronic* training collar,

3. Ignoring the pet – and this includes not chasing it!

In a general sense, the techniques that should be employed for each command are as follows:

Sit   You can use either a training collar or an electronic training collar.

Stay   You should use only a training collar.

Come   You can use a training collar or an electronic training collar, or you can ignore it.

Heel   You should use a training collar or electronic training collar.

Lie Down   You may use a training collar or an electronic training collar.

The technique that you use will depend on the circumstances of the misbehavior. For example, if your dog is in the house, the method used could be different than if it were romping in an open field.

Suggested Training Techniques By Command

Command	Training Collar	Electronic Training Collar	Ignore
Sit	✓	✓	
Stay	✓		
Come	✓	✓	✓
Heel	✓	✓	
Lie Down	✓	✓	

TRAINING METHODS AND EQUIPMENT

The Training Collar

The basic tool used in training a pet, or in correcting a misbehavior, is the training collar.

A training collar is like the training wheels on a bicycle. Once a child learns to ride the bike, the parent discards the training wheels. Similarly, when your dog learns the proper responses to your commands, you may also abandon the training collar. But until that time, keep it on your dog at all times when you're working with him.

Simply stated, the approach is to firmly tell your dog...**ONCE**... what you want it to do. For example: "Come."

If your dog doesn't come within two seconds, correct it with one of the methodologies we've dicussed.

The technique you choose will depend on why your dog is not responding. It will also depend on which you can implement at the time.

For example, if you tell your dog to come, and it doesn't do so, it would be difficult to yank its collar if it's 30 feet away. In that case, use a remote training collar.

Obviously, teaching commands demands planning. You have to equip your dog properly to get results.

On the other hand, if your dog is misbehaving because it wants *attention*, do **not** chase it. Hold your ground and wait for it to come to you.

That's what you do whenever your dog does not obey your command. But when your pet does obey, reward it. You should always use both verbal and physical praise.

Only use food rewards in specific situations. If you use food all the time, you'll condition your dog to expect it...and you may not always have food with you.

Proper Use Of The Training Collar

The first thing you need to do is to get a training collar that fits your dog properly. Then you can leave the collar on your dog 24 hours a day. This is essential for proper training, because misbehaviors can occur anytime, anywhere.

The training collar is **THE** one most effective dog training tool. It works because it's what a dog is used to. The effect of the collar – the quick, temporary collapse of the trachea – is the way dogs show domination over other dogs in their natural environment.

Actually, the inventors of the training collar probably didn't design them with this in mind; nonetheless, that's the reason they work!

Training collars will not hurt your dog as long as they are used according to the techniques outlined in this book. Your dog will not be harmed physically, behaviorally or emotionally from a proper correction with the training collar.

Dogs don't even shy away from training collars. Yet if you were to smack your dog in the face with your hand (and I know that you wouldn't), he would instinctively shy away from that hand motion. The same is not true of a hand movement towards a training collar.

Some owners have had a bad experience with training collars in group training classes. As a result, they don't feel that this method works. Only rarely, it seems, do the trainers tell the owners **why** the collars work. Therefore, most people assume that the collars work because they cause pain (they do not), they make noise (they are soundless) or they simply startle the pet (startle yes, simply no).

If you have had such an experience with a training class, I ask you to think logically – as a human you can – and follow the guidelines set forth in this book. You'll be pleasantly surprised with the results.

Other owners have very different concerns. They worry that their dog might accidently hang itself wearing the collar all the time. Yet these same owners may also leave their dogs tied or chained-up in the back yard while they're gone all day! In either case, the chances of harm are equally unlikely.

With the right size training collar, about the only way a dog can harm itself is if it's kept in a fenced-in area, where it might jump up and get caught.

You also need to watch out if you keep your dog in a cage or kennel. The secret here is to remove the training collar when you put your pet in the cage, and put it back on when you take it out.

__Teaching Your Dog To Sit__

"Sit" is the easiest command to teach a dog, because it naturally spends so much of its time in the sitting position. Most automatically sit while waiting for something to happen: while waiting for food or water; while waiting to be petted; while waiting for their owner to finish reading the newspaper, so they can go outside together. Therefore, it's an easy position in which to place them. Maybe that's why dogs hear the "Sit" command more than any other.

And teaching a dog to sit is, quite frankly, one of the most basic rules of canine etiquette. It teaches a dog that there are consequences to its actions.

Humans, too, have rules...and consequences if we do not follow those rules:

- If we don't show up for work, we get fired.

- If we badmouth a policeman, we get arrested.

- If we walk in front of a car, we get hit.

A good example is when a person learns to drive. If you go through a red light, you may have an accident. But you can avoid that accident if you obey the rules and stop for the red light. We all follow human rules like these to avoid unpleasant consequences.

As an owner, you must teach your dog the same respect for dog rules, because they represent appropriate behaviors.

Your dog must learn to touch its butt to the ground on command to avoid unpleasant consequences (a correction) and to receive a reward (your praise).

Sounds simple, doesn't it? Actually, it isn't too difficult to accomplish.

You must first learn **how** to give an obedience command. You need to know what to do with your hands and body. As important as it is to use the same command in the same tone, it is equally important **NOT** to "act" exactly the same way every time.

Most people, when teaching a dog to sit, will stop whatever it is they were doing and say "Sit." With this technique, the dog may only obey the command when the owner isn't moving.

Or, worse, the dog may "Come" first and then "Sit" (next to the owner). In some circumstances this may be undesirable. For example, an owner may not want the dog to come to them, but rather to sit wherever it happens to be. If a car is coming, for instance, the dog should not cross the street to sit at the owner's side.

So it's important to vary what you're doing, while remaining rock-solid with the command itself.

Say the word "Sit" **one time**. Do not repeat the command. Then, silently, count two seconds to yourself: "one thousand and one, one thousand and two." If your dog sits, verbally praise him and give him a nice touch.

If he does not sit, correct him **only once** with the training collar in the following manner. This correction should be an immediate and quick jerk and then complete release of the collar.

If, after the correction, the dog does not sit, go back to square one and begin again.

First, your dog will learn that the word "Sit" means she will receive a jerk on her training collar. After the first three or four attempts, your dog will react to the command (and the corresponding correction) in one of the following ways:

1. She will turn and growl.

2. She will act submissive by:

    • running away;
    • lowering her head;
    • looking over her shoulder;
    • making noises like she is hurt.

3. Or she actually may even sit!

During that first lesson, most dogs learn that "Sit" means they're about to have their collars jerked.

Their reactions vary. But one thing is consistent, they'll try to find ways to avoid the jerk on their training collar. Some may try to bite their owner's hand. Others run away. Some might go around back and urinate. Others will take a firm stance, becoming rigid.

They'll try just about anything to avoid the correction.

What you must teach them is that there is only one way to do so, by touching their butt to the ground wherever they happen to be.

Another characteristic reaction, usually later in the training session, is when the dog reacts as if his collar was already jerked before his owner even gets that far. Be prepared for this. It can actually be quite funny! But don't let it sway you from your ultimate goal.

When you persist, you will find that most dogs will sit within 10 training tries, if only by coincidence. When this does happen, praise your dog profusely. Under such circumstances he will sit every time. It is a conditioned response.

But before you achieve the success you're after, you may be sorely tempted to vary your approach. You'll want to repeat the command. Don't. You'll want to yell the command. Don't. You'll want to jerk the collar and *then* say "Sit." Again, don't. You'll only frustrate yourself...and your dog.

But remember, as easy as these instructions sound, you may not find them as easy to follow in practice. But persevere.

And remember, the technique itself never changes. Always apply it in the same way. This teaches your dog that you are consistent, and that his response must always be the same: to sit. This predictability is what finally gains control of your pet.

Once your dog has learned the concept, teach it to do the same thing no matter where he is. Use the command in as many situations as possible – in the dining room, the basement, the kitchen, the bath, the backyard, the park, on sidewalks, when the mailman comes, when he is excited, at the neighbor's house and at the front door when the bell rings.

You'll also probably find that when you use the command in new circumstances, it can be a bit distracting to both of you; but doing so strongly reinforces the concept for your dog.

Ultimately, your dog must know that no matter when he hears the word "Sit," no matter what is happening around him, or what he is doing at that time, you will either correct him or reward him based on his actions.

But once he learns, he'll always want to receive the rewards, and not the correction. So he'll sit when told. Be consistent, persistent and patient, and you will receive the proper response from your dog.

It does take some dogs longer than others to learn certain commands, but I've used this technique successfully for every dog except two in 14 years. Some need as few as five trials to learn the response; a few need as many as 200 (not in a row, but possibly over a two week period).

Ironically, I've found that in most cases where 200 trials were necessary, it was actually the owner's fault! Sometimes the owner doesn't jerk the collar hard enough. In other cases, the owner jerks the collar, and then she looks down into her dog's face. And, of course, the dog looks sad and hurt. So the owner changes her behavior because she interprets the look as the dog thinking, "I hate you. You're hurting me. Stop doing this."

Actually, what the dog is probably thinking is this: "I don't want you to jerk my collar. I'll teach you to stop jerking it. I'll teach you by looking sad." This is a dog that has gained control of its human – a clever trick to teach its master!

The fear of making a correction too firmly is largely based on emotion.

On occasion, I've come across owners who worry that training will ruin their pet's personality. But this just doesn't occur. Happy, my contented, well-adjusted Mix-Breed, looks extremely pleased when asked to sit because he's been rewarded for doing so about 50,000 times!

Never give up. Take a break if you wish, but don't give up. If you give in, or you don't jerk the collar hard enough, your dog will never learn.

Another consideration is what actually constitutes "sitting." Sometimes when a dog is trying to avoid correction, it will back into something, like a couch or wall. If it does so, **do not correct it** because the dog has touched something with its buttocks.

To a dog, touching her posterior on the ground is the same as touching it to a sofa or wall. Thus, she's carried out the command. To get back on track, gently pull her away from the object and ask her to sit again.

On the other hand, some dogs will walk backward six steps to touch a wall! Don't reward your dog for this behavior. Instead, begin again. If she backs up again, hold her from touching the wall, and then correct her.

And if you see your dog sitting on his own, reinforce the concept by saying "Sit." Eventually, he'll associate the word with the position. This type of reinforcement is not quite as important as with other commands.

Once your dog has learned to sit on your command, it's important to monitor the sitting position she maintains. Some sit with a hip turned in. For larger dogs especially, it is vital that they sit properly to avoid a hip problem in the future.

Allow your dog to learn the concept of "Sit" first. Then, while he is sitting, adjust his hips with your hands. Eventually, your dog will make the adjustments on his own.

Just to review, you can easily undo hours of work if you change your technique, or use it inconsistently. Often, frustrated or impatient owners do one or more of the following:

- Say "Sit" more than once, in a voice that grows louder and louder.

- Push down the dog's buttocks.

- Require that the dog look at them.

- Become angry and get too physical with their pet.

- Yell at the dog.

- Just walk away and give up.

All of these behaviors inhibit, even prevent, teaching the command to your pet. In fact, over-verbalization – yelling, screaming, and repetitive command – is a severe deterrent to teaching your dog.

Regardless of how hard you might try, you just can't have a shouting match with your pet! Shouting will never change a misbehavior. It *may* stop a misbehavior at the time, but you'll be right back yelling at your dog for the same thing soon afterward.

Try cutting verbalization to a minimum, and concentrate on the specific technique of jerking the training collar in order to teach the command. It's important for you to learn how to deal with your emotions during training. Be calm and consistent.

The Dummy Leash Effect

Sometimes it can be useful to actually set up some troublesome situations or circumstances in order to help train a dog. Many *Specialists* use what is called the Dummy Leash Effect to help correct inappropriate behaviors. I'd like to introduce an expert in this area, Happy, to explain it in more detail.

I'm no dummy. So I don't mind telling you it's not too smart to put a leash on a dog for the first time and start yanking away.

But I've seen many owners do just that. They want instant control. What happens? They yank on that leash and their dog goes berserk — barking, jumping, biting. What results is a terrible tug-of-war that nobody wins.

What the dog learns is this: "Hey, the leash is on now. I have to behave."

But when that leash comes off, they're not under control, they're uncontrollable.

The answer is a little planning...and The Dummy Leash Effect.

It doesn't matter whether you're training a new puppy, or correcting the misbehaviors of a crafty old canine, it works every time.

Put a leash about a foot long on your dog's collar for several brief, 10-minute periods a day. Keep this up for about a week. But don't do anything with it. Just put it on, then, ten minutes later, take it off.

Your dog will learn that when the leash goes on...nothing happens. It doesn't mean anything special. So the leash doesn't represent your control, and your dog will behave when the leash comes off.

*Now if we can only find a way to keep you **owners** on a short leash!*

Many pet owners, knowing that their dogs behave badly in certain circumstances and at certain inopportune times, strike a defensive posture: "I can't do anything about it right now."

What you should do instead is to reproduce the problem situation and work with your dog to eliminate the misbehavior. After all, most human training sessions take place under controlled circumstances, so why should your dog be any different? Why should they have to perform flawlessly without training in the field under fire?

What you need to do is to create – and execute – a training plan. Attach your dog's training collar and leash. Then (for example):

- If your pet always misbehaves while a family member is speaking on the telephone, pick up the phone, dial an incomplete number and begin talking.

- If your dog becomes uncontrollable every time the doorbell rings, ask a friend to visit. Have them make a lot of noise outside the door and then ring the bell. Working with the dog then is much less embarrassing than it would be with someone arriving who is unaware of the problem.

- If your dog runs away every time you take its leash off, why take it off the leash at all? Leave it on. Eventually your dog will learn that the leash isn't coming off at all. Then you're likely to see some misbehaviors with the leash on. At that point, you can effectively address the problem, leash in hand. This may take a couple of weeks, but it's worth the wait.

Teaching you not to sit around waiting for misbehaviors to happen, but to set up correctable situations instead, is an important part of this lesson!

In general, owners should be more prepared. Make sure you have a leash tucked over the doorknob which is available all the time. I know some owners who have as many as five leashes, all hanging in convenient locations for when visitors arrive and they need an added advantage with their dog.

Teaching Your Dog To Stay, To Come, To Heel And To Lie Down

After "Sit," the four other major commands – "Stay," "Come," "Heel" and "Down" – can be taught by much the same methodology.

In fact, you use the exact same training techniques as you do with the "Sit" command. All you have to do is change the word for the command, and the behavior your dog must exhibit to avoid a correction or receive a reward.

Even the sequence of events is the same. The only difference is in your dog's behavioral response. It must correlate with the proper command: the one which you are teaching.

Hand Signals

The motions that you go through are very important to your training techniques. Whether you're aware of it or not, you do certain things with your hands and body whenever you're working with your dog. It helps if you have a plan for these movements...especially for your hands. Many, many people punctuate their sentences with their hands. These hand motions can either reinforce the command that you're teaching...or they can confuse your dog.

That's why hand signals can be a very useful training tool – for both pet and owner. They offer your dog the consistency she needs to understand your commands.

Each command has a specific hand signal that you can teach to your dog. This is like a universal sign language that most dogs can be taught to understand...and to obey.

Hand signals aren't difficult to teach. All you have to do is pair the proper hand signal with the single word used for each command. What follows is a brief description, along with a graphic depiction, of the hand signal you should use for each of the five major commands:

Sit   Stand with your arm straight out from you, parallel to the ground, with an open hand, palm facing down. Move your hand away from your chest, passing it over your dog.

Stay	Stand with your arm straight out from you, parallel to the ground, with an open hand, palm facing down. Push your palm toward your dog. (This resembles a police officer motioning "Stop.")

Come   Stand with your arm straight out from you,
                  parallel to the ground, with an open hand,
                  thumb pointing up. Move your hand along
                  a small plane towards your chest.

Heel   Stand with your arm straight out from you,
parallel to the ground, with an open hand,
palm down. Lightly slap it against your leg.

Lie Down   Stand with hand closed, finger pointing down at the ground.

These signals are simple. And if you use them in conjunction with your voice commands, your dog will probably catch on quickly.

But be careful not to confuse him. There are a number of commonly used motions that will send your dog the wrong signal. For example, avoid the following:

- **Do not use with the "Come" command.**

  When you command your dog to "Come," don't squat down and move your arm toward yourself. If you do this, your dog will learn to come to you only when he hears the appropriate sound paired with this body movement. But if he only hears the sound, or sees this inappropriate signal, he will not come. And if your dog is running away from you, he will never see your body movement or "hand signal."

- **Do not use with the "Sit" command.**

  Many owners have a complicated pattern to their commands that will only confuse their pets. Avoid this. Don't feel like you have to sit directly in front of your dog and force him to look you in the eye, while you point your finger at him and say "Sit." If you do, your dog will correlate all of this activity with the command. Keep it simple. Keep it direct. Keep to the hand signals used in this book.

It's important that your dog obeys you at the sound of a single word. That way, she'll respond in any situation.

Usually, when you most need the proper response, your dog will be running away from you, distracted by something off in the distance. When he's doing this, he's not looking at you.

This is why hand signals are never a critical addition to any animal's training. But they can be a convenience for you, and eliminate some of the confusion for your dog.

If you definitely want your dog to respond to a one-word command, and not rely on hand signals, you still need to remember what you're doing with your hands. Remember to vary your body movements every time, while remaining consistent with your command. That way, your dog will pick up only on your verbal signal.

OTHER TRAINING METHODS AND EQUIPMENT

Electronic Training Systems

The emergence of electronic equipment for use in pet training has been extremely helpful in developing well-behaved companions.

But all products, including the electronic ones, are only as good as the people who use them, whether they're pet trainers or they're owners. Using this new equipment involves much more than simply pushing a button to improve your pet's behavior. You have to recognize that the equipment is only a training *tool* – a means to an end – and not the end itself.

Since the early 1980's, electronic training devices have become more and more popular. And it's easy to see why. Pet ownership has increased, creating new markets. This new equipment provides a faster, more convenient method of training pets for all those new owners. This is especially necessary because today's owners are spending less and less time with their pets.

Also, these days, people expect to train pets to do things that have never been expected of pets before. And finally, new laws are forcing our citizens to train dogs in new and different ways.

Of all the electronic equipment available today, the most effective are:

1. Remote Training Collars

2. Bark Limiter Collars

3. Buried-Wire Containment Systems

This equipment, if used properly, will not worsen a pet's behavior, change her personality or disrupt her demeanor.

Depending on breed, you should only use such equipment on dogs four months of age or older, and weighing a minimum of eight pounds. If you want to use this equipment on younger or smaller dogs, you should consult your veterinarian or *Pet Behavior Specialist* first.

Remote Training Collars

A Remote Training Collar system usually consists of two separate components: a hand-held, remote control unit for the owner to carry, and a small, lightweight box on a separate collar for the dog.

When you press the button on your remote, your dog receives a quick, harmless corrective stimulus – similar to what you feel when touching a television screen after shuffling your feet on the carpet. It is **NOT** the type of jolt you'd get if you were shocked by an electric outlet. I've never heard the feeling described with the word "pain." Some dogs even adapt to this uncomfortable vibration, something they wouldn't do if it were painful.

There are many Remote Collar brands from which to choose; pick one with adjustable intensity levels. Test the correction on your finger before using it on your pet. (But remember that human fingers are much more sensitive than a dog's skin around the neck area, and that we don't have hair to act as an insulator.)

When you do use a Remote Training Collar, be cautious. If you're not careful you could exacerbate certain common canine problems.

For example, if two dogs in one household are acting aggressively towards each other, you can make the situation worse by "zapping" them every time. You might even set off a fight if they think that the other dog is at all responsible for the correction.

You should use a Remote Training Collar to:

- improve certain obedience responses off leash ("Come," "Sit," "Heel," etc.);

- teach boundaries (staying in the yard, or keeping out of the garden or specific rooms);

- eliminate destructive behaviors (like hole digging, chewing, or excessive scratching);

- inhibit miscellaneous misbehaviors like car or bicycle chasing.

Owners should resort to this type of training collar when:

- training off-leash has failed;

- original training methods are no longer effective;

- you need improvement in a short period of time, as when a neighbor complains about the pet's demeanor, or a misbehavior becomes expensive;

- eliminating an aggressive behavior (a trainer or *Pet Behavior Specialist* **must** be involved with this as the dog must understand *why* it is being corrected).

In a few situations, using a Remote Training Collar is the **only** way to train a dog. This is true if your pet misbehaves only when you don't have her on her leash, or if she misbehaves when you're not around (digging holes in the yard only when you're in the house!), or if you've tried everything else – or the wrong things for too long!

This collar can be very convenient. Used properly, it can reduce the time needed for training. It can also give you peace of mind. With the remote control in hand, you can take your dog for a stroll in the park off-leash, virtually eliminating the chance of misbehavior in any situation. Often, an owner needs the assurance of the device long after the dog's need for the collar has disappeared.

Remote training collars are usually available for purchase or rental. I recommend those that are made from a durable material which is also water-resistant (extremely important) and will not be set off by TV remotes, garage door openers or the like. You should be able to adjust the intensity of the correction, and have a signal range of at least 75 feet.

The Dummy Equipment Effect

The most effective way to use the Remote Training Collar is by the "Dummy Equipment Effect." This parallels the Dummy Leash Effect Happy described earlier. In this method, you eliminate the equipment as a factor in the learning process.

To accomplish this, you put the Remote Training Collar on your dog, and carry the remote control around for no fewer than three days. During that time, point it at your dog and push the button frequently. But make sure that you **do so without activating the collar.**

Your dog will get used to wearing the collar. She'll get used to the smell of it. She'll even see you pushing the button on the remote control unit. **But during all of this, nothing happens.**

Then, once the collar is activated, your dog doesn't associate it with the vibration received, but with the specific misbehavior that you want to eliminate. Even if you only rent the equipment, it's **vital** to retain this three-day ploy as part of the training.

Unfortunately, many impatient owners put the Remote Training Collar on their pet, punch the button on their control, and "zap" their dog out of sheer frustration. What the dog quickly learns is that when the collar is on, and her master points the remote, "I get a correction, but when it's off, he can't do a thing to me, so I can misbehave as I please!"

Bark Limiter Collars

Bark Limiter Collars were created for use on dogs to encourage them to curb their vocal activity when inappropriate. The equipment looks similar to the Remote Training Collar, but it operates with a sensor on the collar which detects your dog's barking. When barking is detected, it delivers the same harmless correction as the Remote Training Collar. It's actually quite ingenious.

Buried-Wire Containment Systems

Buried-Wire Containment Systems consist of a wire buried in the ground around the perimeter of an area marked to contain your pet. Your dog is equipped with a special collar. If she comes within a pre-determined range of the unseen "fence," the box on her collar delivers a corresponding electronic correction.

There are many brands on the market today. The one you choose should have at least the following features:

- a water-resistant receiver;
- variable correction levels with optional warning tone;
- signal range adjustment capabilities;
- lightning/surge protection.

Citronella Spray Collars

As mentioned earlier, when used properly, electronic collars can help you to develop a better relationship with your pet. But there are owners, and trainers, who do not believe in the use of an electronic correction. If you are of such an opinion, I highly recommend that you use a Citronella Spray Collar.

These spray collars are available for remote trainers, bark control devices and containment systems. These ingenious devices use similar technology to that employed by electronic correction devices. However, the static correction is replaced by a short, distracting spurt of citronella spray.

This spray is totally harmless to your pet's sight, hearing, smell and taste.

Legal Questions About Electronic Training Equipment

Generally, if you follow the manufacturer's instructions for the use of the electronic training product in question, you can achieve the desired results. Of course, not all dogs react the same way to different types of training.

But if you fail to follow the training instructions, you can count on training problems, just as you would with more conventional methodology. The tricky part is that with electronic equipment, there are fewer historical precedents to help get you back on track.

Because electronic training technology is still relatively new, there are a lot more questions than answers. Questions like the following:

- Is the use of a Remote Training Collar while walking your dog the equivalent of keeping him on a leash?

- Is a Buried-Wire Containment System a legal option when a fence is required to confine an animal by law?

Just as important are questions that arise if the equipment is used improperly, creating misbehaviors – especially aggression. Who is responsible? The manufacturer? The trainer? The owner?

All of these questions are legally unanswered as of yet. One thing is certain, however. Within the next five years, the electronic equipment used for pet training will astonish us all!

7

Eliminating Dog Destructiveness

Destructiveness can include any form of digging, scratching or chewing; in fact, just about any activity that damages your personal property. Even improper elimination qualifies. In short, dog destructiveness is just about any misbehavior that destroys your home.

Because housebreaking and chewing misbehaviors occur so frequently, we've set aside separate chapters for them. After this chapter, you'll find *Correcting Chewing Problems* (Chapter 8) and *Correcting Dog Housebreaking Problems* (Chapter 9).

Destruction doesn't have to be significant to be considered a misbehavior. Even minor property damage can be frustrating, if not costly, especially if it continues over a period of time.

But no matter how small the damage is, it's important that you never let your dog get away with it – even occasionally. Because this type of situational permission only serves to draw out the destructive behavior, by teaching your pet that there are times when it is appropriate. And because this behavior is, by and large, already fun for your pet, this is the last thing you want to do.

If your dog scratches around on a $10 throw rug, it may not be a problem to you; but if she damages a $15,000 Oriental Rug, I'll bet you think it's a misbehavior. Immediately. (Notice the dichotomy?)

THE CAUSES

So why do dogs dig? Why do they scratch and chew? All of these activities, it seems, are Stress Relieving Behaviors; an excellent way for your dog to vent any excess energy or emotion he may have. Excellent for him, that is!

More specifically, dogs usually dig to have something to do. It's almost therapeutic for them. It's an opportunity to put their nose to the ground, to seek something out – and then to uncover its secret.

Sometimes dogs really do dig to bury their bones, like they do in the cartoons. Or they'll hide away a tender tidbit for some later time.

Dogs may also dig for reasons of comfort, to create a cool or warm place to lay down in. Or, on rare occasions, they may even dig to attempt escape from a situation making them uncomfortable.

Mostly, though, digging indicates anxiety, stress, frustration or confusion on your dog's part. It's her way of dealing with these emotions.

You'll usually see signs of destructiveness in connection with something else that's going on in your dog's life. It can be just about anything. If you'll remember, we humans are a very inconsistent breed. But in my experience, a dog's digging usually occurs in one of three very specific areas:

1. in the yard, more often than not, in a fenced-in back yard;

2. at the base of a door, especially when the dog is confined in a room or left alone in the home;

3. inside the house on carpeting or flooring, usually causing scratching damage.

Pet owners commonly think that their dog is digging to escape the yard (which is often true) or, classically, to get back at them (which is certainly not true).

THE SOLUTION

So what can you do to correct this kind of dog destructiveness? Well, first you have to catch your dog in the act. This alone is a difficult-enough assignment. The chances of catching your dog in a destructive act, and then correcting it, are much more likely inside your home. It's much more difficult to catch a dog digging outside in the garden.

Either way, when you do catch your dog in the act, there are three steps you must take to correct the situation:

1. Use a training collar for the correction.

2. Redirect your pet's attention, and behavior, using the "Sit" command.

3. Make your dog's digging area as undesirable as possible.

First you must discipline your dog using the training collar and basic "Sit" command described in detail in Chapter 6, *How Dogs Learn.* This technique will enable you to control your dog's behavior and break her pattern of destructiveness.

You should use the "Sit" command since this is both a basic position, and a natural stance for your dog. If you need a refresher course on the use of the "Sit" command, you'll find it in Chapter 6, *How Dogs Learn*, under the heading: "Training Methods and Equipment." (Remember to use the Dummy Leash Effect, described in the same chapter.) You'll find that using the "Sit" command is the solution to many objectionable pet behaviors.

If you do find the opportunity to discipline your dog with the training collar during a destructive binge, it will probably be the last time you ever see this misbehavior! But such interventions are extremely rare. So what else can you do?

Well, the next step depends largely on why the dog is doing the digging. But redirection is always a part of the solution. In this case, you should redirect your pet's attention to a spot in the yard where digging is less objectionable to you. Or, if this is unacceptable, you can redirect his focus to a more appropriate behavior, like chewing a rawhide or a beef shank bone (or some other "pet-safe" alternative).

If you choose the latter course, make sure to introduce the proper chewable only in the situation where your dog exhibits the misbehavior. If he digs destructively in the back yard while you're away, make sure that when you **do** go away, you leave him there with the rawhide. And that this is the **only** time he has access to the rawhide. By limiting the circumstances in which your dog receives a chewable, it makes that chewable more desirable.

The premise behind this approach is to redirect your dog's destructiveness onto the substitute which you have furnished. Further, because you've provided an acceptable alternative, the more time your dog spends with the rawhide, the less energy she'll have left to burrow under your begonias.

To ease the transition, it's often helpful to make your dog's favorite digging spot somewhat less desirable; in fact, downright avoidable. To do so, apply a small amount of any pet-safe substance with a repelling smell anywhere your dog has been digging. By that I mean repelling to the dog. Lysol Spray has worked for Happy, and the many dogs we've seen over the years.

It's best to apply this "repellent" just before you let your pet loose in the yard. That way, the potency of its odor will be at its highest.

Your dog will instinctively apply her chief sense, that of smell, to any area before beginning to dig. So be sure to cover all of your bases. If she digs in more than one spot, make sure you spray each of them.

Once your pet is repelled by the first spot, she'll move on to the second...and then to the third. The process is very methodical. The trick is to position your acceptable alternative, the rawhide, in an area of the yard away from the offending sites. Eventually, she'll find it, and then your conversion is underway.

If you precisely follow this routine for two consecutive weeks, you'll usually break your dog of her digging habit.

By the way, our focus has been on a dog's digging activity, but the same basic principles apply inside the house, for just about any destructive behavior.

SUMMARY

Again, there are three steps you need to follow when dealing with dog destructiveness. These are: get your dog's attention, redirect her behavior, and make the destruction zone as undesirable as possible.

The most difficult of these steps may just be the first one. As we've noted before, the best way to get your dog's attention (if you can catch her in the act) is to use the "Sit" command. So we thought we'd take time out here to review this all-important command. But this time we thought we'd give you the perspective from the other end of the leash. Here's Happy with the details.

Actually, I've been on both ends in my time with The Master. And I'll tell you, looking up that leash is a lot tougher than looking down it. But what it all comes down to is love. Tough love, sometimes, but love all the same.

*If you love the dog that you live with, you'll try to provide an environment he can be comfortable in. Free of stress. You see, we can take our place in the social structure of the human household. What we **can't** take is not knowing exactly where we stand.*

So, from a dog's-eye-view, there are lots of dos and don'ts for corrections following an obedience command in a destructiveness case. The most critical of these is consistency. Don't even think of this in human terms. Your ultimate goal should be to achieve the very highest level – canine consistency.

This starts with the basic command itself:

- *Say the sound, "Sit," only **once**.*

- *Don't repeat this sound. It will only confuse us.*

- *Follow this command sound with either a correction or praise. Hey, we'll take praise every time, believe me. But be consistent, and deliver the appropriate response, depending on how the dog responds to your command.*

- *Don't ever change the sequence on us. We're still trying to catch on to it as it is.*

- *You know that sound you use to call us? What you call our name? (I haven't met a dog yet who'd admit that his human-given name was "Snippy.") If you* **have** *to use this human name,* **only use it before** *the command, never after.*

- *Try to use the same tone of voice each and every time you use the "Sit" noise. Anything else will distract or confuse us. Remember, we're under a lot of pressure to perform.*

- *Yelling, screaming, running after us, and throwing things at us will not help the situation. They'll only make us more nervous than we already are about your mental health. And please, no startling noises. Then we really know you're beyond canine help.*

- *Remember to reward your dog whenever she gives you the appropriate response. The Master recommends that you do so at least 75% of the time, with verbal praise or petting. I suggest even more than that. Give me a good stroke on the chest 100% of the time, and I'm as happy as can be.*

- *Now here's where it really gets important. Be sure you make a proper correction if your dog doesn't respond properly. Every time. Consistency really counts here. Without it, we dogs just don't understand where you humans are coming from.*

- *If you do see your dog doing a behavior similar to the appropriate obedience response, say the obedience com-*

mand! Sometimes we can catch on that way. Remember that we have more than two different languages going on here. We have two substantially different frames of reference. And ours is much lower to the ground.

Finally, to us dogs, there's a big difference between "Sit" and "Stay." "Sit" simply means for us to touch our heinies to the ground for a few seconds, before going about our business. "Stay" means, well, to stay.

ALTERNATIVE METHODS OF CORRECTION

There are other ways to make a dog's digging spot less desirable. One good alternative is to use an *aversive stimulus*; this is a behavior modification term which means, simply, to create conditions that a dog will want to avoid, and then cause him to associate those conditions with the destructive behavior.

Watch your dog closely from a window inside the house. Each time he begins to dig, blow a gym whistle as loudly as you can. An airhorn is another good *aversive stimulus*.

Your pet's perception of this chain of events is one of association. When he digs in the yard, he hears a loud, offensive noise. And the only way to avoid the noise is not to dig.

There's an obvious problem with this technique, however. It sure isn't convenient for you. For this to work, you can never leave your dog outside unsupervised. To be effective, the *aversive stimulus* must occur each and every time your dog begins to dig. If the offensive noise occurs only every fourth or fifth time, the procedure won't work.

There are other considerations as well. For example, it's a good idea to notify your neighbors of what you have in mind...beforehand. Airhorns can be quite obnoxious. That's their purpose in life. So if your neighbors don't know what you have going on, they're likely to send you some unwanted visitors in black-and-white squad cars, lights flashing and sirens blaring. Talk about aversive!

As effective as the airhorn is in the retraining of pets, if you're forced to stop mid-week it can really let the air out of your program.

If you don't want your neighbors up in arms, the most convenient aversive stimulus may be the remote training collar. This electronic device enables you to provide a safe, harmless *aversive stimulus* from a remote location. Operating distances vary by manufacturer.

When working with such devices, it is helpful to create a Dummy Collar Effect. (For details see Chapter 6, *How Dogs Learn,* under the heading "Other Training Methods and Equipment.") That way, your dog won't associate the stimulus with the collar itself.

Once the regimen is underway, you must correct your dog using the remote trainer every time she starts to dig. Again, this is hardly convenient for you. To facilitate matters, you may want to set up a situation that produces the problematic behavior. That way, you won't have to wait around trying to catch your dog in mid-dig.

Set up the situation by burying something desirable to your dog in the areas where she usually digs. Remember that smell is her primary sense, so such odiferous delicacies as milk bones or scraps of human food are ideal. Then, when the digging begins, correct her with the electronic training collar.

In order for the training to be successful, you'll have to correct your pet consistently every time she digs. The number of corrections will vary with the personality and persistence of your dog; how well-ingrained the habit; and the number of desirable digging areas in your yard. So if you can set up situations on a daily basis, you can shorten your training time considerably.

Eventually, your dog will catch on. And when you do catch your dog chewing on the furnished rawhide, be sure to give him some quality time. Talk to him. Praise him. Pet him. All of this positive attention will reinforce his wise decision to turn to the rawhide.

One last helpful suggestion, when it comes to alternative measures, is exercise. Exercising your dog can certainly help when you're attempting to break her of a misbehavior. But exercise is not a cure-all. There isn't an owner in this world who can exercise a dog out of her misbehaviors.

Nonetheless, exercise can be a wonderful complement to most training programs, if you choose to do it at the right time. The secret is to control your dog's energy level.

When you have to leave your dog unattended in the back yard for many hours, exercise her **first**. This leaves behind a low-energy dog, and reduces the chances that she'll expend energy digging or destroying things.

PREVENTATIVE MEASURES

As with most misbehaviors, the easiest solution to digging or other destruction problems is to prevent them from occurring in the first place. And, also as usual, this is easier said than done.

Most such problems start very early, because most owners treat their dogs differently while they're puppies. And the fact of the matter is, all those behaviors that you find so endearing in a six-pound puppy won't be so lovable in a full-grown, 60-pound dog.

It's so much easier on your dog when you teach him appropriate behaviors at an early age. Happy and I know a 10-week-old English Setter named Louis, who's already on the right track. He's a bundle of energy now. All fur and fun. But his owners recognize that a properly-behaved dog is an assest in the long-run. And this isn't a selfish stance to take, either. More than anything they want to give Louis a comfortable, low-stress lifetime.

The truth is that you can teach the easiest training methods at an early age. The procedures are simple:

• Set the rules.

• Correct your pet's misbehaviors each time.

• Use the same type of correction each time.

• Give a consistent reward.

Again, consistency is the key. To ignore your pup's amusing antics while she is small is to tell her she can get away with them once she grows, especially when her owners are busy, or tired after a long day at work.

TECHNIQUES THAT DON'T WORK

For every effective training approach out there, there are 10 more techniques that just don't work. How do you tell the difference? Start by listening to your own common sense.

One old pet training book offers a simple "solution" for dogs digging holes in the back yard. It suggests that you dig a hole, fill it with water, and then hold your dog's head underwater for 10 seconds.

Barbaric! It's incredible that any owner could see this as logical advice. How cruel! Not only would this be life threatening for the dog, it would make him fearful of his owner...and with good cause.

Moreover, even if it wasn't all of these other things, it would be ineffective. Why? Because the intervention doesn't relate to the digging or destructive misbehavior. Sure, education is an appropriate step. But overeducation can do more harm than good.

Here's Happy again to illustrate this premise with another anecdote from our time together on the road:

The Master and I were visiting a friend in Chicago – an Airedale – who was living with two other dogs and a human couple. I won't use their real names to protect the inconsistent.

One of this dog's housemates was a Water Spaniel. He was friendly enough, I guess...but his easy-going personality was no match for the Airedale's other housemate, a Doberman Pinscher named Reggie.

Reggie, it seems, was all his human beings could handle. He was like a four-pawed wrecking ball, destroying everything in his path. Digging. Chewing. Scratching. If you humans consider it a canine crime, he was chest-deep in it. And aggressive didn't even begin to describe him.

He also had his share of health problems, serious internal problems that baffled his veterinarian.

All-in-all, the whole household was in a sorry state when we arrived. Every member was at a loss for what to do. The Water Spaniel kept to himself, pretty much, always with a wary eye out for Reggie. Our friend the Airedale, a well-balanced old bone-chaser, watched out for the poor Doberman as best as possible. But there are some things that are just out of our paws.

At the heart of this situation were the two humans, who loved the three dogs very much. So much, in fact, that they'd acquired almost 40 books on dog training and pet behavior. And, because Reggie was their problem pooch, books on Dobermans. A lot of them. They were voracious readers.

What was happening was that Reggie's humans were getting conflicting information from these books. This isn't a rare ailment for humans. With so many sources to choose from, and so many techniques to try, overeducation is fairly widespread.

Inevitably, Reggie's humans got confused by all this information. They didn't know which end was up and which end was down. And if you think the humans were badly off, you should've seen poor Reggie.

We've discussed consistency before. But the only thing consistent about the techniques these humans tried was the regularity of change.

My advice to you humans is always pretty simple, otherwise we lose something in the translation. Choose one technique and stick with it. You just can't try one technique for four days, read another book and try a second technique for the next week.

If you pick one and stick with it, even if it's wrong, at least you'll give your dog the consistency she craves.

But back to Reggie. The disgruntled Doberman was downright confused. He'd been through so many opposing training methods that his head was spinning. Naturally, that's what made him so hyperactive.

He'd bitten two trainers. Each told the humans they should put Reggie to sleep. This made the female so afraid, that whenever someone reached for Reggie's leash, she would jump back for fear of an attack.

So that's the situation The Master and I walked into, without so much as a sniff. But once we got a whiff of what was going on, The Master went to work.

He approached Reggie with the air of confidence and authority he usually commands. Immediately, Reggie responded with respect. To him, The Master was a breath of fresh air, the most consistent human he'd ever met.

The human female was amazed that Reggie didn't try to bite.

"He actually looks like he's enjoying himself," she exclaimed!

The human male was equally astonished.

"Do you know what you're handling?" he asked. "At the vet it takes four people to hold this dog down, and that's just to clip his nails."

That's when he decided to make things interesting.

"I'll bet you can't clip Reggie's nails," the male challenged. "In fact, I'll bet you can't even clip one nail in 15 minutes!"

With the gauntlet presented, we now needed a prize. Success meant two tickets to the Chicago Bulls/Philadelphia '76ers playoff game! (The Master can't resist watching a good ball game. Me, I prefer playing them.)

"Okay, but you can't use cheese (Reggie's favorite treat) as a reward," the human male added quickly.

The Master made a quick phone call to tell another friend, "I'll be late, but I'm bringing two playoff tickets with me!"

The human female went to get the clippers. She returned hiding them behind her back. She was convinced that as soon as Reggie saw them, he would go for the jugular. He didn't.

The Master taught Reggie how to sit and stay. Every time he acted aggressively, moved his feet, or made a noise of protest, The Master corrected him with the training collar. But when he obeyed, The Master petted and praised him.

Then The Master showed Reggie the clippers. He was fine. Next he was allowed to smell them. Still he was fine.

All the while, The Master stroked Reggie around the ears and legs. And all in all, he was one fine dog.

But now came the big test. The Master touched each of Reggie's paws, spreading his toes. Occasionally the dog would move, and once he even curled his lip. But each time he was corrected. And The Master moved at a very fast clip.

With the humans watching the clock, their pet had his pedicure in under ten minutes, start to finish. They were still awestruck as they handed the playoff tickets to The Master.

But it's our philosphy that it's best to learn by doing. So we had the female clip Reggie's nails next, followed by her husband. And all the time Reggie was fine!

Another of our rules is that human behavior reflects pet behavior and vice versa. Nowhere was this truer than in Reggie's case. So many people were convinced that Reggie was dangerous – aggressive and destructive – that they treated him like he was rabid. When all the time, the poor pup just needed a little tough love, consistency and discipline.

Unfortunately, this story has a sad end. Eventually, Reggie had to be put to sleep anyway. His internal problems had him in too much pain to go on. It was a classic case of stress-related ailments causing a pet's death. We were all sorry to see him pass. We met him too late in his life to save him.

Pick a single *Pet Behavior Specialist* or trainer, and read only what he recommends. If you do, you'll probably find training techniques with a common foundation. Still, make your choice carefully.

Some pet trainers have no formal background; they read a few books and decide to start their business. When you choose a *Specialist* or trainer, here are a few important questions to ask:

1. Is pet training their full-time job?

   A full-time trainer or specialist is the best choice for you and your pet.

2. How long have they been in business?

   Look for people with at least five years in the business. A few years of experience usually indicates that they know what they're doing. After all, if they're still in business, they must have enough clients to prove they're doing something right.

3. During the first telephone conversation, do they offer some idea of why the problem exists and estimate your chances of successful re-training?

   If so, you're on the right track. But watch out. If they're willing to spend more than 15 minutes with you, they're probably not very busy. That's not a good sign.

4. Ask for references.

THE REBELLIOUS PERIOD

Any time you impose your will on your pet, you're going to come up against the rebellious period. The last thing your dog wants to do is to succumb to you, but eventually that's just what she will do. She'll see the futility of furthering the fight. And that's when you win.

The secret is to get through the tests your dog will present, to bear with your pet when his behavior takes the inevitable turn for the worse. This is a natural part of the process, when things get worse before they get better. It happens with all obedience command training, for example.

This is not a sign that the techniques you're using aren't working. Rather, it's the opposite. Your dog is fighting you because she knows it's going to work. But with a little consistency, and a lot of perseverence, you and your dog will make the breakthrough.

For more information on "The Rebellious Period," see Chapter 14, *Handling The Occasional Relapse.*

8

Correcting Dog Chewing Problems

Although a dog's chewing behavior is technically a component of destructive misbehaviors (see the previous chapter), there's more than enough of it going on to warrant a separate section here.

You may be surprised to learn that dogs are equal opportunity chompers. Their prowess for punching holes in our finest footwear is legendary. They've torn apart enough socks to eliminate the dryer as the number one suspect in the missing member derby. When it comes to clothes, they may not like to wear them, but they sure do love to tear them. And they can shred the sports section in the time it takes you to read the headlines.

All that is yesterday's news. But what you may not know is that dogs may also develop a taste for furniture, carpets, eye glasses, remote controls, books and record albums. One dog we know even eats money. Exclusively. Now that's a dog with the kind of taste that makes cents to me!

Sometimes it's amazing to discover what a dog will choose to chew. Happy has a few choice stories to whet your whistle.

Mandy is an outgoing Black Labrador from Columbus, Ohio. She lives there with an enterprising young human couple.

One day, these humans came home with two enormous pieces of etched glass and accompanying wood frames. The humans had purchased them at a local movie theater's auction. Once they got the glass home, they converted it into a pair of sliding doors which lead from their living room to an outdoor patio. The entire project cost well over $10,000.

But dollars mean nothing to a dog. Heck, we don't even have pockets.

So one evening, the humans returned home to find that Mandy had been munching on the wooden frames. By the time they arrived, she'd virtually destroyed them. Worse yet, she'd also actually managed to leave tooth marks on the glass!

Now, whenever both humans know they're going to be away from home, they confine Mandy just to be safe.

Happy and I have heard some mighty strange stories in our time. But fact is always stranger than fiction. And two tales in particular take the cake. Here's Happy with the icing.

A German Shepherd we once worked with had a panty fetish. Her name was Angie, and she would burrow in the dirty laundry pile until she came away with her quarry. Then she would lay there, contentedly chewing the underwear.

Well, Angie's human was red as a fire truck when she gave us the specifics, but her embarrassment ran out with her supply of skivvies. The Master quickly deduced that the panties were the only item in the house that Angie ever raided. And once they were made inaccessible, the problem was resolved. Simple enough!

The other story wasn't so simple. It involved a Toy Poodle named Fancy. She arrived for a consultation with her owner, a human female. The woman was well-dressed in fur and diamonds. Fancy matched her, in her own fashion, with a poodle sweater and cubic zirconium sparkling everywhere.

As her human described the situation, the Poodle just rolled her eyes. The woman was worried because Fancy had a nail-chewing problem. The problem was, it wasn't Fancy's nails she was chewing on...it was her human's. It happened while they watched soap operas together each weekday afternoon.

The problem was that we didn't see any evidence of destructive chewing. And we couldn't duplicate the situation for ourselves. It was all a big mystery for awhile.

But in the end, it wasn't much of a nail-biter after all. The Master finally coaxed a confession from the femme fatale. It turned out that the human didn't want to own up to her own problem, so she framed Fancy, cleverly covering her tracks with exquisitely painted, false fingernails.

Humans are so hard to fathom sometimes!

THE CAUSES

Though it may be difficult to pinpoint in specific instances, ultimately, owner negligence is the root cause of most destructive chewing by dogs.

Not that it's intentional. In today's busy society, we simply don't take the time to work with our pets; to teach them how to live a happy, healthy life in the human household. So they'll do what comes naturally to dogs. They'll run and they'll rough-house, they'll howl at the moon (and just about everything else) and they'll chew.

Many dogs prefer something new to chew on rather than something that's "all chewed-out." Unfortunately, when human emotions enter the mix, sometimes this canine need to chew on something new gets a little skewed.

One day, Happy and I were invited to visit an elderly couple, and their tiny, white Miniature Poodle, Cuddles. Cuddles and her owners took this basic tenet and twisted it beyond all repair. Here's the story, as Happy likes to tell it.

The couple started by telling us that Cuddles was the smartest dog in the world.

I looked over at the little dog, standing dimly, but determinedly, across the room, and I could just hear the "but" coming.

Sure enough, the old female added, "but she does this one stupid thing. Occasionally she chews on things she's not supposed to."

I translated this immediately into, "Cuddles chews on everything all the time." But I didn't know yet how right I would be, because we still had to work our way through the playful side of this story.

Apparently, Cuddles' favorite thing to chew on was whatever new toy the humans gave her. The problem was that they gave her a new toy each and every day!

Cuddles had literally hundreds of dog toys. They were strewn everywhere throughout the home. Not just your everyday balls and bones either. We're talking clever little items, like a squeaky toy in the shape of Ronald Reagan (there's nothing like gnawing on the leader of the free world), wicker baskets with her own name on them, and a toy box for all the toys.

Not that it helped. The toys were piled high in the wicker baskets, which were stationed all around the living room. The toybox itself was brimming over. But Cuddles didn't seem interested in any of them.

What she did seem interested in was us. She jumped around the room, yapping, biting ankles, and pulling at pant legs. She even gave me a haughty little sniff or two. All this was bad form, no matter what company you're keeping.

And all the while the two humans sat calmly, not seeming to notice the theatrics, as they discussed Cuddles' "one little problem."

As they saw it, the problem was that each time they left the house, Cuddles chewed their personal belongings to bits. Worse yet, the primary target of her tiny little teeth was usually something tail-waggingly new; something they'd just brought home – a shopping bag, a box of clothing, or a new book. It didn't matter, except that she'd never seen it before.

*The Master, with a great deal of patience and understanding, explained to this elderly couple that Cuddles couldn't discern the difference between her new toys and **their** new "toys."*

185

Unfortunately, they weren't able to understand the concept either. Or rather, they were unwilling.

To Cuddles, even with her toys literally covering the floor, every one chewed once and then discarded, everything new in the house was fair game. Everything was chewable.

The sad thing is that this situation would have been a snap to solve. All the humans needed to do was to eliminate the toys, the baskets and the box included. Just throw them all away.

But when The Master told them his Master Plan, they recoiled in horror. Really! I saw it with my own eyes.

*"But Cuddles **needs** all her toys," the old man stammered. "She can't survive without them."*

To which The Master replied, "If Cuddles needs all her toys, why doesn't she chew on them?"

The elderly couple hemmed and hawed a bit at that.

"Why don't you just give her a small rawhide?" The Master suggested.

With that the room erupted in an array of emotional protestations. I think there were tears in the woman's eyes as she said, "Oh, my goodness, that would be dangerous."

"What if Cuddles were to chew a piece of the rawhide off and swallow it?" the gentleman added. "She'd choke on it."

"She'd get an intestinal block," the woman continued. "She might die!"

At this point, it was obvious that our services weren't needed here. And The Master did his best to part this company with dignity all around.

Believe it or not, this kind of response is not unusual. Many owners resist the switch to rawhide. In Cuddles' case, though, the circumstances were pretty extreme. They allowed their dog to chew on rubber, nylon, cloth and wood, not to mention toys with bells, ribbons and elastic string on them. These aren't exactly the most digestable delicacies in the world.

I've had other owners complain that their pet has just eaten three towels, two padlocks and five pounds of tinfoil. All incredible, and inedible, objects.

Why, then, do some owners worry about feeding their dog a digestible rawhide?

The truth is that many owners feel the need to baby their pet. And that's okay. But you need to recognize that this is **your** need, and not your dog's. And you need to be willing to live with the consequences.

If you really want results, you need to remember that your "baby" isn't a **baby**. This dictates a very different course of action. What you really need to do is **puppy** your dog.

In Cuddles' case, her owners refused to remove all the toys. They were willing to live with the destruction, rather than to take the steps necessary to stop the chewing. They sacrificed their own peace-of-mind – and their personal property – to retain their humanized perception of Cuddles' happiness.

Actually, Cuddles was too confused to be happy. She didn't understand what was a proper chewable and what was not. Her owners then compounded her confusion by correcting her after the fact, whenever they arrived at home.

Their unwillingness to correct Cuddles' situation was rather inhumane, adding undue stress to her life.

THE SOLUTION

A dog is going to chew. It's in his nature. But that doesn't mean it has to be your new Nikes. As you discovered in Chapter 7, redirection is the proper procedure for eliminating dog destructive-ness behavior. But for chewing problems, the solution is usually a lot tastier for your pet.

What you must do is give your dog the right-sized rawhide whenever you leave him home alone. How do you find the right size? When you're in the store, find one that looks proportional to the size of your pet. If you're in doubt, ask someone there.

When I'm talking about rawhide, I mean the real thing: the untanned hide of an animal. It's made specifically for dogs to chew on and to digest. In fact, its contents may be familiar to the discriminating owner. They're actually the same ingredients found in many hot dogs.

But many people offer a rawhide to their pet indiscriminately throughout the day. This won't work when you're trying to eliminate an improper chewing habit.

Only give your dog a rawhide when you have to leave her home alone.

Remember, the purpose of the rawhide is to distract her from her usual chewing patterns with something more enticing. If absence makes the heart grow fonder, imagine what it does for her tummy. Limiting availability increases the desirability of rawhide as a chewable.

Pets, too, have their limits. So never discipline your dog unless you catch him in the act; that is, in mid-chew (*gesundheit*).

Remember that your dog cannot reason. When she finds an old shoe, she'll always associate that scintillating smell with that most pleasant of pastimes: chewing.

The tragedy is that many people willingly hand over that first "old" shoe for their new puppy to chew. And what is their reaction when the pup goes after it with gusto? Praise!

Then when the same puppy gets into the closet and gums on another shoe, they get a reprimand. Well, which is it? "Good dog" or "bad dog?" Can't the "dumb dog" tell the difference between an old shoe and a new shoe?

No, it can't! They both look the same. They both smell the same. And they both taste the same. One is just aged a little longer.

Your puppy is **not** human; she's a dog! You told her the shoe was a proper chewable when you happily gave her the first one. So she thought she was doing the right thing by chewing up all the shoes in the house. The last thing she was expecting was a correction!

Is it any wonder that people are a paradox to their pets?

You can't treat your dog like a child. Dogs can't reason the same way. So when your dog misbehaves, you just can't sit down and talk to it. This just won't work with your dog.

Oh, he may put his ears back when you scold him. He may look dejected when you read him the riot act. But that doesn't mean he understands what you're saying. That remorseful look and cowering posture are actually in anticipation of the inevitable correction. They may also correlate directly to your dog's confusion.

For a detailed description of why you should discipline your dog during the act, rather than after the fact, please refer to "Non-Solutions" in Chapter 9, *Correcting Dog Housebreaking Problems*.

ALTERNATIVE METHODS OF CORRECTION

There are instances where the techniques described in this chapter won't solve your problems by themselves. For example, if your dog chews when you're home, but out of sight, then you may need to add some form of confinement to your methodology.

The best way to do this is to incorporate a kennel. Please see Chapter 13, *Other Dog Misbehaviors*, under the heading "Escape Behaviors," to find out more about determining the proper size for your pet.

The purpose of confinement is to force your dog to chomp only on the appropriate chewable that you've provided (e.g., a rawhide), and to prevent further destruction to your house.

After 3 to 5 weeks of this routine, used in conjunction with the techniques previously described, you can gradually eliminate the confinement from your regimen.

THE REBELLIOUS PERIOD

In the early stages of correction, your dog may actually increase her chewing misbehavior before she eventually comes around to your way of thinking.

Again, this increase in misbehavior is something that you must see before your training is successful. This Rebellious Period occurs not just while you're trying to eliminate improper chewing, but when you're training to eliminate **any** misbehavior.

Be aware that you're in for a fight. As long as you understand this, you won't be worried when the relapse occurs.

It's a good thing, really. If your dog is struggling against your will, it means she understands the implications. So stand firm. If you set the rules, and stand by them, eventually your pet will learn to do so, too.

PREVENTATIVE MEASURES

Start to teach your dog the difference between a proper and an improper chewable when you first bring him into your household. If your pupil is a puppy, you should begin before he enters his teething period. If you start when your dog is as close as possible, but not less than, eight weeks, you'll improve your chances of successful training.

Never allow your dog to start chewing on old socks or shoes. This sends her all the wrong signals; specifically, that anything which smells like you is fair game for a good chew! And the same is true for anything else you own, from your favorite T-shirt to your cellular phone.

9

Correcting Dog Housebreaking Problems

As difficult as it is to housebreak a new puppy, correcting an older dog's housebreaking problem can be more difficult. The difference is that with a puppy, you don't have to contend with months or years of established "mistakes." With an older dog, many bad owner habits must be broken – and this is a much more difficult proposition than breaking in a new owner.

Happy sat with me during one very unusual request for housebreaking advice:

We were expecting a visit from Fifi, a white, Toy Poodle. At the appointed time, an elderly human female arrived, but the dog was nowhere to be seen. The Master invited the woman inside, and she came right to the point.

"I want Fifi to go poopie and wee-wee on the floor of my shower stall because it's so easy to wash it down the drain the next morning!" she squealed delightedly.

She talked about Fifi for 20 minutes, all the while acting as if her little dog was right there in the room with us. It gave me the willies.

We were all seated in a simply-furnished room. In it there were a table and several chairs – that's all. And from my position on the floor, I could easily see under every one of them.

Finally, tactfully, The Master asked the female if she thought Fifi was there in the room with us.

"Certainly," she said, opening her purse. A tiny poodle head emerged. Fifi looked around, and quickly ducked back in to safety! Fifi's woman closed her purse and continued the conversation as if this sort of thing happened every day.

Unphased, The Master went on to explain to her how to train Fifi to use this unique toilet area. And she did! Hey, it doesn't matter to us dogs where we go!

Perhaps this story illustrates a human idiosyncracy more so than a problem of pet behavior. But as we have suggested, many so-called pet behavioral problems begin and end with the desires of their human counterparts. It is the role of the *Pet Behavior Specialist* to educate you so that you can best achieve the objectives that you're after, and that means changing your pet's behavior to meet those ends.

The goal is to build a good relationship between you and your pet. So, really, what you say, goes. And anything goes, as long as your plan isn't detrimental to your pet. Of course, your definition of what you consider to be a "good dog" is different from everyone else's. Sometimes very different!

Some people believe their pet knows that its actions are wrong, yet it misbehaves anyway to "get back at them." This is especially easy to believe regarding housebreaking problems. But, again, dogs have no power of reasoning to allow them to retaliate.

When a pet's good housebreaking habits go bad, its owner is sometimes angry, usually upset and almost always a little hurt – as if the owner takes the pet's mistakes as a personal humiliation.

What it comes down to is that when a dog has to go, it has to go. And without proper maintenance of learned habits, dogs of any age will break from their training.

THE CAUSES

An eight week old puppy eliminates whenever and wherever the need arises. It just doesn't know any better. You have to teach it to use an appropriate place, just as you would a baby.

So the primary reason a puppy may exhibit inappropriate behaviors is that it has not been taught – at all, or, perhaps, properly.

Another common cause is that humans have a tendency to feed their pets too frequently and without a set pattern. And what they feed them! Dog biscuits. Beer. Table scraps. Just about anything goes with owners, it seems.

A dog that eats whatever it wants, whenever it wants, wherever it wants, is much more likely to develop a housebreaking problem than a pet adhering to a regular daily diet of healthy pet food.

To control when your dog urinates and defecates, you must control what, where and when it eats and drinks.

There are many other causes to be considered, too. Inappropriate urination and defecation may also be caused by frustration or excitement. And, of course, these states may be brought about by just about anything:

- being left alone frequently;
- seeing another animal through a window;
- the excitement of a ringing doorbell;
- the mailman clanging the mailbox.

Finally, unusual circumstances may impact your dog's system as well. Leaving your pet at the kennel, for example. This may cause diarrhea, because your pet is frustrated, anxious and stressed. This situation speeds up her internal chemistry, and stimulates the bowel and bladder.

NON-SOLUTIONS

We've already shattered the myth that you can discipline your dog after it makes a mistake. Discipline after the fact does not work. Ever. Nor does rubbing your pet's face or body into the "mistake." Ever.

All this teaches your pet is that when you find a "mistake," you will give it a correction.

Another non-solution is the use of a leash or training collar for correction in this situation. Although this may seem appropriate, the truth of the matter is that you can rarely catch your pet in the act once, much less on a consistent basis. Since this is a vital part of a successful leash or collar correction, this method, too, is ineffective.

It is important to learn when – and when not – to discipline your dog in these circumstances. It is actually quite simple. If you can't get your hands on the animal **while** it is urinating in the house, do **not** discipline it in any way.

Yet time and again, when owners find a "mistake," they do the same thing. They seek out their dog, drag him to the mistake, rub his nose in it and discipline him.

Not only will this approach **never** work, but in my experience it makes the problem worse.

Most owners assume the dog knows it is being disciplined for urinating or defecating in the house, but it is impossible for the pet to understand. They do not possess the necessary self-awareness, or the thought processes, to enable them to put number two and number two together. In fact, as I mentioned previously, a dog's memory only allows him to associate any discipline with what happened within 1.8 seconds of that event. Again, Ivan Pavlov proved this point many decades ago.

So when you return from a hard day's work, and discipline your dog after finding a "mistake" in the living room, you're sending it the wrong signal. Especially if you drag your dog over to the "mistake," and discipline it well after the fact. Your dog will soon learn that when you come home, it must cower in a corner because your arrival signifies discipline. This is the most natural connection your dog can make for the correction.

And because it cowers or hides, you will probably assume it knows exactly what it did wrong.

But a correction when you get home does not teach your dog what it did wrong...or the proper place to urinate or defecate.

Instead, it learns that to avoid the discipline, it can't let its owner find the mess. To accomplish this, a pet may try several tactics.

1. It acts submissively when its owner finds the mistake, in hopes that the owner will not discipline it.

2. It tries to hide the tell-tale signs of a "mistake" from its owner. But a dog doesn't do so as people would, by sight. Instead, it does so as a dog would, by smell. So it searches out an area in the house that doesn't have its owner's strong scent.

    If dogs had a reasoning process, they might logically think: "I don't want my owner to find this, because then I'll be disciplined. I'll try to hide it. I'm going to find a place he doesn't go often," (by searching for an area that doesn't have the owner's strong scent on it).

Oftentimes the "hidden" toilet area appears along walls or behind furniture...even in a frequently used room. More often, it will occur in a room that isn't used often, like a guest bedroom.

But, ultimately, even the owner's poor sense of smell leads her to the "mistake," forcing the dog to find a better hiding place next time.

If your dog runs out of hiding spots, it may even eat the "mistake" in its desperation to keep you from finding it. (Corrections for this inappropriate "eating" behavior can be found in Chapter 13, *Other Dog Misbehaviors*, under the heading "Unique Problems.")

Owners correcting their pets after-the-fact is one of the most common reasons dogs sometimes do eat their own defecation.

This may seem extreme. But many owners admit that their dog has had this problem for two-and-a-half years without improvement. Since they still have the problem, perhaps they should concede that disciplining after the fact ***does not work!***

Even if you do catch your dog in the act two times out of 10, and discipline it with the proper use of a training collar, it will not work. There's just not enough consistency in the approach. Unfortunately, it only teaches your dog not to go in front of you.

To be effective, the correction must be given ***each time*** the dog misbehaves. Therefore, physical intervention is rarely an appropriate housebreaking technique.

REAL SOLUTIONS

Before embarking on any program to correct a housebreaking problem, it is vital that you make sure your pet is healthy. Take your dog to a veterinarian to rule out simple problems like bladder infection, worms and parasites. This is an important step, and it shouldn't be omitted for any reason.

Once you have established that your dog is otherwise healthy, you can begin to address a number of issues that may contribute to housebreaking problems.

Consistent Routine

Create a consistent, daily routine for your dog, one that doesn't allow it to be stimulated for urination or defecation except when you are home. The ultimate purpose of such a routine is to develop a new habit: You want your dog to wait until you are home before it develops the need to go outside to do its business.

In their natural environment, dogs do not care where they go; but in the human world, they must have consistency in order to learn what you want them to do.

I cannot overemphasize consistency, for it is the key factor in retraining a pet.

This means **all** family members must be willing to follow through with the new routine. And this can be difficult. It's hard not to give in to a begging pet. But if just one family member departs from the plan – sneaking snacks to the dog because he or she feels sorry it is receiving limited meals daily – the family is fighting a battle it is destined to lose.

Now, I understand that taking a dog outside at the same time every morning and evening can be difficult in today's busy world. Especially after you've come home from an arduous day of work. But without consistent follow-through, the retraining process will not "take."

Dogs do understand, and desire, a predictable routine, rather like children who thrive when parents set appropriate limits for them.

Regular Feeding Schedule

The goal of feeding is to establish bowel movement predictability so that the dog defecates at about the same time each day. For adult dogs, one feeding per day is proper; for younger dogs, provide two meals per day.

Each feeding should last no more than 20 minutes. Your dog may eat all or none of the food during that 20 minute period. At the end of 20 minutes, pick up the food bowl and put it away. Also, make sure your dog gets no food in between meals.

Why is this feeding schedule so important? Because it is important for you to control your dog's defecation.

Three specific events will stimulate a dog to have a bowel movement:

1. eating;

2. exercise;

3. waking from a deep sleep. Usually, dogs are more stimulated to defecate when first waking in the morning.

To correct the housebreaking problem, you must control when the dog defecates; therefore, you need to establish a good routine. Most dogs are stimulated to defecate approximately 20 to 40 minutes after eating. This eliminates not the food it just ate, but the waste developed from the previous meal.

Dogs average one or two bowel movements each day – usually one large and one small. The bigger one usually occurs after eating or during the morning or evening walks.

Many people feed their dog as they are walking out the door to go to work in the morning. That means their dogs are alone in the house for 8 to 10 hours. And twenty minutes after they leave, the dog is stimulated to defecate.

Most dogs cannot wait 8 to 10 hours after eating to go outside and defecate, no matter how well-trained they are. So how can those with a housebreaking problem be expected to do so?

When your dog wakes up, take it outside and let it do its business **before** you leave for the day. **Do not feed it afterwards.**

When you arrive home, your dog is excited to see you. Because excitement encourages bowel movement, take it outside again, providing it the opportunity to defecate. Then bring it back inside.

The best time to feed your dog is when you're having dinner. That way, you're more likely to be home for the next several hours. So after your dog has finished eating, you'll be available to attend to its needs.

A side-benefit is that you'll find that this also reduces begging from the table!

Exercise is another excellent stimulation for defecation, so exercise your dog after dinner. Take it for a 5 or 10 minute walk. Most dogs will not defecate during exercise, but they will very soon after the activity has stopped. Let your dog roam calmly for a few minutes after the walk, and wait for it to go before bringing it back inside.

Please note that it is a mistake to run a dog extremely hard, and then bring it directly into the house. If you do this, more likely than not, your dog will provide you with an odoriferous mistake of its own several minutes after you let it back inside.

Then, about one hour before bedtime, exercise your dog one more time to stimulate a bowel movement.

The Menu

The type of food that your dog eats is also important. Some dog foods aren't always what they seem to be. They may appear to be less expensive. They may have fancy packaging and clever slogans. But it is important to compare more than the price and weight of the package. You should also examine the recommended amount to feed your dog each mealtime.

A 20-pound bag of one food may seem to be a better bargain for $10, than a 20-pound bag purchased for $15.

But there's a reason for the cost difference. The manufacturer of these "less expensive" brands adds filler to their products. Filler may consist of vegetable matter, cereal, and meat by-products.

Is this bad? Not necessarily. But if your ultimate goal is to feed your dog a pet food that results in fewer bowel movements – and of less volume – you should consider a different product.

If your dog is passing a large pile of brown mush that is never quite firm, she is eating a pet food with 40-60% filler. A dog's body cannot absorb these foodstuffs. To provide the daily nutritional requirements for a 50 pound dog, you might have to feed her 4 cups of food per day. And most dogs will eat what is put in front of them.

But their bodies will only absorb about two and one-half of these four cups. The rest is waste material going right through the dog's system. This waste contributes to the housebreaking problem, because the dog is forced to defecate what its system can't absorb.

Actually, the same is true of humans. A person who eats junk food has more bowel movements than one eating meat, vegetables and fruit. The body doesn't need the excess, therefore it eliminates it.

Owners should check with a veterinarian or other pet professional to determine which dog foods have fewer fillers. These will help alleviate the situation, and will allow you to feed your dog a healthy meal limited to one and one-half cups of food.

Then your dog will find it easier to control its bowels because there is less pressure inside pushing a large quantity of waste out.

Watering Schedule

Helping a dog to develop a consistent bladder routine parallels the procedures used for eating and defecating. But a dog with a urination problem must be given water on a more regular basis than they are given food. Allow your dog to have water as long as you are home and awake. Water should not be available at any other time. Most dogs will be ready to urinate 10 to 20 minutes after drinking.

The long term goal of housebreaking or retraining is to change your pet's behavior and ease the household back into its routine. But each owner is different, so there are many different resolutions to this common problem, as Happy and I once learned.

The Master and I were out to see another elderly human female, who said that she had never heard of housebreaking a dog! She thought asking a dog to relieve itself in public in front of other pets and people was utterly inhumane. Sandy, her Cocker Spaniel, just winked.

This woman had accepted Sandy's behavior, limited it to one area and was quite content. I can't imagine that she had many human guests in that house, though!

Quite a different situation involved a four-year-old Sheltie named Mandy. She called one day, irate because her humans wanted to change her housebreaking habits. They were both professors at a well-known university. And, apparently, they were upset that she was going in the same spot in the back yard each day.

"So what's the problem?" I asked.

"That's just it," she cried, "my humans want me to go in the park, because they don't want to clean up the mess."

Eventually, The Master taught these humans to use a daily routine. They walked Mandy to the park immediately after she ate. And they didn't allow her to stop moving until she arrived there.

Mandy thought that this was a super solution – she was quite comfortable with the routine – until a local pooper scooper law was passed, and she was forced to return to the yard.

"I'm right back to where I started," she told me soon afterwards!

Other families focus their efforts not on the problem, but on hiding it from the outside world. Some are so demoralized that they don't even clean up the mess every day. Embarrassed as they are, they live with the odor.

Another such Cocker Spaniel case cropped up in Cincinnati. Happy and I were on the trail together.

Mork and Mindy could be quite obnoxious. They ruled the roost of their Cincinnati home, jumping on human houseguests, while coming and going as they pleased.

Worst of all, for their humans anyway, they peed with impunity everywhere in the house. But after battling these little black balls of fur for years on this issue, the family had given up.

Now they addressed the problem with liberal doses of aerosol air fresheners, and open windows...even when it was below freezing outside.

Fortunately, they drafted The Master to come in and help them solve their situation. He worked with them to strengthen their obedience training. This, along with a basic daily routine, enabled them to solve their housebreaking problems.

Have faith, humans, giving up need not be an option.

ALTERNATIVE METHODS OF CORRECTION

There are some situations where controlling what and when a dog eats and drinks is not enough to solve a housebreaking problem, as Happy can tell you. Take the following case for example.

The Master and I met a married human couple, mates without a litter yet, living in their first home together. They'd lived there for about two years.

During their first six months there they "rescued" a 2-year-old dog, Sandy, from the local humane society. As it turns out, a housebreaking problem was the reason Sandy was put in the humane society in the first place.

Well, when it came to feeding and watering, Sandy's humans did everything that books told them to do. But Sandy still answered nature's call inside the house. He made most of his "mistakes" in the living room.

Sandy's humans tried everything, including discipline, distracting chemicals...even aluminum foil over the mistake area...everything. But by this time Sandy was one confused canine. His humans finally called The Master.

After a lengthy discussion, The Master had an inkling as to why Sandy was doing his tinkling in the house. We suspected that Sandy had made so many mistakes inside, there was an outside chance that he'd developed a habit. And as undogly as it seems, he now believed that the indoors was his toilet area.

This seemed a likely explanation. But what was the solution?

Our Master Plan was simple. We figured that the only way to break this habit was to force Sandy to "go" outside often enough to form a new habit. So The Master prescribed a strict regimen of confinement and supervision.

Sandy's humans were instructed to buy a cage. Some humans seem to have a problem putting us dogs in cages, but we really don't mind. As long as it's large enough to stand up in with our heads erect, and wide enough so we can turn around without bumping the sides.

Anyway, Sandy spent many hours a day in this cage for about a month. When he wasn't in the cage, one of his humans had him on a leash, except when he was outside. That's the only time he was actually "free," as humans define it. So he started to take advantage of his time out there.

When he "went" outside, his humans praised him verbally and physically. And if he even looked like he was thinking of "going" inside, they immediately took him outside.

After about four weeks of this routine, Sandy snapped out of it. He started to show some consistency, going outside at the proper times. Over the following four weeks, the confinement and supervision were gradually eliminated and everything was fine.

TECHNIQUES FOR PUPPIES

Housebreaking a puppy (age 8 to 22 weeks) incorporates all of the techniques described in this chapter. You need the correct food, a consistent routine, and the use of confinement and supervision. But with such a young dog, you also need to account for the following:

1) **Type of Food.** Consult your veterinarian or other pet professional. A young dog has different nutritional requirements than older dogs. The proper food for your pet may be very different than that for another dog you may know.

2) **Feeding Routine.** Adult dogs can be fed just once per day. But younger dogs must be fed 2 to 4 times per day. Once again, consult your veterinarian for a recommendation. However, like an adult dog, the time food is made available should be limited. That is, your puppy should have access to food for only 20 to 40 minutes at a time...and then it should be removed. This teaches the puppy to eat it all at once, and not "pick" at its food.

3) **Watering Routine.** Puppies need a more constant supply of water than an adult dog does. But there are still times that water should be restricted, such as when your puppy is in her cage at night. Your veterinarian can tell you more about the specific routine for each breed.

4) **Use Of Confinement/Supervision.** A young dog needs much more supervision and confinement than an older dog. Picture your dog as a one-year-old child. You wouldn't let that child wander unsupervised in your home – so don't let your puppy. Your puppy should be confined when you aren't at home, or even when you are, but you can't provide supervision.

And even when you are at home, and supervising your puppy, you shouldn't let her out of your sight for the first month. Soon you'll build enough trust in her ability to interact with her environment that you can relax the supervision somewhat.

THE REBELLIOUS PERIOD

As with any misbehavior, your pet's actions will deteriorate at some point before they improve. This Rebellious Period will test any owner's convictions and resolve. They're not a sign that the techniques aren't working. For more information, see "The Rebellious Period" in Chapter 12, *Changing Dog Disobedience*.

Occasionally, an unusually stubborn dog will decline to deal with a new routine. He may even entirely refuse to eat. But the biggest mistake you can make is to give in too soon.

Wait 72 hours before becoming concerned. Or consult a veterinarian if you're uncomfortable with the situation. Generally, short-term fasting won't harm your animal, especially if he is still taking in sufficient water.

In order to build a lasting solution, you must be strong enough to withstand these assaults!

PREVENTATIVE MEASURES

Besides following a consistent plan, there are few preventative measures you can take in regard to inappropriate urination and defecation. Fewer still are successful.

The most common measure owners attempt is neutering. This surgery can be successful only if it is done at an early age, before the pet has begun to establish bad habits.

Under these circumstances, neutering can prevent the habit of territorial marking from forming.

CLEANING UP AFTERWARDS

While dealing with a housebreaking problem, owners must also address how to clean up and eliminate the odors that are its tell-tale signs.

Remember Sandy, whom Happy told you about earlier in this chapter? Well, during his period of confinement and supervision, his owner had to use a chemical to remove the odor Sandy had left behind. This had to be done so Sandy wouldn't maintain his habit of going indoors for scent-related reasons.

No matter how hard his owners worked with Sandy... no matter how successful the Confinement/Supervision regimen...it would all have gone for nought if they didn't also do an appropriate clean-up.

Here are some tips that you may find useful while you're cleaning up after your dog.

Eliminating Odors

A dog's well-defined sense of smell gives it the ability to track down even the most subtle, to humans, urine scent. This wreaks havoc with the retraining regimen.

Dogs determine where to urinate and defecate through scent. When a dog is ready to go, she will seek out spots that already contain dog scent, her own or that of another dog.

This may be a bit disconcerting for multiple dog families, because if one dog decides to go in an inappropriate spot, all the others are likely to follow suit!

So it's a good idea to keep your dog away from the improper areas that it has used until those areas have been treated – and retreated, if needed – to remove the scent.

Often, desperate owners turn to old wives' tale "solutions" to rid their homes of these odors. And there are many:

1. *Vinegar*. This helps camouflage the odor from humans, but not from pets.

2. *Carpet Shampoos*. Urine seeps through the carpet, onto the padding and wood floor beneath. So carpet shampoos only scratch the surface of the problem.

3. *Repellent or Neutralizer*. Again, these products appease the human nose rather suitably, but do not eliminate the scent from the nose of the dog.

4. *Ammonia*. This is an extremely poor selection when treating odor because, to a dog, the smell of urine very closely resembles the smell of ammonia, thus drawing him to return to a spot.

Don't try to mask the odors. Doing so only hides the smell from your own nose. The dog's nose, which is much more sensitive, will lead it right back to the spot in question.

Instead, when a "mistake" is made, soak up all the urine or pick up solid matter as soon as possible. Then clean the area by applying a bacteria-eating enzyme solution according to the directions on the bottle.

Although a mixture of tepid water, baking soda and vinegar will work well enough to suit you, your dog's keen sense of smell will whiff its way right through this concoction. And your dog will continue to make the same old "mistakes" in the same old place.

Only bacterial cleaners will remove the scent sufficiently so an animal doesn't return to the scene of the crime.

There are hundreds of products on the market which claim to eliminate or neutralize the odor or repel a pet from the spot. But be wary. Most are ineffective. Those claiming to eliminate odor usually just mask it. And if they do address the cause of the odor itself, it is to the human nose and not the pet's nose. And now you know which nose is more important!

Still, don't expect miracles. It's certainly possible to treat a small area. But if you want to treat a large area, or one that has been used hundreds of time and thoroughly saturated, you'll probably have to replace carpet and padding while you treat the floor with the proper solution.

The story of Happy's friend Sandy had a happy ending. But it wasn't over yet. About a year after we'd worked with the confused dog, we got another call.

Sandy's humans called us when he started making mistakes inside the house again. And everything had been going so well, too.

For the past six months, Sandy had been so "low-maintenance" his humans were convinced he was a different dog! All they'd had to do was let him outside on occasion, and he did the rest.

But the problem resurfaced when the weather turned. During a two-week stretch of very, very cold, slippery weather, Sandy's humans were less willing to take him outside...and Sandy himself wasn't keen on the idea either.

With the regimen broken, Sandy slipped quickly into his old habits.

It took a visit from The Master, and a reapplication of the regimen to put Sandy – and his humans – back on the straight-and-narrow. But this demonstrates the need for consistency on everyone's part.

10

Correcting Dog Aggressiveness

One day, The Master and I were visiting a Boxer named Tyson, who was having some difficulties with his humans. They hadn't yet provided him with an appropriate chewable – so he had contented himself with his human female's shoe closet.

While we sat in his living room, listening to his humans tell his tale, we watched a most curious progression of events.

First, Tyson got up and moved away from the human couple's precocious two-year-old child. By human standards she was an adorable little girl, but as we watched she followed the young Boxer around, twisting his ear and hitting him with a red plastic hammer.

Again Tyson moved away. The child chased after him, pulling his tail. Finally, the dog trotted off into an adjoining room with the little girl hot on his heels.

Just as the toddler's parents were telling us how good their dog was with the baby, we heard growling – and then a sharp cry of pain, followed by the wailing of the little girl.

Tyson was immediately banished to the back yard, while our conversation changed completely to focus on this unhappy incident. I went outside to get the Boxer's side of the story.

Tyson was already on edge because of our visit, he told me. But that wasn't the reason for the little nip he gave the human child.

Apparently, after six months, he had realized that ignoring her aggressive play wouldn't work if he wanted any peace at all. If anything, she was persistent.

Once we'd arrived, he'd tried holding his ground and growling, just to save face. But the little two-year-old had never heard a dog growl before. So she had no idea how to translate this new message, and blithely maintained her approach.

The dog, cornered, finally decided to challenge the little aggressor.

"I had to increase my aggressive behavior and bite her, or she would have run rough-shod all over me for the rest of my life," the distraught dog related.

This particular little girl was lucky because the Boxer only nipped a little at her hand. But most children in a similar situation are bitten on the face because it happens to be on the same level as the dog's mouth.

I could tell that Tyson was leveling with me, so I passed the information on to The Master, who explained the situation to the stricken parents.

"Oftentimes, this is all the education both injured parties need," he said. "But rarely does a pet bite a child out of the clear blue."

Any breed of dog may exhibit the aggressive behavior characteristics exemplified by the Boxer in Happy's story. Fortunately, these misbehaviors can usually be corrected.

The bulk of this chapter is written to help guide the average owner through the "normal" aggressive misbehavior patterns associated with the average pet. The dogs in this discussion include common house pets like:

- *The Cocker Spaniel.* The breed owners most commonly complain about. The complaints may indeed be justified – but in some cases the aggressiveness can be reduced or eliminated.

- *The Doberman.* With its fierce appearance and history as an attack or guard dog, the Doberman has one of the worst reputations among non-dog-owners. This reputation is not deserved.

- *The Rottweiler.* Its ferocious look makes it the most intimidating to work with. And, in fact, it may act the toughest of any breed. But what is "act" and what is "fact?"

- **The Springer Spaniel.** When it acts aggressively, it can be one of the "meanest" breeds, intense and prone to losses of control.

- **The English Sheepdog.** This may be one of the most unpredictable breeds. At the same time, it also exhibits the strangest aggressive behavior. As large as it is, the English Sheepdog almost always initially bites people on the feet or ankles.

- **The Miniature Dachshund.** This dynamic five-pound package may be the most comically aggressive breed. But if you've ever witnessed all that angry yapping, you know you couldn't expect more out of a 120-pound Rottweiler. Owners might back away laughing from this intense little dog, but they are confronted with a problem.

- **The Chow Chow.** Again, reputation is the reason that many Chow Chow owners worry about the possibility of aggressive behavior.

Over the years, I have found that owners who come to me for help in cases of aggressive behavior generally fall into one of four categories:

1.   Those who recognize an undesirable characteristic and seek assistance when a puppy begins play biting.

2.   Those who call when their dog is finally frightening them, but hasn't actually bitten anyone yet.

3.   Those who make contact when their dog has bitten them.

4.   Those who have ignored all the warning signs, and whose dog has bitten several times. They may finally call when their pet bites someone special (in many cases a child or grandchild) or someone who threatens legal action.

Whichever of these categories your dog may fit into, a *Pet Behavior Specialist* will first try to determine whether the aggressiveness exhibited is an "understandable misbehavior" or a "normal" aggressive behavior.

Like any good detective, he'll start by asking a lot of questions...starting with an explanation of the circumstances surrounding the alleged aggressiveness. He might uncover an example of an "understandable misbehavior" if an owner answers: "Every time I go to hit my dog, she growls at me."

The dog, of course, does not want to be hit, and is telling the owner so in a language she knows her owner will understand.

Another example of "understandable" or "normal" aggressive behavior would be a dog that reacts to teasing by children...especially when the dog is confined, or tied up. In fact, Happy has a story that illustrates this point very well.

I know a Border Collie named Harvey who lives in a southern Ohio town. It was common for Harvey's humans to leave him tied on a ten foot chain in his back yard when they left the house.

225

He enjoyed the fresh air, and all the freedom he could romp out of a circle with a 20-foot diameter.

What he didn't enjoy were what he called "O.P.K.s" – Other People's Kids.

Apparently, for many years teasing children often ran around him in a circle just outside his outstretched paws. Then, one day, an O.P.K. finally stepped inside his circle. Harvey promptly chomped him on the leg.

"I was just releasing some frustration," said the Border Collie, his long, dry tongue planted firmly in cheek.

Naturally, Harvey's owners called in The Master, who taught Harvey that it was O.K. to ignore the teasing of the O.P.K.s.

Aggressive behavior is normal for canines in their natural environment. It is part of the day-to-day interaction of the pack. But for a dog to fit comfortably in the human environment, this inappropriate behavior must be trained out of them. The "normal" types of aggressive behaviors to which I refer may occur for the following reasons:

- Avoidance of correction or control by humans or other animals. Aggressive behavior is often exhibited in order to force a rival (or an owner) to back off.

- Stress or confusion which has built up over a long period of time. A dog which bites without warning is not necessarily abnormal or unpredictable.

- Deterence of rivals (or humans) used as a last resort when the usual techniques haven't worked.

- Escape from a hopeless situation. Unable to extract itself from unusual circumstances, a fearful dog may act aggressively in order to get away.

- Physical illnesses, such as a sore hip that someone touches.

All the reasons for individual instances of aggressiveness rarely come to light. But, by the same token, the original explanations for them rarely hold water either.

Whatever the cause, it is best for you to seek assistance at the first signs of an aggressiveness problem, rather than to sit back and wait for your dog's misbehavior to take root.

Happy has an excellent example of the seeds of misbehavior being planted, nurtured, taking root, and growing quite out-of-control.

One day, we got a call from a terrified young woman, who asked for an appointment to discuss her Doberman Pinscher, Brutus. When she arrived at the office, she claimed that she needed our assistance because Brutus was making it impossible for her to arrive at work on time in the mornings!

Although at first we thought this story far-fetched, The Master listened carefully. The problem, it seemed, was that the Doberman had become more and more aggressive.

It had started one night when he entered her bedroom, stood over her on the bed and woke her from a sound sleep with a ferocious growl. Understandably, this forced her to retreat to the living room, where she spent the rest of the night on the couch.

For Brutus, this was just the starting point. Each night afterwards, he would sprawl on her bed, not allowing her to return.

To her further dismay, he grew increasingly aggressive. By the time she called The Master, Brutus refused even to allow her to enter the room in the mornings to dress for work. Not, anyway, until he was good and ready to rise from her comfortable bed.

The Master wasn't much of a comfort to her either, at first, prescribing what turned out to be a harrowing month of work with the dog. But the regimen did end the poor woman's nightmare. Brutus now sleeps contentedly under the bed, while she's back to being the early bird at the office.

THE CORRECTION

In cases of aggressive behavior, a *Pet Behavior Specialist* often works with the owner to produce the misbehavior under controlled circumstances in order to correct it. To give the owner the greatest advantage, the dog wears a training collar and six-foot leash.

It will not harm the pet to wear a leash continually for a period of time. Normally, while trying to break a pattern of aggressiveness, it is left in place until the owner has not used it to correct a dog for 60 consecutive days. Only then may the owner remove the leash.

The leash is used to help force the dog to sit, stay and to make necessary corrections. It also allows you to feel less fearful about correcting your pet.

The first step in working with an aggressive dog is to teach it to sit and to stay, so that it knows what is expected of it. It is also necessary so that the owner learns how to correct the dog.

In a classic case of aggressiveness, a dog might grab a shoe and carry it under the dining room table and chairs. Black Labradors are notorious for this hide-under-the-table behavior.

When you approach to retrieve your shoe, your dog might growl intensely to induce you to back off. Because this aggressive behavior is inappropriate, you must confront your pet to convey that you aren't afraid of its aggressiveness.

You need to do several things immediately:

1. Reach under the table, grab the leash and pull the dog out.

2. Correct it with the training collar. The methodology is simple. While your dog stands there looking and acting aggressively, grab her collar, say "sit" once, and firmly jerk the collar.

    If your dog remains belligerent and standing, repeat the "sit" command and jerk the collar again. Continue to repeat this procedure, using the word "sit" only once and then jerking the training collar.

    Only when the dog finally sits is this step completed.

3. Command your dog to sit and stay until called. In the proper sit and stay stance, she won't move or make noise.

A dog should always understand *why* it is being corrected. If an owner were to reach under the table, jerk a pet out by the collar and then smack it, what would be the message? Perhaps that when its owner approaches, he's going to be corrected. Instead, a dog needs to associate the correction with the improper misbehavior of aggression. By first bringing it into the sit and stay position, the owner connects the correction with the prior behavior.

Unfortunately, when a dog attempts to make its owner back away, some dog trainers will tell you to reach in and physically intimidate the poor animal. This is unfair and inhumane advice. Although a beating might eliminate aggressive behavior in a very small percentage of dogs, it may also create an extremely withdrawn, timid animal.

This isn't exactly the warm, loving dog most pet owners want in their homes.

The correct technique is actually the very simplest method of correction. But actually learning it may take many hours, because the *Pet Specialist* must teach the owner as well as the dog, and old habits are difficult to break.

In addition, human emotions often get in the way of the learning process:

1.   Owners are frequently fearful because they are working with an animal they are convinced is dangerous to their well-being.

2.   Most owners start out repeating the word "sit" over and over before each correction...often without realizing they are doing so. They must work to become aware of their words as they relate to their actions.

3.   Learning the correct strength of the tug on the training collar is a difficult assignment. It differs by dog and by owner. Small dogs require only a little pull. Medium-sized dogs need a stronger jerk to receive the same message. Large dogs may need a very strong hand.

The intensity of this correction is also somewhat dependent on the dog's temperament. That is, strong-willed dogs need a more intense correction than a more timid dog.

4.   Owners tend to adjust the weight of their corrections to the situation. If, for instance, their dog is acting aggressively towards them, they may give a mild correction; but if the dog is acting aggressively towards a neighbor's child, the correction may be more intense.

In the end, it is your dog's perception that counts. It has to know when and why it is being corrected. If the methodology is consistent – if it **never** changes – then you can eliminate aggressive behavior, sometimes with only five to ten consecutive corrections.

But owners are often afraid they will harm their pet while correcting it. This can be difficult for a *Pet Behavior Specialist* to understand after listening to an owner describe her dog's aggressiveness.

"I'm afraid he'll bite me" just doesn't correlate with "I'm not going to correct him because I'm afraid I'll hurt him."

I have found this to be particularly true of owners of the toy and miniature breeds. As illogical as this is, many owners live in fear of their yappy, nippy, biting, aggressive little charges. They may even fear them as much as they do a larger animal; yet, while the loss of a finger tip is certainly possible, they are seemingly unaware of their dog's diminutive size.

Rarely does an owner correct a dog as firmly as required. It's much easier for a *Pet Behavior Specialist* to walk into a home and correct a growling, 100-pound monster with exactly the correct amount of tension to return her to the status of common housepet. Why? Because he is not attached to the dog as the owner is. The *Specialist* is merely teaching it not to be aggressive.

But most owners instinctively hold back right at the critical moment during the jerk of the leash on the training collar. The result is an ineffectual correction.

Using this faulty technique, an owner's corrections may stop the misbehavior temporarily, but it will not end the pattern of aggressiveness. Owners might have to subject their dog to 300 or more of these too-mild corrections before the message finally sinks in. On the other hand, if they had corrected the dog at the proper intensity just 20 times, they could have saved 280 yanks of the collar and months of work.

Owners, for the most part, approach their dogs too timidly. In fact, there are probably just 15 seconds out of each day during which you need to rethink your approach to your aggressive pet. You have to meet its intensity with some resolve of your own.

Many people won't ever get as intense as they need to with their corrections, but they'll come close enough to save perhaps 100 corrections and end the misbehavior.

How you feel about your dog is vitally important. You need to begin training an aggressive dog with a positive mental attitude and a physical plan. The mental plan is to enter the situation thinking, "I'm calm. I have a plan and I'll follow through with it. Dog, if you bite me,

I'm going to grab your collar, yank it, tell you to 'sit' and 'stay,' and stick with you until you do so."

If you approach the training thinking that your dog will bite you, you're fighting a losing battle. On the other hand, if you develop the mindset that you **will** handle your dog, you stand an excellent chance of eliminating the misbehavior.

Having the correct mindset is important in correcting most common behavioral problems – overexcitement, hyperactivity, excessive barking, and many others. You need this positive foundation, especially when working with an animal that can elicit extreme human responses such as fear, frustration, impatience and anger.

When you lose your mindset and give way to those emotions, you lose control of your actions...and the training that you seek to instill.

Another classic example of overly aggressive behavior may occur when you walk your dog down the street. As an unknown dog approaches, your dog may begin to growl and act excitedly.

You may think, "Oh no, there's going to be a dog fight here. I don't know what to do."

This fear may quickly reveal itself in your reactions to the situation: quicker, higher-pitched commands; greater use of the leash; pushing, pulling and impatience.

The results can be devastating to all the hard work you've done with your pet. Your dog responds to your reaction with, "I'm going to act more aggressively to make any unknown dog back off before my owner goes completely irrational again."

As excited as your dog may get in such a situation, you must remain calm. Someone has to correct your dog and tell it what it must do. That person is you. And your pet must clearly understand your meaning, spoken and unspoken.

Ultimately, your calm control and comfortable patterns will make it easier for you to communicate what it is that you're after: "Dog, this is what I want you to do. Do it no matter what the situation. If you do so, everything will be just fine." This is the bottom line.

Regardless of the cause of your pet's aggressiveness, you must **always** follow these steps:

1. Make your dog sit and stay, so it knows what is expected of it.

2. Once your dog sits and remains calm for five to ten seconds, move in close and pet it on the chin. This is often difficult to ask, especially if you've recently been on the receiving end of aggressive behavior.

3. Verbally and, occasionally, physically praise your dog for sitting, staying and remaining calm. Do **not** reward your pet with food. You may not always have food on hand, and it is unnecessary.

A third example of aggressive behavior occurs when one dog attacks another. Happy has been the referee for more than his fair share of canine counterparts. Sometimes, such attacks even occur within the same household, as they do in this story.

The Master knows a pair of Springer Spaniels, Abercrombie and Fitch, who own a human doctor.

Abercrombie, a male, and Fitch, a female, would usually sit quietly around their house, enjoying each other's company. But on occasion, Fitch would suddenly look around wildly, and quickly run out of the room.

Within seconds, Abercrombie would attack her. There would be no warning signs. This would initiate an ugly fight, which always resulted in drawn blood.

Although Fitch was apparently capable of sensing these onslaughts, it was virtually impossible to determine their cause. Complicating this situation was the fact that it is very difficult to eliminate attacks like these unless you're actually right there when they occur.

Fortunately for Abercrombie & Fitch, with a little training, this aggressive behavior was eliminated...but it took a great deal more than conventional methodolgy.

THE TIMETABLE FOR CORRECTION

Training times can be as short as 30 days or as long as six months. Your actual training time will vary, but you should know that they are dependent on several factors, including: breed; why the dog is acting aggressively; how long the aggression has been in existence prior to the start of training; and how consistent the owner is with the techniques.

236

Here's how each of these factors can impact your timetable for correction.

Breed

Certain breeds take longer to "retrain" than others. Even within a specific breed there can be variation. We will concentrate on the breeds mentioned earlier in this chapter. What also may be helpful is a frank discussion by Happy of his reaction when first meeting each of these breeds.

Happy, On Cocker Spaniels: *Although it's a bit embarrassing, The Master has asked me to describe my action to each of the various breeds when I met them for the very first time. So I'll give it to you straight, even at the risk of alienating some of my close friends.*

Many Cocker Spaniels gave me the willies. You can smell the aggression on the little rogues. From what I'm told, this is no fault of their own. But it sure can be disturbing, at first. (I'm told that on occasion I actually whined!)

My hair was up when I got in range. I sure wasn't going to make eye contact...let alone physical contact. But I was very much aware of what that Cocker Spaniel was doing every second of our encounter.

Today, Cocker Spaniels are some of my best friends. And to a pup, every one of them tells me they still have to work hard to overcome their aggression.

Dr. Andrysco, On Cocker Spaniels: This is one of the most difficult breeds when it comes to eliminating aggressive behavior. The Cocker Spaniel's aggressiveness usually starts at an early age, and can be very intense.

It is my opinion that this aggression is somewhat "inherited." Decades ago, this breed became very popular (right about the time Disney released its animated classic, "*Lady and the Tramp*").

The demand for the Cocker Spaniel dramatically outpaced the supply. Breeders initiated poor breeding practices to increase the supply. This eventually resulted in an aggressive behavior first reported in the late 1960s, called "Cocker Spaniel Syndrome."

Even into the 1970s, there were many published reports of this breed acting aggressively for no reason at all.

Since then, breeding practices have improved, and the "Syndrome" has disappeared, but what remains is a breed with aggressive tendencies.

I am not saying "don't buy this dog" or "this dog is untrainable." I'm saying this breed has a history of aggression and you need to be very consistent with it from the first day you bring one home.

The average time for successful non-aggressiveness training is 2 to 3 months.

Happy, On Doberman Pinschers: *All dogs look up to Dobermans. They're a dog's dog. A role model. They inspire confidence in all of canine kind. And the word gets around.*

So when I met my first Dobie, I met him head on. Perhaps this was naive on my part, but I don't think so. Dobermans return respect for respect. So I made it obvious that I respected him. My hair was up...but just a little. And my tail, well, I gave that Doberman a weak wagging salute...which he seemed to accept graciously with a sniff of my underbelly.

Dr. Andrysco, On Doberman Pinschers: I've always considered the Doberman the "easiest" breed from which to eliminate aggression. Perhaps that's because they're the most misunderstood.

These dogs are easily trained in many areas, including obedience, security and protection. They are also easily "modified," and this includes the elimination of aggressive behavior.

It is actually the owners of this breed who tend to need more work than their dogs. They need help overcoming their fear of their dog breed's reputation.

Once the owner is trained, consistent and assertive, the dog will change within a relatively short period of time.

Generally, you can modify aggressive behavior in 30 to 60 days.

Happy, On Rottweilers: *A Rottweiler is like a Doberman on steroids. But like the Doberman, they seem comfortable in their role. So they don't need to flaunt any aggression they may have.*

When I met my first Rottweiler, I was wary but unafraid. In fact, I let my hair down. And so did he. Still, because he was so big – and I was just a pup – I made sure my movements were slow. That way, I didn't startle him, and, at the same time, I could react very quickly, if necessary.

Fortunately, it wasn't. But I did a good deal of territorial marking all the same. It was my turf, after all, and I wanted him to know it. I'd let him approach me. It was only neighborly. But when he go too close, I gave him my most intimidating look.

Looking back at the incident today, I'd say he probably found this very amusing from a little mutt like me.

Dr. Andrysco, On Rottweilers: Rottweilers are very similar to Doberman Pinschers in terms of modifying aggressive behavior. Their owners are similar, too.

In fact, Rottweiler owners usually take longer to train than Doberman owners, because their dogs tend to look even more menacing.

But in reality, Rottweilers are very quick studies. You can usually modify aggressive behavior in 30 to 75 days.

Happy, On Springer Spaniels: *When I met my first Springer Spaniel, we were both kind of stand-offish, though I didn't feel any fear. Neither of us got our hair up. So I guess it was more awkward than anything.*

We were both interested, you know? Very aware of each other. Hey, in my youth I was a prime specimen! Eventually we sniffed each other out, and went our separate ways.

Dr. Andrysco, On Springer Spaniels: I tend to see the Springer Spaniel less for aggression than I do the three previously-mentioned breeds, but when I do, it often proves to be a difficult case.

These dogs are normally very "explosive." They may skip the normal warning signals and go right to the biting stage.

I may tend to spend a lot of time with these owners, discussing the "downsides," and in some cases they would choose not to work with this breed.

When attempts were made, they usually resulted in longer services and a greater number of training sessions. The success rate is generally less than 40% with Springer Spaniels. And it usually takes 4 to 6 months to achieve the desired results.

Happy, On English Sheepdogs: *I don't ever remember paying much attention to big ol' English Sheepdogs. They were just there, if you know what I mean. Not a mean bone in their bodies, was what I'd always heard (although I've seen a couple of good stories firsthand since then).*

These big balls of fur always seemed willing to play. But sometimes their size would get in the way. So I'm sorry to say, I'd often just ignore them. Or pretend they weren't there.

Dr. Andrysco, On English Sheepdogs: I never have seen the English Sheepdog as frequently as these other breeds. But when I do, they can be difficult to work with, if only because of their size.

Also, this dog's long hair hides its eyes. That means it's sometimes difficult to pick up the dog's warning signals, which, in turn, makes it difficult to predict its behavior.

Still, I've never met one that was "dangerous."

Training an English Sheepdog to eliminate aggressive behavior usually takes 30 to 60 days.

Happy, On Miniature Daschunds: *My first meeting with a Miniature Daschund didn't amount to much. In fact, I had to be reminded later that I'd met one at all. I never had much interaction with the little guys. At first blush, there isn't much there more than a little mischief. But looks can be deceiving.*

These little dogs are very loyal, and prone to being overprotective of their human charges. Personally, I can't find fault with this attitude. I only wish there was more of it out there these days.

Dr. Andrysco, On Miniature Daschunds: When they're aggressive, Miniature Daschunds are very noisy. Their aggression usually is directed at non-family members just as they enter the Daschund-owner's home.

The most interesting aspect of retraining the Daschund is that most of their owners have a difficult time overcoming their fear of hurting these little dogs when correcting them with a collar.

Nonetheless, the rate of success is very high in just 2 to 3 months.

Happy, On Chow-Chows: *I'm happy to say that I've never met a Chow-Chow I didn't like. Perhaps that's because I avoid them whenever I can! Actually, I've got a Chow or two for friends. And good friends they are, too. But when I come across a strange Chow, I don't go out of my way to meet them. That way, I won't become chow myself!*

Dr. Andrysco, On Chow Chows: These large dogs have the reputation for being willing to use their aggressive nature. This reputation is deserved.

They're more than willing to bite their owner, given the right opportunity. Chow Chow owners need to be very assertive, and willing to "correct" at any time.

And it certainly helps if an owner "plays aggressive" and wins.

Training for aggressiveness takes 3 to 6 months, on average.

Why Is The Dog Acting Aggressively?

Is the aggression learned? What is the stimulus that caused the dog to be aggressive? How has the owner responded in the past? These are some of the questions that must be answered before a prediction can be made as to how long it will take to modify a dog's aggressive behavior.

Most aggressive behavior has been learned by the dog or, in other words, accidentally taught to the dog. If it is a learned behavior, you can usually retrain your dog in 30 to 90 days if you're consistent with the techniques.

If aggression is the result of outside stimulus, but still learned (e.g., the postal carrier coming to the door) the behavior can still be modified in 30 to 90 days as long as you can apply the proper techniques in the situation that causes or contains the stimulus.

If aggression is not learned – if it is genetic or the result of some physical problem – the chances of completely eliminating it are less than 30%.

How Long Has The Dog Exhibited The Aggression?

Simply put, the longer the behavior has manifested itself, prior to training, the longer it will take to eliminate it.

Basically, the improper or old habit must be broken first. Only then can the new behavior be taught to your dog. Owners who call me at the first sight of a misbehavior experience more success more quickly than those who wait months to call. For each week you wait to call, add 2 to 3 weeks to the retraining period.

How Consistent Are You With The Technique?

The more consistent you are, the quicker you'll see positive results. If you make a "mistake" once every ten or fifteen interactions with your dog, you won't ever be successful. You must perform the technique properly every time. If you do, you will be successful in a relatively short period of time.

ALTERNATIVE METHODS OF CORRECTION

There are a number of alternative methods for eliminating aggressive behavior that you can try if the *Sit, Stay and Collar Correction* technique doesn't work for you after a reasonable period of time. These include:

<u>1. Ignoring It</u>

This method may sound silly, but certain types of aggressive behaviors are employed solely for the purpose of getting your attention. Toy breeds especially are prone to doing so.

A dog that isn't getting enough attention may give you a small growl. When you come over to reprimand it ("Now, you stop that!") your dog has already accomplished his objective ("This is great. I finally got her out of her chair. I'll just growl again the next time I'm feeling bored").

This type of behavior should be totally ignored.

But how do you decide if your dog's aggressiveness is simply an attention-getting behavior?

- *Observe.* If aggressiveness ceases once you give your pet any type of response at all, the behavior is most likely utilized just to get your attention.

- *Ignore.* If you're still unsure, try ignoring the behavior. If your pet goes out of its way to track you down, and *then* acts aggressively, it is probably seeking your attention.

- *Monitor.* Watch your dog when it is without an audience...perhaps while it is alone in the back yard. If you see no signs of aggressive behavior, then its misbehavior might be of the attention-getting nature.

2. Pre-emptive Rewards

Rewarding your dog before it becomes aggressive is another excellent technique. As you walk your dog down the sidewalk, you'll usually spy another dog approaching before your pet will. This is only natural. Your dog is excited just to be out spending some quality time with you. Then there are the thousand sights and sounds...and smells.... that she's already busy with, so that even with her superior senses, you're likely to spot Spot before she does.

Put you dog on "sit" and "stay" and pop a food reward, such as a very desirable, and small, piece of cheese or hot dog, into her mouth every two or three seconds until the other dog passes by. What will this teach your pet? That when a strange dog comes near, it gets a wonderful treat!

In other words, put your dog into a situation where aggressive behavior is most likely to occur. But preempt the aggressiveness with a reward *before* the stimulus for misbehavior ever even comes into view. Continue to reward your dog until the stimulus for misbehavior is completely out of sight – and out of your dog's mind.

3. An Electronic Training Collar

You should use an electronic training collar under any of several sets of circumstances:

- When you are fearful of physically correcting your pet, this collar is a good starting point.

- When you need to correct the aggressiveness of a fenced-in dog. Or a dog that is acting aggressively toward children passing down an adjacent street or sidewalk.

- When you need to use the proper measure of force to correct a very large, very strong, very intense dog which is not responding to the correction of a traditional training collar because you may not have the herculean strength necessary to administer the appropriate collar "jerk."

  You may even want to time the stimulus of the electronic training collar to coincide with your pull on the collar to give the dog the perception that you are now somehow stronger.

But one thing that I can't stress enough in instances of aggressive behavior is that owners should only attempt to correct their animals after consultation with their veterinarians or *Pet Behavior Specialists*. That way, an expert can help them with their pet's specific situation and idiosyncracies in mind.

4. **Medication**

Prescriptions such as phenobarbital will sometimes have a mellowing effect on an aggressive animal, while still allowing it to remain functional. The medication may actually make it more receptive to learning. Such dogs are usually the over-responder type. They are overwhelmed by the daily stimuli of the human environment, becoming over-excited. They are often bothered by small distractions, which may in turn produce aggressive behavior.

But you should never medicate your pet without guidance from a veterinarian. Especially when it pertains to animal behavior modification, ask your veterinarian to work in consultation with your *Pet Behavior Specialist.*

A CAUTIONARY TAIL

Finally, a word of caution. Correcting aggressive behavior is not necessarily something you should take upon yourself. Elimination of this misbehavior is often particularly difficult and dangerous, and it doesn't work for everyone. If you find yourself in need of assistance, please consult with your local *Pet Behavior Specialist.*

Understand that a qualified *Pet Behavior Specialist* has seen every aggressive behavior characteristic there is to see, and is comfortable working with dogs of all temperaments. These experiences allow your *Specialist* to judge your pet against all the others with which he has worked.

In most instances, your pet's misbehavior will be one that is commonly exhibited. The advantage that you have with a *Pet Behavior Specialist* is that they will recognize a unique or uncommon problem, and they'll know how best to deal with it.

Occasionally I've come across dogs so violently aggressive that I had to offer to remove them from the home and put them to sleep.

One Springer Spaniel I went out to see had bitten a very young child more than half a dozen times, breaking the skin on each occasion. Although its owners were exceptionally fond of this dog, repeated instances like these often dictate direct action. Still, many people try to keep their pet, and avoid the problem, but they always risk the chance of recurrence.

In many cases this attitude is understandable. Dogs are usually considered part of the family. And family members may be more tolerant of their pet because they knew it when it was lovable. But when it acts aggressively, they are forced to back off just the same.

Obviously, under such circumstances, the family will be unable to work with their dog. And you just can't find another home for an animal with such a background.

Although this situation occurs infrequently, when an exceedingly aggressive animal cannot be controlled even by a *Pet Behavior Specialist*, euthanasia may be the only solution.

11

Modifying A Biting Dog

Technically, biting is an aggressive behavior, part of the previous chapter. But because of the seriousness of the situations where this misbehavior occurs, we've chosen to present it as a separate section.

Dogs *do* give warning signals when they're about to bite, but most people don't seem to recognize them. It's not that these people are so unaware. But perhaps they don't know what to look out for.

When a dog is building toward a bite, it will growl, curl its lips and bare its teeth. If you watch out for these warning signs you'll find that it's easy to predict – and therefore to prevent – a bite.

Other indicators are more subtle. Only experience can offer you an accurate "feel" for what's going on inside the animal's mind. Sometimes a dog will raise the hair on her back. In other situations, she may eye her antagonist suspiciously, with her nose to the ground at a 45-degree angle, and her head turned slightly away.

But usually, you have an "out," a way to diffuse the danger. Or, at the very least, a path of retreat, enabling everyone to regroup.

If your dog shows any of these warning signs before biting, the chances are good that he can be retrained.

In fact, in most cases, the situation isn't even the dog's "fault" at all. Oftentimes it's not the biter, but the "bitee" that is to blame. Or the dog's owner, if he and the bitee are not one and the same. Sometimes dogs are just plain mistrained. Even through the pain, you can hardly blame the poor pups for that!

And don't forget that there *are* legitimate grounds for a dog to act aggressively. These reasons are explained in detail in Chapter 10,

Correcting Dog Aggressiveness. To recount briefly, they are as follows:

1. an animal avoiding correction;

2. behavior as a result of stress or confusion;

3. last resort actions when evasion does not work;

4. a fearful pet backed into an inescapable situation;

5. physical illness.

Fortunately for us humans, most normal dog bites aren't severe.

In fact, it's only when a dog bites for no apparent reason that its owner may have a real problem on her hands. The dog may have an unpleasant personality or a nasty disposition. (Still, it is highly probable that *someone* originally trained the dog to be mean, either intentionally or through neglect.)

But should a dog bite without showing any of the **warning signs** described earlier, it might be best to put the dog to sleep. It's just not normal for a dog to bite without forewarning.

And a dog that bites repeatedly and intensely, or one that holds onto and shakes its victims, isn't even worth working with. It has a neurological problem, a mishandling problem, a genetic problem, a chemical imbalance or a mean personality. Get rid of it for your own safety and for that of your family.

Try to take an unbiased look at the situation in your household, and how the biting effects you. How many people are in your family? In what situations does the dog bite? If it bites children, are there children in your family? If so, again, euthanasia may be the answer.

THE CAUSES

A pet that bites is, usually, the creation of its owner. Now please don't take offense. It begins, innocently enough, with aggressive play. Most people roughhouse with their dog from the day that it enters their lives.

In other situations, biting behavior is the result of an imbalance of power within the domestic "pack." Some pets are allowed to rule the roost right from day one. They're allowed to strut and cluck without restriction. When this occurs, the pet presumes that her agenda has top priority, and that she can do as she pleases.

Happy is standing by, on all fours, with a story about how priorities can change, for pets *and* their owners.

Max was a seven-year-old Lhasa Apso who lived with a young human family in Cincinnati, Ohio. He'd been a brute for most of his life, biting his humans and their visitors at will, though never badly.

But then, all of the sudden, there was a baby in the house. Immediately, the dog sensed a difference in the attitudes of his housemates. So he eyed the baby suspi-

ciously every time she bobbled by. He'd growl at the little gal, and try to get in a good bite whenever she was between bottles.

His humans never let him get close enough to succeed, but they both agreed it was time for them to do something about Max. So they called us in for a consultation.

They explained the situation. Then The Master spent some time with Max, so he could fully understand the bully's behavior.

Finally, The Master sat everyone down again. And what he said startled everyone in the room, Max included.

"You taught Max to bite," The Master began.

"We did not!" interrupted the male. He was clearly shaken. So was his wife.

"I know you didn't do it on purpose," The Master continued. "But you did teach him to bite by not setting rules for him that had any teeth to them."

By now, they were beginning to catch on. And as they did, the whole story came out. The humans had always allowed Max to do whatever he wanted: climb on the furniture, steal food, jump up on people...anything. They assumed this meant they were being good "masters."

But without the discipline, Max had no way of defining appropriate action. Because he was never challenged, he thought he was allowed to behave the way he did; even to the point of biting.

"But what can we do about it now?" asked the female.

"Oh, that should be easy," answered The Master. "We'll just put him on a leash and correct for aggression."

And do you know what? It was that easy.

Oh don't get me wrong, some of the changes were hard for Max. All the rules were rewritten. And they were enforced, too. That took some getting used to. No longer was he allowed up on the furniture. He wasn't allowed to steal anything off the table. And if he was feeling belligerent, his family never let him get away with it.

But Max was a smart dog. He learned his lessons well, and he adjusted to his new social standing with grace. Now the whole family lives together in perfect harmony.

To preserve the harmony of your household, don't wait to correct your dog for aggressive behavior. Don't delay your decision to do something until the dirty deed is done.

Pre-empt this problem by setting rules for your dog, and then enforcing them. Most biting cases arise as a dog pushes against the limits that you set. If you don't push back, she'll assume she has the right to act as she wishes.

This error of omission on your part is taken as permission on her part. And as she usurps more and more power in her adopted pack, she'll continue to exert it, on you. Unless you fight the bite by standing firm on the foundation that you've built for her.

THE SOLUTION

If your dog bites, you should correct him the same way you would any other form of aggressive behavior. (Please see Chapter 10, *Correcting Dog Aggressiveness Behavior.*) Most dogs that bite are also aggressive, so the rules are the same. Correct it right then and there so you'll never see the same behavior again.

Put a leash on your dog, and keep it on him for the duration of the training period. Verify that he obeys both the "Sit" and the "Stay" commands; if he's a little rusty, retrain him. (See Chapter 6, *How Dogs Learn,* for more information on teaching these commands.)

Whenever he bites, immediately grab the leash and jerk it hard enough to send him the message: "This behavior is improper and will not be tolerated."

Then command your dog to "Sit," just once. If he continues biting, or he goes back to the biting behavior, hold the collar, say "Sit," and then jerk it.

Then tell your dog to "Sit" and "Stay" until called. Sometimes a little quiet time can be beneficial in settling everybody down. Oftentimes these circumstances can be confusing, if not emotional.

And when the message does get through to your dog, it may not be a revelation, but it **will** probably revitalize your relationship.

This isn't the case in every instance. Occasionally, I've come across a dog that just can't be re-conditioned.

I know a young married couple who owned an eight-year-old Springer Spaniel. When their son was seven months old, the Spaniel bit him seven times, breaking the skin on each occasion. This dog was probably incurable. Unprovoked, he bit a defenseless baby.

Why would you want to keep a dog that uncontrollably and indiscriminately bites a young child? Most people don't. But still they receive a lot of pressure from people outside their immediate family to work with the dog; or to place the dog in a new home.

And it's understandable that people who have owned a dog for many years want to give it every chance possible to reform itself. They love their dog. But their child's welfare must come first. Under such circumstances, breeders, veterinarians and *Pet Behavior Specialists* suggest that the animal be put to sleep.

That's not to say this is a common end to the story of dogs that bite. Rather, it's the exception to the rule. A far more common case would be that of a young Chow Chow I worked with recently. Here's Happy to share some insight in this next bite.

One day, we got a call from a family which was having problems with its "Bear." Bear was a stray that they had taken in; a Chow Chow who was more than living up to his name.

When we arrived, we were greeted at the door by a female. The male and their five children – one male and four females – awaited us, sitting politely on the couches in the living room.

On closer inspection, each child's face had stitches or a bandage. All of this was evidence of the "Bear," now contained for the duration of our conversation in the back yard.

Yet each and every one of them wanted to keep Bear as a member of their family. They felt that he was just confused; perhaps as a result of the situation that had sent him "astray" in the first place.

Finally, The Master asked them, "If it comes down to one thing, what do you think it is that's bothering Bear?"

"I just don't think that Bear likes people hugging him," one of the daughters piped up.

"Okay," The Master said, "to prevent future bites, let's stop hugging the dog."

A little embarrassed, the wife said, "We were wondering about that!"

From there, The Master and I went to work. We set up several situations to test Bear's tendency to bite. We forced him to move off furniture; we startled him; we took objects away from him; The Master overcorrected him; we even placed him in close quarters with other dogs (namely me).

And do you know what? Bear never once showed a hint of aggression, let alone the urge to bite.

So the family was able to keep Bear, and the Chow hasn't bitten anyone since. The children play games with him, run with him and walk him – in fact, they can do anything except hug him!

And the moral of our story? Sometimes you get the bear hug, and sometimes the bear hug gets you!

ALTERNATIVE METHODS OF CORRECTION

The only real alternative for correcting a biting dog isn't training methodology at all, but prevention. It's important to teach your pet when he is very young, or she is first introduced into your household. The message is simple, but it must be made clear: Biting is not an acceptable behavior. Not in any way, shape or form.

Since he was a puppy, my dog Happy has accepted two human fingers inserted into his mouth back behind his canine teeth. Once they're in position, he bites down, but not hard enough to hurt you. That's the way he can play "Tug-of-War." Often, dogs will use their mouth as a human being would their hand. Still, even a friendly game of tug-of-war can lead to something more, so this isn't necessarily a good idea with all dogs.

People find a puppy's playful bite acceptable only because what they're up against is a small, "harmless" dog. Many people think it's cute and allow the pup to bite, but as the dog grows, so does their problem. So it's best to nip the possibility in the bud.

THE ACCEPTABLE BITE

You may, on rare occasions, even hear an owner make reference to a dog that "bites acceptably." The **only** acceptable bite that I know of is the one that occurs when pet and owner are roughhousing, and the play-bite is a nip. The dog doesn't bear down, because the "biting" is just part of the fun. Even so, this type of biting should be thoroughly discouraged because it can so easily escalate into more severe behavior.

An escalation in aggressive activity is the very last thing you want to encourage. But even if it comes to that...even if the biting becomes belligerent...the prognosis may not be so bleak. There are techniques that you can use to re-train your dog (perhaps even professionally). And there are other options that you can use as a last resort, more than ever before.

Nobody knows these options better than my best friend, Happy, who's seen more of them implemented successfully over the years than any other dog on the planet. Here he is with the down-to-earth story of how we were able help a young puppy through a particularly difficult patch.

Chocolate Chip was only four months old, but already the Chocolate Labrador owned a beautiful pair of humans. Show material, he suspected. He wasn't sure if they were mates yet, but he figured he'd find that out soon enough.

Anyway, these three were all living in the same house, and Chip was having a grand old time. His humans always seemed to have enough time for him. And the kind of play they provided was very physical. He enjoyed the challenge. They even allowed him to "play bite." Even at that age he knew better than to hurt anybody.

But when Chip called me he was frantic.

"Get right over here Happy," he said. "I've just got to see you. And bring that human of yours. That Master guy."

During our first visit, "Chip" described his problem. His humans just couldn't keep up with him anymore. And he needed more to do. In a hurry.

About this time, I caught The Master's eye as he left the room to have a word with the young Lab's humans.

As he suspected, they thought Chip might be overactive. Extremely so. They described Chip as constantly on the move. He ran for miles in the park each day; he jumped on people; he never seemed to calm down.

In fact, the more novel or stimulating the situation, the more excited Chip became. He couldn't control himself.

"I'm an action junkie," he said. "You've got to help me, Hap."

I thought this was a good first step. He recognized that he was the one who might have the problem.

So for two weeks, The Master and I tried a battery of training techniques. None of them worked. If anything, Chip's behavior worsened. The more stimulus we gave him, the more wound up he got. He was totally out-of-control. And he knew it.

"Can you try something else?" he pleaded.

We tried an electronic training collar. We administered a drug called phenobarbital, a barbituate. (Sometimes you humans call it a doggie downer.) We even tried the two together. But the dog's active lifestyle continued, unabated.

Nothing seemed to work. I have to admit that Chip is the one truly hyperkinetic dog I've ever known. But the poor dog was forlorn.

Finally we tried a mild amphetamine. Its effect on Chip was to start a chemical reaction inside his brain. I'm told that it can last a lifetime.

And that's a good thing, because it's now enabling Chip to lead a normal life at last. He's become the nice, gentle family pet he's always wanted to be.

"Now I'm acceptable company," Chip tells me.

Chocolate Chip's biting was a result of his medical condition. But "acceptable" or not, I'd recommend that you don't allow biting under any circumstances. Once it starts, it's hard to stop. In fact, it has a way of running rampant.

Sometimes a biting problem even runs in the family; or at least the extended family, as Happy can explain!

Remember Cujo? Earlier in the book I told you about how this little, five-pound Pomeranian lived the life of Riley. Well, it seems he also dabbled in politics.

In fact, Cujo had been busy biting some of the most influential and powerful people in town. His human was concerned about something called liability; something we dogs don't understand much. She was also interested in eliminating what she considered to be a social embarrassment. So she called us in.

264

I, for one, was embarrassed for the dog. It was already apparent that he'd never had any formal training. And I thought that with the proper program behind him, he could go a long way in the political game. The Master felt the same way.

So we started to groom him for office. He was the ideal candidate; patient but persistent. The Master molded him using the techniques we've described for aggressive behavior.

Soon Cujo was the model citizen. His human was ecstatic as the education process proceeded. Believe it or not, she'd never been trained in the proper etiquette either. And do you know what? They graduated together at the top of their class!

But the story didn't end there. Because The Master was able to convince them that consistency was critical to Cujo's continuing career. So the human also had us train her housekeeper, her masseusse, her manicurist, her errand person and her gardener...even her exterminator!

Cujo's popularity soared in the polls. He was a wonderful host, and in no time at all he was the toast of the town.

But pets and politics rarely mix. And soon a new challenger surfaced. His human's 18-year-old son brought home an eight-week-old Pomeranian named Terry.

Terry was a political troublemaker who, for some reason, insisted on biting Cujo...on the fanny.

Cujo maintained his composure. But with his hectic schedule, and all the public exposure, a breakdown was inevitable.

One day he was lapping at some water when Terry came up and took a nip at his hind quarters. Cujo, tired of the aggravation, whipped around to put the pup back in its place. Unfortunately, someone caught him in the act.

They jokingly referred to the incident as "Waterdishgate." And that's all it took to land him back in the doghouse! The electorate is fickle, isn't it? Well, I guess that's what you have to expect when you're born to run. But I doubt that's the last we'll hear from the little Pomeranian!

12

Changing Dog Disobedience

Dogs are "disobedient" when they do not respond to an owner's verbal stimulus or body signal.

Usually, when owners request assistance with a dog that doesn't obey – or one that is committing misbehaviors – they have more than one problem. If your pet seems out of control, jumping on people who visit your home, knocking your kids over and dragging you down the street when you're out for a walk, you probably have a "multiple" disobedience situation on your hands.

We once worked with a woman in Ohio who certainly had her hands full. Happy has the details for you.

We took a call from a woman, about 40 in human years, who said she sometimes had a problem with her yellow Labrador Retriever, Honey. When we arrived, we discovered that she did indeed have a problem. A big problem: ninety pounds worth of disobedient dog.

Now don't get me wrong. Honey was a nice dog...not aggressive at all. But from what we saw, she was totally out-of-control.

In fact, she gleefully described for me the trouble she put her owner through – jumping up on houseguests, sleeping on forbidden furniture. Honey even outlined an elaborate game she played where she scored points by bowling over her owner's kids.

When I asked her why she did all this, she replied simply, "Because I can."

Caninely, I think Honey was just "spoiled." We dogs need discipline (in reasonable amounts). It gives us a set of rules...a sense of order.

But Honey was never disciplined, even though she was controlled. It took The Master to show Honey's owner the difference.

Once her owner learned the proper use of the training collar, and she used it consistently, Honey became a well-behaved, well-mannered dog. In fact, she was well-adjusted in just 60 days.

For some reason, *Black* Labrador Retrievers, more than most any other breed, love to hide out under dining room or kitchen tables. And not just under them, but in the very center where they're unreachable.

Perhaps this is because these tables make such good retreats; a place where these Labs can be underfoot during dinner, where they can beg for food scraps, or where they can hide away while their owners find their latest mess. These sanctuaries are also easy to defend...or to start on the offensive when the game gets rough.

All-in-all, they're an excellent place to make a stand in a disobedience stand-off. In other words, hiding underneath a table is a very bad habit for any dog to establish!

While you may find this behavior cute in a new Lab puppy, remember the ramifications. A year and a half down the road, you'll be fighting a very determined, full-grown dog.

It's a lot easier to teach an eight-week-old puppy not to go under that table at all, or to stay out of the living room, or to avoid that neighbor's yard. You can eliminate months and months of headaches and frustration by teaching your pet at an early age using the techniques described in this chapter.

THE CAUSES

Dogs develop disobedience for several reasons, just as they develop other misbehaviors. These reasons include:

1) **Owner Inconsistency.** This is by far the number one reason disobedience develops. No matter what techniques are selected, if you don't use them consistently, they won't work. Once a dog learns that you will vary your responses to its behavior, it will test you every time.

2) **Unique Situations.** Many owners have dogs that do very well off-leash at home, or on-leash in public. But off-leash in public, given the right distraction (i.e., a running squirrel), they will forget all their training.

3) **New Significant Stimuli In Their Environment.** If you're bringing a new puppy or a newborn child home, if you're moving to a new home or to an apartment, you may want to be on the look-out for disobedient behavior. All of these are stimuli significant enough to force their training from their fuzzy brains!

THE SOLUTIONS

There are several solutions for the dog owner who wants to transform a misbehaving pet into a well-adjusted, obedient one. These include:

1. sending it to a professional for training;

2. group obedience classes;

3. individual sessions in your home with a *Pet Behavior Specialist*; and,

4. self-instruction with the assistance of books, video-tapes, etc.

Only you can decide which method is best for your particular needs. But there are several important considerations you'll need to take into account.

- **Cost.** A *Pet Behavior Specialist* would come to your home for 6 to 10 one-hour sessions at $75 to $150 per hour.

  The next most expensive method would be to send your pet to a professional for training. This might cost $600 to $1,500 for a two to three-week period, depending on where you live. In a large city – like Chicago for example – the cost may be $1,000 per week.

  Group obedience classes total approximately $50 to $75, with 8 to 12 one-hour lessons.

- *Time and convenience.* Allowing your dog to be trained elsewhere is the least time-consuming method for you. Participating in group sessions is the most time consuming.

  Lessons may take less time at home with a *Specialist,* where both you and your dog may be more comfortable.

  Finally, reading books or listening to videotapes to learn the correct procedures is relatively costly in terms of time.

- *Degree of disobedience.* How disobedient is your dog? If only one member of your family is experiencing disobedience problems, this might dictate turning to a *Pet Behavior Specialist.* The probability is that this family member is handling the pet differently than everyone else.

- *Effectiveness.* The best success rates occur when you are a part of the training. That's because owners often have just as much to learn about the new preferred behaviors as their dogs do.

Overall, you need to select the best, most effective and most convenient method for training your dog on your own terms. But remember that training is a 24-hour a day job. Just as with children, you must intervene promptly, properly and consistently whenever your pet is disobedient. You can't sit there in your comfortable chair and think "I'm just too tired tonight. I'll let him get away with it just this one time!"

Obedience training is an ongoing process. It must be done all day, every day, for the lifetime of your dog. Dogs learn new habits; so you must become habitual about responding to them.

The true key to a well-trained pet is consistency in responding to disobedience each and every time it occurs. Without fail.

THE BEST SOLUTION

Teaching your dog to sit using a training collar will give you the control you need to correct disobedience in almost all instances.

As stated earlier, "Sit" is the easiest command to teach. It is a very basic position, and dogs spend many of their waking hours in this posture naturally.

The use of the standard "Sit" command will solve many problematic pet behaviors. To teach your dog the "Sit" command, please see Chapter 6, *How Dogs Learn,* under the heading "Training Methods and Equipment." Remember to use the Dummy Leash Effect, also described in Chapter 6.

Information provided in that chapter is extremely important in teaching your pet a broad range of new and preferred behaviors. But you must work with your pet; practice the techniques, and use them in different settings under varied circumstances. The more practice you give your pet, the more automatically he will respond to your commands. And, ultimately, that is what you're striving for.

The "Sit" command, like all obedience techniques, may be taught using verbal commands or hand signals. Hand signals are an acceptable methodology, but they are limited in their effectiveness by several variables. For example, they work only when your dog is looking at you while you're using them, or if your dog is expecting you to use them. This may not be the case under all circumstances.

Some training schools will teach your dog to sit on command and then, for an extra cost, to sit for hand signals.

Learning a hand signal is not difficult for most pets. When you say the word "Sit," you simply use the corresponding hand signal at the same time.

The most commonly-used hand signal consists of a single, simple motion of the hand and arm. You start with your arm straight out, palm facing the ground. Then you bend your arm at the elbow and move it in a motion that resembles passing your hand over your dog's head.

It won't be long before your dog will pair the voice command with the hand signal, and after enough repetition, she'll respond to the hand signal alone.

One case that demonstrates how "easily" this is done involved a young college student with a deaf Dalmation named Polka. When I first met her, she wanted to teach her dog hand signals, but she said she didn't know how to use the proper techniques. During our initial consultation, it surprised me to see Polka respond to the appropriate hand signal for "Sit." It turns out that Polka's owner was unconsciously doing the right technique, and she didn't even know it.

SUMMARY

Although the specifics of teaching a dog to "Sit" are contained under that heading in Chapter 6, *How Dogs Learn,* it is important to review the highlights here. Generally, the "dos and don'ts" to remember when correcting for disobedience include:

- Say the command ONCE. "Sit."

- Do not repeat this command.

- Follow the single verbal command with correction or praise, depending on the appropriateness of your dog's response.

- DO NOT correct your dog by yelling, running after it, throwing things at it or making startling noises.

- DO use your dog's name BEFORE the command, if you must use it.

- DO try to use the same – or a similar – tone of voice. Always.

- DO reward the appropriate response with verbal or tactile praise (petting your dog on the chest) at least 75% of the time.

- DO make a proper correction if your dog does not respond appropriately.

- DO use the obedience command if you see your dog engaged in a behavior similar to the appropriate obedience response.

- NEVER change the appropriate sequence.

FINAL NOTE: "Sit" does not mean "Stay." "Sit" means for your dog to touch the ground or floor with her buttocks for a few seconds, after which she is free to go about her business.

ALTERNATIVE METHODS OF CORRECTION

Although the training collar is currently the most widely-used method of correction, there are a number of alternatives which are growing in popularity. Most notable is the electronic remote training collar. Each of these may also be effectively employed in teaching the discipline necessary to control disobedience. Please examine the information in Chapter 6, *How Dogs Learn,* under the heading "Other Training Methods and Equipment," to learn the techniques specific to this type of equipment.

As with the training collar, it is important that you work with your pet, practice the techniques and use them repeatedly and consistently in a wide range of settings and under different circumstances. An automatic response to your commands is still the desired outcome.

THE REBELLIOUS PERIOD

Some dogs will become rebellious in the early stages of their training regimen when they learn that "Sit" means they will receive a correction if they do not comply. Instead, they might lay down or run away.

You may experience a rebellious reaction in response to any obedience command. It is actually the distinctive sound and tone you make to which your dog is responding. Few pets actually pick up individual words like "Sit."

Owners sometimes brag that their dog can sit. When asked "Will your dog sit whenever you say the word?" they answer in the affirmative. Meanwhile, their dog is walking around, examining its surroundings, nosing through the flowers and **not** sitting, even though the word "Sit" has been used at least 20 times during the conversation.

"Well, of course he's not responding," retorts the owner. "I wasn't talking to him."

Then he gets up, stands in front of the dog, stares at it and says, "Sit." The dog sits on cue.

What this does demonstrate is that very few dogs actually do pick up such commands under normal situations. The command must be a very distinct word, in a definitive tone, self-contained and sometimes containing the dog's name. Often it must be accompanied by a hand signal or body movement.

It is important that your dog learn to respond correctly to the single word "Sit" (or any other distinct obedience command).

MISCELLANEOUS

Occasionally, a member of the animal rights movement will suggest that using a training collar (or more often, an electronic training collar) is an inhumane way to train a dog.

"Train a dog only with rewards," they recommend. "When it does something right, reward it. You never need to correct a dog. There's no reason for any living thing to live in fear of a correction."

That is rather like suggesting that children do not need correction. And any parent will attest to the fact that children not only **need** correction, but that they **desire** parentally set parameters. Limits show concern and caring and love. These guidelines provide the rules that we must follow to live in today's society. It is because we have learned to avoid improper behaviors that we live happy lives.

By using training collars, we're doing the same thing for our pets. That is, teaching them the proper (animal) behaviors to serve as guidelines for happy (animal) lives.

13

Other Dog Misbehaviors

The last five chapters covered the most common concerns that owners are likely to have with their pets in the typical household. This chapter is dedicated to the rest of the list. It's a kind of catch-all for those misbehaviors that may not occur as frequently, but cause just as much frustration for both the dog and the owner.

But as broadranging as these behaviors are, the first thing you need to do is to determine whether the problem deserves the time. You need to weigh the nature of the problem, and its impact, against the cost in time, money and emotional commitment needed to change it.

Some misbehaviors just don't warrant a lot of effort. For example, if you're faced with a hyperactive hound for a three-hour car ride once every six months, you shouldn't subject yourself to a sophisticated training sequence. It's just not worth it.

A simpler solution would be for you to seek out your local veterinarian before the trip, and ask him to prescribe the appropriate medication.

In other words, you need to know how to deal with the unique challenges you'll come across in your day-to-day life with your dog. Generally, you'll face what amounts to a short-term challenge.

Here are several guidelines for you to follow when determining whether or not you'll want to try to change your pet's behavior:

1. Consider the liability involved.

2. Judge the size of your dog.

3. Calculate the cost involved.

4. Find out how much time it will take to change the behavior.

5. Identify the type of intervention needed.

6. Weigh the involvement of children.

7. Calculate the risk to your dog.

8. Review the age and health of your dog.

9. Factor in your dog's breed, and where you got it.

Let's review these guidelines one-by-one to give you a better idea of what to look out for.

1. *Consider the liability involved.*

Is your dog's behavior aggressive? If so, you may risk a lawsuit if she bites someone; because these days, whether the person bitten is a neighbor or visitor, friend or stranger, his lawyers are probably just as aggressive...especially if the "bitee" is a child.

2. *Judge the size of the pet.*

How large is your dog? (Aggressiveness is the main consideration here.) If you're dealing with a five-pound dog, you're more likely to succeed than if you are working with a 120-pound dog. Smaller pets are just easier to work with. No matter how aggressive a diminutive dog is, he just can't cause the physical damage that larger dogs can.

3. *Calculate the cost involved.*

What will it cost you to modify the misbehavior? Can you afford it? Can you afford not to? After all, you'd never put money above the love you have for your pet, but you have to draw some limits. What are they? Can you risk the damage your dog may do to your domicile? What are the trade-offs?

If your dog is destructively chewing, and doing hundreds of dollars in damage each day, how does this compare with the cost of a *Pet Behavior Specialist* who estimates it will take two months to correct the pet?

4. *Find out how much time it will take to change the behavior.*

A financial estimate is a good starting point, but where will it all end? You also need to get an accurate estimate of the time it will take to correct the problem. Will it fit right into your family's routine? Or will you have to make adjustments?

If your dog is acting aggressively, and your *Pet Behavior Specialist* tells you it's because he needs more exercise, what will you do?

A corrective program may include an hour of exercise each day, plus 30 minutes of training time. Do you have the time to spare? If not, you might as well not make the commitment, because your dog's behavior won't change.

5. *Identify the type of intervention needed.*

    Do you know what you have to do to modify your dog's misbehavior? You need to make sure your *Pet Behavior Specialist* gives you a good, thorough understanding of the steps necessary. Then you have to decide whether or not you can apply these techniques.

    What if the procedure involves the use of medication? Are you willing to administer it? Some owners will; others won't.

    What if the methodology means you must confine your dog in a cage 8 to 10 hours daily? Can you do it? Many owners just aren't willing to put their dog into that situation.

    Or if the program calls for you to confront a very aggressive dog, are you up to it physically and emotionally?

    You need to determine in advance whether or not you're willing and able to implement the necessary intervention.

6. *Weigh the involvement of children.*

    If you have children – or there are children around – are they old enough to understand the need for the training at hand? Are they physically prepared to protect themselves, if need be, as they apply these techniques?

As an owner, you should take special care to keep babies, infants, toddlers or young children safely out of harm's way...especially if an animal exhibits an extraordinary degree of aggressiveness.

7. *Calculate the risk to your dog.*

   Whatever direction you decide on, don't allow anyone to carry out a correction that you feel will be harmful to your pet.

   Unfortunately, there are some so-called "expert trainers" out there using an array of improper intercessions. I've had to intercede myself on several occasions when I've caught some charlatan hanging a dog in the air by its leash; hitting or kicking it; taping its mouth shut; or hitting it with various objects.

   These kinds of things happen out there, so be aware. Techniques like these cannot be tolerated. You'll know the difference, even if someone holds himself up as an expert in the field of pet behavior.

   If you **ever** feel that your common sense is being assaulted – if you ever have any doubts at all – **get a second opinion.** Don't allow the interventions to proceed. It will be harmful indeed to the dog you love.

8. *Review the age and health of your dog.*

   Is the misbehavior you're monitoring the result of old age? If so, you may not stand a chance of changing it. You may even have to accept the offending action until the pet passes away...or you decide to have it humanely euthanized.

But for the sake of argument, let's assume you have an old dog that does have a changeable behavior, but that it will take 3 to 6 months to correct, and it will cost $1,000. If that same dog has only about a year to live, do you really want to go through it all?

Further, is your dog physically fit enough to follow through with such a program, from start-to-finish? Should you go forward or should you forego the modification drugs, confinement routines or electronic collars that may be too much for your more mature pet?

You have to be prepared to make decisions like these in the interest of your pet.

9. *Factor in your dog's breed, and where you got him.*

Some behaviors in specific breeds of dog generally signal a significant problem...and substantially lower success rates for behavior modification. If your pet fits into this category, you may decide not to try to change it.

We've already described the Cocker Spaniel Syndrome, and the effects of inbreeding back in the early sixties. (Please see further information on this topic in Chapter 10, *Correcting Dog Aggressiveness Behaviors,* under the heading "The Timetable For Correction.") Even today this little dog's aggressive behavior towards children is difficult to change. Often, it's easier not to deal with these cases.

If you purchased your dog from a reputable breeder, rather than a pet store, your chances for successful modification are greatly enhanced.

These are all factors you need to be aware of when you pick your pet out in the first place. This is another good reason to get a *Pet Behavior Specialist* involved early on.

You can never change behavior if the breed you choose is incompatible with its new environment. Take the Australian Shepherd. In its natural environment it may run 25 to 30 miles in a single day as it herds.

But if you banish it to a one-bedroom apartment, and leave it there alone for 8 or 10 hours a day, with only 15 minutes of leashed exercise daily, you're bound to see problems. And you won't ever be able to change its behavior because it doesn't have access to an appropriate outlet for its boundless energy.

As a pet owner, you must be able to see the big picture before you decide to pursue a training program for your pet. But when you've explored all of the pertinent information, you'll put yourself in a much better position for successful behavior modification.

Now that you know how to assess a less frequent misbehavior situation, you're ready to address the other categories presented in this chapter:

1. excessive noise;
2. inappropriate attention-grabbing behaviors;
3. escape behaviors;
4. self-mutilation;
5. improper eating habits;
6. stressful situations;
7. chasing cars;
8. unique problems.

Each of these areas is described in detail in the balance of this chapter. All of these uncommon misbehaviors can be corrected with the right combination of common sense and hard work.

1. EXCESSIVE NOISE

You'll know right away when you have an excessive noise problem. If you don't, your neighbors will let you know soon enough. It can include barking, whining, whimpering, growling or howling; just about any sound your hound can create with his vocal chords, in fact.

Dogs usually deliver their highest decibels when they've been banished to the backyard, or some other "remote" location. Sometimes this happens at night; sometimes when you're away during the day.

Excessive noise is typically a frustration-release behavior for the dog. It can be just as frustrating for the owner. But you can solve this "problem" with the help of a bark inhibitor collar or an electronic training collar.

Using A Bark Inhibitor Collar

Bark inhibitor collars work using sophisticated microtechnology that is contained in a small box attached to a conventional collar. Two blunt probes protrude through this collar for contact with your dog's neck. Then, when she barks, a sensor picks up the vibrations from her vocal chords and sends a signal to the box. Another popular solution emits a short burst of citronella spray.

This signal instructs the inhibitor either to warn your dog, or to correct it. Some systems can be programmed to do both. Today's most popular collar emits a buzzing sound as a warning, followed by the same type of correction used in a remote training collar.

The idea is **not** to eliminate barking altogether. It wouldn't be wise to train your dog not to bark under any circumstances. What you want to do is to create a situation-dependent behavior. That is, you want to teach your dog not to bark under one specific set of conditions – such as when you put her in the garage for the night – and that if she does, she'll receive a correction.

Take care not to allow the correction to be associated with the bark inhibitor collar. To avoid this mistake, use the "dummy equipment effect" explained in Chapter 6, *How Dogs Learn*, under the heading: "Training Methods and Equipment." Set up the situation for your dog, but don't activate the collar for three or four days.

After that, activate the collar each time you put your dog into the noise-prohibited situation. Then, every time she barks, she'll get a correction. Ten to 14 days later, she'll have developed the situation-dependent behavior you desire. The conditioned response is that she won't bark in the garage any more.

Some dogs will need a refresher course every few months for the first year; about 10% of all dogs will need to wear the collar every time the situation arises. In these cases, you might find it less costly to buy the equipment rather than to rent it.

Using An Electronic Training Collar

An electronic training collar can also be used to correct excessive barking. It operates on essentially the same principle as the bark inhibitor, but is controlled externally, with a hand-held remote device. Please see Chapter 6, *How Dogs Learn,* under the heading "Other Training Methods and Equipment," for detailed information on this kind of collar and its use.

Some people worry that they'll harm their dog with such a device. Perhaps it's the word "electronic" that concerns them. But actually, when they're used properly, these collars are very humane and quite effective.

It's kind of humorous, really. The first question many owners ask, once they understand the collar's concept, is: "Can I get one for my kids?"

They'll agonize about injuring their animals, but they won't hesitate to strap it on their own offspring! Or their husband! Or their mother-in-law!

I guess it's a good thing that people who have pets with this problem retain any sense of humor at all. Most situations that involve excessive noise just aren't funny. Barking can be extremely intrusive – especially when there are neighbors around.

Happy has a story where this really made a difference to a dog and her owner when they were ready to move into a new neighborhood.

Fritzi was a 10-year-old Chow Chow with an age-old problem. His lifelong companion was now an octogenarian; she was really getting to be an old-timer (even in human years). But he vowed to stick by her. He was a very loyal dog. And he never wanted anything to come between them. But this woman's daughter almost did.

It took some doing, too. His companion had done very well for herself in this human-eat-human world. Yet her daughter claimed that she was running out of money. And that she had to sell her mansion, along with most of her cherished antiques.

"After all, she's an antique herself," the daughter announced one day.

Unfortunately, this younger woman – his human's offspring, mind you – couldn't see the priceless nature of her mother's personal freedom. Instead, she was ready to pack her off to a retirement village.

This was supposed to be a temporary arrangement, but as wise as Fritzi was, he suspected otherwise.

291

"It's just until Uncle Ervin builds mother a house in California," the daughter insisted.

What did seem permanent, though, was Fritzi's predicament. Wherever his human went, he wanted to go, too, regardless of the circumstances. But in this case, there was a catch. He was a backyard barker. And in the retirement village, excessive noise was a no-no.

He'd tried to kick the habit before. He'd even sought professional help. But whatever he did, he seemed to be barking up the wrong tree.

To complicate matters, the daughter wanted Fritzi trained without her mother's knowledge. She stressed that the elderly woman was already under enough strain. And Fritzi felt that this was probably true.

"But it means I have to go behind the old dame's back just to get back into her life," the dog mournfully maintained.

Fritzi felt that an anti-bark collar would've made everything a lot easier, but he suspected that this technique wouldn't work because his human was "too gentle a soul" to follow through.

"I'm sure she disciplined her daughter as a child. And when she did, she probably said things like: 'This is going to hurt me a lot more than it's going to hurt you.' Well it's the same principle. Tough love works...but only if you're tough enough to administer it."

As it turned out, Fritzi's reformation wasn't so tough after all. The daughter boarded him at a kennel, where he was quite *comfortable. There, he was taught **not to bark** whenever he wore a training collar around his neck.*

"What'll they think of next?" posed the pup. "This modern technology's incredible!"

Once he got the hang of the collar, he didn't bark for five straight days. He was actually released early for good behavior.

Then, to maintain his mum behavior, the daughter had Fritzi wear a dummy collar. That way, when he was returned to her Mum, no one would know the difference. All either of them would ever know was that they were back together; and that Fritzi had put his barking days behind him to make it possible.

Sometimes, silence really is golden; especially during the golden years. So fortunately, excessive noise is usually easy to eliminate. Nonetheless, it's never fun to be near it when you first hear it. But there are actually other behaviors where getting closer to your dog is exactly the wrong thing to do.

2. INAPPROPRIATE ATTENTION-GRABBING BEHAVIORS

Many misbehaviors – or what many owners classify as "bad" behaviors – are actually a pet's way of stealing more attention from their owners; sometimes literally.

Some pets will steal just about anything just to get a rise out of their owners: shoes, clothing, newspapers...you name it. But attention-seeking behaviors manifest themselves in many other ways, too.

Some dogs may jump up on people. Others may greet visitors incorrectly. Or they may urinate or defecate in front of their owners. Sometimes dogs demonstrate aggressive behavior. Others make noise until their owner responds, especially when left alone in the yard or in a cage. They may even resort to self-mutilation, chewing or licking themselves excessively.

All of these behaviors can indicate a dog's desire for more attention from its owner.

Ah, but what do we mean by "attention?" Attention is defined here as any response that you give your dog. This includes looking at her, talking to her, yelling at her, touching her in any way, moving towards her, or making a noise, such as banging on the door to quiet her down.

As with most other misbehaviors, what is inappropriate will be defined by your own personal likes and dislikes.

For example, how do you want your dog to approach you for attention in the first place? Should he just come up and sit with you, wagging his tail and waiting to be petted? Should he put one paw on your leg, or rest his chin on your lap? Or should he lay in a corner and wait for you to invite him to approach and be petted?

Each owner has her own definition. And so does each dog. But all dogs seem to know instinctively that sitting still and looking cute won't generate nearly as much attention as a chase through the house. So if stealing is what it takes to get you up off your duff, hot in pursuit, that loaf of bread on the kitchen counter is as good as gone.

Unfortunately, most owners seem to determine the nature of their response by the amount of bread the stolen object cost them...or its relative importance. This is a major mistake!

In a dog's mind, there isn't any difference between a $2 toy and a $200 pair of shoes; even though only an assault on the second might send you out of your mind!

In either situation, you really have only one choice. **Totally ignore your dog.**

This is the proper procedure because the pet is trying to provoke a response. So when you don't respond, you're not giving your dog a reason to continue the behavior.

If you're confining your dog in a cage or kennel, and he's whimpering, whining or barking, ignore him until he's been quiet for 15 to 20 consecutive seconds; then praise him lavishly.

But if he's barking in another room, and you yell or bang on the door, you're giving him a response. And any reaction on your part provides a reason for your pet to continue the misbehavior. By not giving him the attention he's after, you're actually correcting him, because you're not reinforcing the behavior.

Ignoring him *is* the correction. Of course a little positive reinforcement for proper behavior never hurts. So later, when your dog is doing something more appropriate, make sure you give him some added attention.

Some owners have a great deal of difficulty ignoring inappropriate behavior. They become frustrated and impatient. If you find yourself in this position, you should try to separate yourself from your dog. Try going into a different room, for example.

Ignoring a dog always works when you're trying to eliminate an inappropriate attention-grabbing behavior; and it does so in just a short time. But it can be difficult to implement because **everyone** in the entire family must adhere to it.

Here are some examples of specific attention-grabbing misbehaviors, and the techniques you can use to correct them.

Greeting People Inappropriately

Many owners complain about their dog's behavior when someone knocks on their front door. Sometimes they're more concerned with what happens once the door is opened, and a visitor enters their home.

These misbehaviors vary widely, in both action and intensity, but they can include jumping, licking, touching, urinating, pawing or barking. In fact, all excessive, aggressive or submissive behaviors towards visitors can qualify as an inappropriate "greeting."

You may be more familiar with the excessive or aggressive behaviors. But an example of submissiveness would be a dog that waits by the door, but when a visitor reaches down to pet her, she runs and hides; or perhaps she rolls over and urinates.

Most of the time, these behaviors can be classified as "attention-grabbers." But they may also be a conditioned response (i.e., the first thing your pet does when a person walks through the door) or a means of showing dominance.

Once you've identified the behavior as an attention-grabbing device, you can modify it simply enough using the techniques that Happy will outline for you in the story below.

 *Whenever we'd visit Fred and Sarge, two local Basset Hounds, they'd go berserk before we even arrived at the door. We asked their human about it, and he said they overreacted every time the doorbell rang; not just for us.*

Apparently, these two-year-old litter mates fed each other's frenzy, resulting in a crashing crescendo of crazed canines, and an intimidating, united affront to all visitors.

The two pooches were apologetic.

"We just can't help ourselves," Sarge said.

*"Yeah, strangers are about as exciting as it gets around here,"
Fred agreed. "We just get whipped-up about it I guess."*

*For The Master, there was no guess-work to it at all. He knew
exactly what the problem was. Neither dog had ever been
properly disciplined for their dynamic behavior before.*

*"Do you mean we're not supposed to do that?" asked the two in
tandem.*

"No," I whispered. "You're not."

*With the human's help, The Master equipped each dog with a
training collar. Some people call them "choker" collars, but
that's not really what they're for.*

*Then they set up a typical situation, with The Master on the
victim's side of the door and their human inside with them.
When the doorbell rang, both dogs went out-of-control, despite
themselves. At that point, each was corrected properly with the
training collar.*

*Both learned quickly. If their paws came up off the floor, they'd
receive a correction. And the only way to avoid a correction was
not to jump. Ever.*

*During the session, The Master showed his mastery of both the
stick **and** the carrot. So each time the Basset Hounds behaved
themselves, they received a reward.*

*The results were phenomenal. After just one visit, the two
young dogs were on their best behavior whenever a visitor came
to the door. And because their human was consistent, and*

followed through with their training, whenever they welcomed guests from then on, those visitors were more inclined to stay.

Once you've brought the behavior back within acceptable parameters, you don't have to reward appropriate action in each instance. Although an occasional reward for proper behavior should provide all the incentive your dog needs to continue her good behavior.

But no matter what the circumstances, you must correct any inappropriate behavior every time it happens.

Urination

With most attention-seeking behaviors, from the submissive to the excessive, you have a choice of responses available to you. But if you have a dog that urinates to get your attention, your options are limited. All you can do is ignore him.

When your dog makes his mark, it can be very difficult not to react. Most people find this particular behavior both disgusting and frustrating. It can also damage your home, and everything in it. But you still must stick to your plan. It is very difficult to correct **or** redirect this particular behavior. So ignoring him may be your best chance for a solution.

Once you've ignored your dog until he has "calmed down," your next step is to ask him to "Sit" and "Stay." Once she does this, you should praise her. Continue this cycle until the inappropriate urination goes away.

<u>Sympathy Lameness</u>

Sympathy lameness may be the definitive attention-grabbing behavior. Not that it's serious. The sole purpose of your pet's action is to alter **your** response.

Sympathy lameness occurs when your pet favors a healthy body part but there is no cause to do so. The "malady" is entirely a ruse used by your dog to gain attention, or to avoid doing something she doesn't want to do.

Dogs are very perceptive. They're gauging your actions and reactions all the time. So if they ever have a sore paw, or a broken bone, they see the sympathy you give them. And they're adept at using this to their best advantage even after they're fully recuperated.

For example, your dog may begin limping when you give her a classic obedience command. This is a tactic used strictly to try to remove or reduce the control you're exerting.

Or you may be snuggling with a significant other on the sofa, and your dog will approach, dangling a limp paw. He wants some attention, too.

Again the resolution is simple: Have no sympathy.

Ignore your pet completely when he behaves this way. If you give him any attention while he's acting that way – including a physical or verbal reprimand – it will only reinforce his misbehavior. And he'll walk all over you for the rest of his life. Like a Sheltie Happy once knew.

What can you tell us about sympathy lameness, Happy?

Well, I've used it myself, on occasion. No offense to The Master, but there are a lot of humans out there who'll fall for it, depending on how good your performance is. I'm just fair, myself. But then again, The Master's a tough critic.

But one of the best actors I've ever met was a Sheltie named Oscar. He lived in Chicago. Every day Oscar would start to "limp" on his way back home from a walk. He was a method actor, reeling from the feeling of pain down there in his paw.

And his performance really affected his audience. His human, perhaps for artistic reasons, would actually keep the dog outside. He told The Master he felt sorry for his dog, so he kept on walking it.

And that was all Oscar ever really wanted!

That, in a nutshell, is your solution. Only give your dog the attention that she wants when her behavior is appropriate. If she wants your attention, she should lay down on the floor, and look calmly up at you with her tail wagging. (Or whatever your preferred position.)

When she does so, be sure to give her enough attention to satisfy her needs...and to diminish her dependency on sympathy lameness.

3. ESCAPE BEHAVIORS

For a dog, escape can be an exhilarating experience. Everything is new and exciting: the sights, the sounds, and especially the smells.

Sometimes, escape is a dog's intent, especially if they're not content with their situation. Other times they kind of stumble into it. Either way, once your dog establishes escape as a misbehavior, she'll make a break for it every chance she gets.

The most common escape behavior occurs from a fenced yard. Dogs like to dig under fences, but they're just as likely to jump or climb over them. Most dogs will do so only when their owner isn't in the yard with them. It's rare for a dog to escape while together with its owner.

So if you're not going to be around all the time, can your dog be trained to stay within the limitations you set? Yes, via several methods.

- Replace the fence you have with a higher fence.

- Build an addition onto your existing fence, angled at 45° up and into your yard. This will give your dog the perception that the fence is high enough to prevent escape.

- Temporarily use an electronic remote training collar.

- Temporarily or permanently use a buried-wire containment system.

How To Prevent Escapes From Yards With Fences

If your dog has developed an escape behavior even though you have a fence, you can try any of the suggestions listed in the previous section. But what most people really want is to teach their dog to stay in the yard rather than just building, or adding to, their barriers. This is most easily accomplished with an electronic remote training collar or buried-wire containment system.

For full details on these systems, and their usage, see Chapter 6, *How Dogs Learn,* under the sections "Other Training Methods and Equipment." You can rent or purchase these systems.

Basically, a buried-wire containment system – or unseen "hidden" fence – consists of a wire buried in the ground inside the perimeter of the area fenced to contain your pet. Your dog is then equipped with a special collar that sends out electronic warnings or corrections if he comes within a predetermined range of the unseen "fence," (and, hence, your real fence).

Once the wire is in place at the base of your exisiting fence, fit the receiver-collar around your dog's neck, but do not activate the system for three days. This will create "The Dummy Collar Effect" that will prevent your dog from attaching a stigma to the collar itself. Please reread the paragraphs on "The Dummy Equipment Effect" in Chapter 6, *How Dogs Learn,* if you'd like to bone up on the subject.

The second step is to activate the system. Training usually takes no longer than 14 days. When this period is over, your dog will be conditioned to stay approximately two feet away from your existing fence.

The function of the remote training collar is similar, but the correction isn't automatic. Instead, you must observe your dog from inside the house, and push the button that delivers the correction **every time** your dog approaches the fence.

Although this method works just as effectively, it generally takes 30 to 60 days to teach a conditioned response with the remote training collar.

With both of these methods, it helps if you tempt your dog into an escape attempt. You can do this simply enough by walking around the perimeter of the fence. Or you can have a neighbor place her dog outside of the fence. You can even jump over the fence yourself...or throw tantalizing objects back over it. Anything you do to draw your dog over the forbidden line should help to facilitate the training process.

However, under no circumstances should you command your dog to "Come."

The use of buried-wire systems is spreading, both here and abroad. It is now an accepted pet containment method, successful in about 90% of known escape-behavior cases.

But please understand that these systems are not fail-safe. Like any other system of containment, they do have their drawbacks. For example, nothing prevents people or other animals from crossing the fence **into** your yard.

There are some other limitations that you should be aware of before you try relying on one of these systems. Happy has an excellent example of what I'm talking about right here:

Once, we met an escape-artist name Max the Magnificent. Max was a three-year-old Labrador Retriever, black as magic. And he had this habit of disappearing on his assistant, a human who always seemed to be out somewhere tracking him down.

One day, these two decided to install a hidden fence system. Max was very excited about it, because he knew that once it was operational, some of his least favorite things in the world would vanish; starting with the ol' stake and chain.

When the fateful day came, though, the wonder of it all went away...almost right away.

"We turned the thing on, and went out into the yard, and right away this jogger just materialized out of nowhere," Max's human told us.

Max picked up the story from there.

"So I said to myself, 'Hey, there's nothing to stop me from jumping the fence and giving that guy a good run for his money.' And I took off after him."

"Then 'a la kazam,' the guy zaps me," Max told us. "I'd never been up against a force anything like it before. So I summoned all my strength and went after him."

We patiently listened to the obligatory chase scene that seems to drag on in every drama these days. Then it was The Master's turn to perform. He spoke about all the smoke and mirrors that *make the buried-wire electronic system work. It was spellbinding. Then he revealed the secret behind the jogger's power.*

"In essence," he told Max, "you associated the corrections you were receiving from the system with the jogger, because that's what you were seeing at the time."

"That's some sleight-of-paw," said Max.

Max could have connected the correction with anything that was going on at the time, instead of with the fence boundary. I guess it's fortunate that this guy's feet were faster than the eye.

When you try a buried-wire containment system, it's critical for your dog to make the right connection with the correction.

How To Prevent Escapes
From Yards Without Visible Fences

The big difference between containment training with and without a fence is the very obvious visual boundary marker. Without the fence to reinforce your parameters, you need to take special care to identify where the borders are. It may be helpful to use a tree, bush or shrub. Setting these boundary markers will enable both you and your dog to identify the specified area.

Training does take longer without the fence, even though the techniques are the same, because the boundaries are not visible. But you can use this system (with or without a fence) to train dogs that already show a tendency to escape...or to pre-empt an escape on the part of a dog that hasn't tried before.

How To Prevent Escapes
With Traditional Techniques

The most traditional alternative correction method is to use a 30 to 50-foot rope or leash with your dog's collar. Then, every time she challenges her boundaries, grab the leash tightly, and firmly pull her back into the yard. Once she's been back in the yard for five seconds, praise her. Do this **every** time she crosses the boundary.

Generally, you can train your dog this way in three to six months. The drawback is that during this time, you must closely monitor your pet every time she goes outside, and be prepared to correct her whenever she crosses the boundary.

How To Prevent Escapes
From Cages, Kennels And Crates

It's very difficult for a dog to escape from the proper type of cage, kennel or crate. But if your dog has a history of escape, don't use a standard "cage." These have too many accessible parts, and offer too much potential for destruction.

The key to escape-prevention is the correct kennel. The best are plastic, like those used for air travel. Ninety-nine percent of all dogs can't escape from these. That's because these kennels don't have many parts for a dog to destroy. The bars are placed close together, so they can't be bent. About the only thing a dog can really get a grip on is the door. But the door doesn't open into the kennel, so they'll rarely get out, because dogs don't push, they pull using their mouths.

Proper kennel size may be the most important factor. The more comfortable your dog is, the less likely she is to attempt an escape. And remember, dogs are partial to the enclosed environment provided by the kind of kennel in question.

To pick the correct kennel size, make sure your dog can stand inside it, head erect. Also, be sure she has room enough to lie down inside, without touching nose or haunches; and that she can turn around comfortably, without bumping into the sides.

If the kennel meets this criteria, then it fits your dog perfectly, and will reduce the likelihood of escape (or even an attempt).

How To Prevent Escapes When
You're Entering Or Leaving The House

Some family pets will wait patiently by the door for children to enter or depart. Then, at just the right moment, they'll make a dash for freedom...especially on beautiful spring and summer days.

To put a stop to this behavior, teach your dog to "Sit" and "Stay" when the door is being opened; and not to "Come" until you command her to.

Then if she tries to go through the door on her own, all you have to do is make a simple correction by pulling her back into the house with the training collar.

Once your dog has been back in the house for a full five seconds, praise her new-and-improved behavior abundantly.

How To Correct For Escapes
From Confinement Inside The House

Escape from "confinement" usually occurs because the room in question doesn't have the right latch or lock, isn't closed tightly, or doesn't lock at all. Once you've solved your technical problem, you'll cut off your pet's path to escape.

You can also try a pet gate, provided it's the proper kind. It needs to be high enough so your dog can't jump it. These gates do offer some advantages. For one thing, they enable your dog to see and hear you (if you're in the next room), cutting down on his frustration.

Or you can make temporary use of an electronic containment system. These work just as well inside your home; and you don't even have to bury the wire! When you use these systems inside, they can provide your pup with just the right incentive to stay put until their containment period is over.

How To Prevent Escapes From
Collars, Leashes And Outside Ties

Using the proper equipment – and teaching your dog not to pull on it – will prevent escape from collars, leashes and outside ties.

The first thing you need to do is buy something strong enough to handle your dog's weight. Follow the same principle you would buying fishing line. You need the right "test-line" for the situation. That is, you can't expect a 40-test pound chain to hold your 100-pound dog. It may save you money, but it isn't going to save you the trouble of chasing him down.

A collar is the next consideration. It fits properly when you can barely force it on over your dog's head. Their heads are always larger in circumference than their necks, so the collar will hang loosely once in place, but it won't come off easily.

A rock-solid tie is also the right idea. The best kind screws right into the ground. Don't get one you have to pound in; after working on these awhile your dog may be able to pull it out.

The screw variety is one-and-one-half feet long, and when it's in place only the handle is exposed. Attach your dog's chain to this handle. Allow a lead of at least 10 feet; the length you choose depends on the size of your yard, and how much roaming room you want to give your dog. Remember to watch out for objects that your pet's lead may become twisted around.

Whether you're using a leash, a chain, a cable or a tie, it's best to teach your dog not to pull on it. As soon as you feel your dog apply constant tension on her collar (pulling the tie), give her a firm correction by pulling her back towards you. **But say nothing.**

Your dog receives the correction when she feels the tension on the collar. To avoid this correction, and receive an occasional reward, she'll learn not to put tension on the collar.

4. SELF-MUTILATION

A surprising number of dogs will exhibit self-mutilation misbe-haviors during their lifetimes. This self-destructive streak can be attributed to a diverse array of conditions, including frustration, confusion, pent-up emotion, or even a simple need for attention. But whatever the cause, it can develop into a very dangerous and habitual daily ritual.

The most common methods of self-mutilation that a dog will engage in include:

- excessive licking of her forelegs, pads of feet and body,

- severe chewing of his legs, feet and pads.

These behaviors often result in bleeding or bodily damage to the dog, and the result can be quite serious.

Some dogs may even do damage to their claws, teeth, nose or mouth area. They'll do so most frequently when trying to escape from a cage.

There are other causes, too. Tail biting often begins with an innocent chase of the tail. But when a dog is bored, over-stressed, filled with anxiety or excitement, he can make more than a game out of it. And when he does, he'll actually grab his tail, hold onto it and chew.

After a while, this becomes a habit and they chase the tail just to chew on it. This sometimes results in extreme damage to the tail, even its destruction.

Sometimes self-mutilation has physiological roots. The dog may have an allergy (to weeds, fleas, etc.), an insect bite or another irritating problem which causes her to begin excessive chewing or abuse.

The pet's initial instinct is to lick or chew to alleviate the discomfort. But often this chewing can become a habit by the time the canine has returned to the comfort zone.

Watch out for open wounds or sores on the tail or leg area. These are tell-tale signs that self-mutilation may be occuring. People know enough to stop behavior that causes bleeding; dogs do not.

Bare spots are another indicator. They are commonly found on the dog's abdomen, and they're usually caused by an allergy or insect bite. Chewing irritates insect bites, which reinforces the dog's attention to the area. Thus, the cycle begins.

To resolve this problem, be sure to consult your veterinarian first to rule out any physical causes. If these **aren't** at the root of your pet's problem, check with a *Pet Behavior Specialist.*

In the meantime, inspect the wound frequently.

You must first determine whether or not what you're dealing with is an attention-grabbing behavior. If so, your dog will only chew when you're around. If not, your inspections will probably show a wetter, bloodier wound, often with missing hair, which worsens when you're away.

Once you know you're working with an attention-grabbing behavior, your best alternative is the proper use of a training collar. **The trick is to catch your dog in the act.**

If you're unable to catch your dog in the act – and in self-mutilation cases this is common – you're presented with a two-part problem. You must:

1. prevent your dog from damaging himself further when you're not there,

2. entice him into doing so when you are there, so you can teach him the proper behavior with a training collar (or electronic remote training collar).

Turn to Chapter 6, *How Dogs Learn*, under the heading "Training Methods And Equipment," for further instruction on using the training collar to correct your dog.

Step one is easier than it sounds. There is a device called an Elizabethan Collar designed specifically to address this problem (see the illustration on this page). It looks a lot like a bucket cut to fit over your pet's head to prevent him from reaching any part of his body with his teeth or his tongue.

In fact, an Elizabethan Collar looks so much like a bucket with the bottom cut out of it that the latter is, itself, used regularly for the same purpose. Many owners prefer buckets because they're not as big and bulky, and their dogs don't knock as many things over while wearing one. They aren't as functional, though, as they make it more difficult for your dog to eat and drink.

There are also certain medications that can be used in these cases (see your local veterinarian), but I do not recommend the use of a muzzle as a training tool.

The important thing for you to remember is that it's more important to treat the cause than the effect. So when you're home, and able to observe your pet, you should remove the bucket or Elizabethan Collar you're using. This is the **only way** you'll be able to catch your dog in the act of self-mutilation. And that is the path to prevention. Only then can you utilize the proper training procedure.

Here's Happy with the prim story of how we helped a proper little blonde Cocker Spaniel lick her self-mutilation problem.

*When we first met Sandy, she was almost nude. This is a very embarrassing condition for a canine; far more so than for a human. In fact, I don't know how her humans allowed her fur to go so far. More than half of it was missing. Yes, **half!** Sandy licked herself excessively...everywhere.*

Not that she liked herself for it. Quite the contrary. At that time, Sandy led a very sad life. She'd sit in front of the TV, furtively watching the hair transplant ads, licking away.

She had a problem, you see. And it had nothing to do with the bad-hair day she had every day. You see, she was an attention addict. And her humans had taught her that if she licked enough, she'd get all the attention she wanted.

To save Sandy, The Master had to teach her humans how to ignore her. I know it sounds backwards, but the best thing they could do for her was not to give her the direct response she desired.

So they didn't!

Eventually, that took care of the cause. But they still had to eliminate the effect. So when Sandy's humans were away from home, they had her wear an Elizabethan Collar.

I stopped in to see her whenever I could, soothing her by saying that she looked very stylish. (Actually, she looked a lot like the life of a party, lampshade and all!)

*But when her humans **were** home, the party was over for this little "animal."*

They couldn't allow her to get her licks in. So they used a gym whistle to startle her off the behavior every time she stuck out her tongue. And Sandy learned to avoid the whistle by not licking her body.

Soon she was able to make an entirely new fashion statement....with a fabulous new fur coat!

Excessive licking is often owner-directed. It can occur when you give your dog too much attention. In such cases, the more your pet gets, the more she wants. Dogs need attention. And they'll take what you'll give them...for starters. Then they'll go out of their way to get even more!

When you get home from work, your first impulse is to wind down. But that's not what your dog wants. She's wound up! She wants immediate attention. She needs an energy release, and she'll use all of her guile and cute little canine tricks to get the most out of you.

Self-mutilation takes the guile that extra mile. But here's a story about a dog who almost took it from here to eternity. Happy has the details.

Lucky was a black Labrador Retriever. He lived in Indiana with a pair of caring humans. But Lucky was absolutely the worst self-mutilation case we'd ever seen. He'd been licking his left front leg for three or four of his eight years.

His owners had consulted veterinarians, Pet Behavior Specialists, dermatologists – even a neurologist – and spent thousands of dollars trying to solve Lucky's lamentable problem. All to no avail.

No matter what they did, he did them one better. Once he was out of sight, Lucky went out of his mind, licking away like his leg was a popsicle. But his luck was about to run out.

His veterinarian was actually talking about amputation.

He had all the attention a dog could ever want, but his leg was in such bad shape that he could barely walk.

That's when we entered the picture.

"Lucky's about to lose his leg, I'm afraid," the male human offered after describing the dog's disposition.

"No, he's not," said The Master. "All Lucky's going to lose is the extra attention you've been giving him."

*Lucky's leg was saved by adjusting his **humans'** behavior. He thought it was all right to lick because when he did, he got more attention. Eventually, this behavior became an attention-grabbing device. And then it became a habit.*

To make matters worse, his humans – who were genuinely concerned – had created too many ways to try to correct the behavior. And when they did intervene, they didn't do so consistently. All this only confused the limping Lab.

But do you know what? Lucky's leg had a new lease on life less than two months later!

The Master had his humans stick to a strict regimen. When they were away, Lucky wore a "poor dog's Elizabethan Collar." It was just a bucket with a hole in the bottom for his head.

"I looked pathetic," Lucky laments. "But it sure beats a prosthetic. And I was on my last leg...figuratively speaking."

But we broke Lucky's habit when the bucket came off. Whenever his owners were home, they replaced it with an electronic training collar. As soon as Lucky went to lick his leg, he received a correction.

He knew it was for his own protection, so he had no objection. Especially when, after 30 seconds, his humans gave him verbal or – better still – physical praise.

Lucky didn't lose his leg; or any attention he loved! All-in-all, he was one lucky dog!

The key to modifying this misbehavior is to adjust your response. After making it impossible for your dog to do while you're away, you must act consistently when you're home. But whatever you choose to do, make sure your reaction is aversive enough for your dog to want to avoid the self-mutilating behavior. And reinforce proper behavior with appropriate rewards.

5. IMPROPER EATING HABITS

In the wild, a dog's eating habits are developed on a catch-as-catch-can basis. But in the human home, what a pet consumes should be closely regulated. When it isn't, problems can develop. This is a subtle way of saying that when a pet exhibits improper eating habits, the paw points to the provider.

Human beings are basically warm at heart. We give in easily to feelings of guilt, especially when it comes to the "withholding" of food from our dogs. They give us one little "hang-dog" expression, and we break down, offering anything they ask for. When we do this, we're just asking for problems. Most improper eating habits are caused by:

•overfeeding dog food,

• too many "human food" scraps (overtly or covertly),

• an improper, inconsistent diet.

Many people unwittingly teach their pets to be overeaters, undereaters or beggars. This is not an unimportant subject. Both overeating and undereating can be life-threatening.

Overeating

Your dog will not beg unless he knows he'll be given a treat, even if it's only every once in awhile. You can be sure that he's not begging because he's hungry, but because he knows he can get food, or perhaps, more attention.

319

It's very easy to find out if you're overfeeding your dog, or if he's being fed table scraps, even under the table. Just put him on the scale, the same as you would do for yourself. Check his weight. Does he look fat?

Stopping this destructive habit is solely up to you. Essentially, you have to do the dieting for your dog. You've got to have the will-power, or your dog won't lead the long and healthy life he deserves.

You have to be the one who determines what you need to do...and then you must follow through. Of course, it helps to know what is normal when it comes to intake.

The proper proportions for the average dog depend on a number of factors. But here is a typical feeding schedule, according to age:

- 6 months or less .... three times per day.

- 6 to 18 months .... twice per day.

- 18 months and older .... once per day.

Quantity depends largely on the quality of the food that you choose to use. See Chapter 9, *Correcting Dog Housebreaking Problems,* under the heading "Real Solutions," for more information on how to select a dog food.

To determine the proper serving size, read the recommendation on the package. Divide by one, two or three times per-day according to the above table, and feed your dog **only** that amount.

Do not feed her between meals.

Snacking between meals is a trait that isn't limited to human beings. A dog will do it too, when she can get away with it. But it's a bad habit to get into. And one they just can't get into without help.

Most humans find this hard to understand. In fact, we'll go to great lengths to pamper our pets.

Happy loves to tell the story of the owner who tried to cook up her own solution for her dog's snoring problem. It just goes to show you how irrational we humans can be when it comes to our pets.

At a year old, Duke easily weighed 220-pounds. Of course, he was an English Mastiff, so he was supposed to weigh that much. His diet wasn't his problem. His problem was snoring.

One morning his human called to see what The Master could do about her big ol' buzzsaw. She'd just spent another sleepless night stewing about her situation.

"Dukey's snoring so loudly," she yawned, "that he's vibrating my bed. You've go to do something!"

The Master had just the recipe. He suggested that she go to the grocery store for a beef shank bone to give him before bedtime. The idea was to wear the dog out, so he'd be less likely to snore.

But Duke's human thought The Master meant something more. Around 9 o'clock that evening she called back to check on her *main course of action. She wanted to know how to **cook** that beef shank bone! Her butcher had suggested one way, and her friends had told her to try another!*

Well, The Master set her straight. And I must say the retraining was well-done. At least it put a stop to the snoring.

But as funny as it was, this case isn't rare in one regard. When it comes to feeding us, humans will go to almost any length without even thinking. And that can be bad for our well-being.

Pets That Refuse To Eat

Overeating is an overwhelming problem in the pet population, though this isn't much understood. Undereating is by no means as big a problem – but it seems to strike more fear in the hearts of dog owners.

The fact is, it's an easy problem to resolve.

Undereating is, more often than not, a rebellious response. Usually, it occurs during a period of change in a dog's daily eating schedule. You may be trying to ween your dog from people food, for example; or even from one brand of pet food to another. Or it may be as simple as a change in the feeding schedule.

Whatever the cause, your dog resists the change, insisting (by her refusal) on a return to her old routine.

When your dog refuses to eat, don't make the mistake of giving in too soon. Most owners do, and they suffer the consequences of a continuation of the inappropriate eating habit.

Wait 72 hours before becoming concerned. As long as your dog is still taking sufficient water, she won't come to any harm. Dogs that refuse to eat rarely go beyond this 72-hour limit. In fact, if you don't blink, you'll usually find that your dog will be back at her bowl before the time you set is up.

Here's Happy with another example of a pampered pet, and an owner who sought a solution she was unwilling to implement:

Dinky is a King Charles Cocker Spaniel. He holds court in a household with a sweet old human female. And talk about your royal treatment! He eats only chicken or tuna fish; and even then only out of her hands or from a spoon. It's a wonder he doesn't have a taster, too!

"I've got a taste for the finer things in life, Happy," he tells me.

Well, one fine day, we got the call. His human wanted to know what she could do to end Dinky's reign. The Master knew exactly what she had to do to dethrone the little dog. He told her to put dog food down in Dinky's bowl and leave it there.

"Dinky won't let himself starve to death," The Master explained. "Eventually, he'll eat what you put out for him."

But the woman was convinced that Dinky would die before deigning to eat what the common dogs do. So she continues to hand-feed the little dog, when all it would take is a little willpower on her part to put him in his proper place (beside her).

And to this day, Dinky remains the king of his castle.

6. STRESSFUL SITUATIONS

Many situations in the human environment are stressful for our pets. Almost anything that a dog doesn't know how to deal with instinctively is a potential problem. This leads to many different kinds of "misbehaviors." This section features only a few of the most common stress situations, specifically:

- fear of fireworks/thunderstorms,

- fear of riding in cars,

- loss of a family member or another family pet.

Situations like these can be very stressful for your dog, which may react by hiding, backing off, acting fearful, chewing or even excessive noise-making.

When you see such behavior, you must be careful **not** to positively reinforce it with your correction. Instead, ignore it. Wait for your withdrawn pet to recover some. Then, reward her with all your love and attention.

When you coddle your canine in a stressful situation, you may think you're reassuring her. But from your pet's perspective, you're **rewarding** her when she acts that way, so she's more likely to repeat her wrongdoing.

Fear Of Fireworks Or Thunderstorms

Always try to look at the circumstances surrounding your dog's actions. Some dogs respond to loud, unexpected noises – like fireworks bursting or the occasional thunderclap – by hiding.

As noted in the introduction to this section, it's important for you not to comfort your dog under such circumstances. It will inevitably reinforce this misbehavior.

Other times, a dog's response to loud or frightening noises is to attack and destroy.

Your proper response would be to apply the appropriate correction for aggressive behavior. Teach your dog to "Sit" and "Stay." Then, if your dog reacts aggressively to a stressful situation, correct him with the training collar.

Say "Sit" only once, and firmly jerk the collar. Repeat this procedure, saying "Sit" only one time; jerk the collar if the dog does not obey.

Please read Chapter 6, *How Dogs Learn,* under the heading entitled "Training Methods and Equipment," for full details on teaching a dog to sit.

Fear Of Riding In Cars

For a dog, a ride inside a car can be a joyful experience...or it can be a real mess. It all depends on how the dog has been taught to deal with the stress.

Automobiles are alien to all animals. So it's only natural that dogs approach them with a certain amount of fear and apprehension. Especially if a visit to the vet is on the other end of the trip.

Still, almost every dog acts differently in the face of this situation. Some become overactive, constantly jumping from the back seat to the front seat, and then to the back again. When they do so, they often climb right into the driver's lap, or even under her feet, an extremely perilous place to be!

Other dogs get carsick. So you must first check with your veterinarian to ascertain whether or not your dog's problem is physiological. It may just be motion sickness. If it is, a doggie "Dramamine" prescription will take care of this problem. But follow your vet's instructions closely, because it contains a mild tranquilizer, so it should only be used occasionally.

If your dog still becomes sick when the car is in motion, the malady is something more. It is habitual or behavioral, and probably caused by overexcitement. This typically results in vomiting.

To counteract all of these problems, you need to teach your dog to be calm in the car. The best way to do this is to teach her to "Sit" and to "Stay." See Chapter 6, *How Dogs Learn,* under the heading "Training Methods and Equipment," if you need to review your skills in this area.

Practice these commands with your dog in the back seat of the car. Do so **not** when you're driving 55 mph down a major, six-lane highway in five o'clock traffic, but with the car standing still in your driveway. This makes all the difference in the world.

Once your dog comes to grips with the concept of the car, and she remains calm, cool and collected, you can start to accelerate your training. Have a friend actually drive the car, while you sit in the back seat teaching your pet to be still when the car is moving. Once around the block is good for starters. Then, each time out, take a longer test drive to gradually give your pet the "driving" experience she needs.

But remember that the goal is not for your dog to be a robot on the road, frozen in the "Sit" and "Stay" position. Rather, you want her to generalize the calm backseat behavior.

Ideally, this means she'll remain in one small area of the seat, lying or sitting. Standing is a dangerous position for any pet in the car. So if she tries to stand, teach her that this is the wrong way to go. But do so only under controlled conditions.

Find an empty parking lot or a side street with no traffic. Command your dog to "Sit" and "Stay" in the back seat. Then adjust the rearview mirror so you can watch your dog the whole time without turning around to look at it.

You might also want to remember to warn other riders in advance, to ensure that they're wearing a seatbelt (even at that slow speed). Most eventually volunteer to get out of the car!

When dog and mirror are in position, drive a reasonable distance at no more than 5 to 10 miles per hour. While the dog is sitting or lying down, drive the car smoothly and offer verbal praise. But if your dog stands up at any time during the exercise, stop the soothing talk and slam on your brakes. This action will unbalance your dog, delivering him headlong into the padded seat in front of him, and, ultimately, to the floor. When he's recovered his "sea-legs," he'll scramble back onto the back seat and lay down. Always.

It rarely takes more than three brakings to teach a pet to remain seated in the car. Yet you're not subjecting your dog to a great deal of damage; far less than the free-flying experience he'd have in a car going typical traveling speeds.

Ultimately your dog will conclude that the safest thing he can do when you're at the wheel is to stay put in his seat. When your dog does remain calm in one small area of the car, you should always reinforce the behavior, with occasional verbal praise and physical contact (when prudent).

Driving your dog should never be a full-contact sport. So only use this technique under the conditions described above.

This is a foolproof training method that won't harm your dog, and gives pet and driver alike a lifetime of peace-of-mind. But, remember, never drink and train!

Frustration At Being Left Alone In A Car

A far more common car complaint arises when dogs are left alone inside them, usually in parking lots. Feeling deserted and abandoned, they release their frustration in a number of unwanted behaviors. These can include excessive noise, destructive chewing, urinating or defecating in the car, or acting aggressively when people pass by.

For owners, the seriousness of these stressful situations can range from nuisance to not-allowable-under-any-circumstances. And the correction usually varies according to traditional training techniques by the complexion of the crime.

But none of the misbehaviors listed above can even begin to compare with that of Bigsby, an English Bulldog with whom we had some relations some years back. Bigsby was unique. And so was his solution to a stressful situation, as Happy will explain.

Like many dogs, Bigsby was left feeling frustrated whenever his humans left him behind, locked in the car. He always wanted to go with them, and he just couldn't understand their unwillingness to have him along.

*When they did leave him behind, he did miss them — but he wasn't about to miss out on an opportunity to do **something** physical. In fact, he was a fine physical specimen himself.*

But what could he do inside the car? It was so hot. It was so claustrophobic. Geez. He couldn't even do his aerobics. Or could he?

One day, Bigsby, left to his own devices in the parking lot of a regional mall, developed his own unique method for releasing stress when all cooped up in an automobile.

How did he do it? He brought back-seat behavior up front and center. Without beating around the bush too much, Bigsby sexually mounted the steering wheel.

Once in place, he looked a bit like the Club, clutching at the steering column. But the way he was honking the horn, he sounded more like a five-alarm intruder alert system.

His first performance drew a crowd from all corners of the parking lot. It turned out to be quite an affair. The police were summoned, regarding this indecent exposure, and his humans were left wondering what they'd done to deserve this.

But that wasn't the last of Bigsby's escapades. He followed up with multiple performances at locations all over town. His embarrassed humans didn't want to leave their home, for fear that Bigsby would steer them wrong again.

When they did venture out, they lived by an unspoken credo "When the car was a rockin', they came quickly to unlock 'im."

But the climax of this story happened when the retired couple decided to take a trip out West; and of course they took Bigsby with them. But by now, he was really in the driver's seat. When he wanted attention, they gave it to him. And when they left the car, he left with them. He enjoyed the new arrangement.

But there's no wrath quite like that of a Bulldog scorned. So when they finally stopped somewhere along the interstate, to grab a quick bite to eat, and they left him alone in the car, he picked right up where he left off. But this time, the thrust of the matter actually damaged the steering column.

When they finally arrived home a week later, with their ruined car in tow, the first thing they did was call in The Master. When we arrived, they brought Bigsby from back behind the house. He give me a nudge and a wink. I could barely keep a straight face!

The Master then "set-up" some situations to encourage Bigsby to repeat the behavior. But the Bulldog didn't need much in the way of encouragement. We put him in the car while we all walked around the corner of the house. Within minutes, the car and canine concerto was in full swing!

Even The Master had to admit he'd never seen anything quite like this before...and he's seen it all. But within minutes he'd developed a plan to help get Bigsby over the hump. In fact, the "dismount" wasn't difficult at all.

The Master used what he called an electronic Doctor Ruth. This turned out to be an ordinary remote training collar. He placed it around Bigsby's neck. The Bulldog was corrected if he made so much as a pass the steering wheel. And each time, after Bigsby had calmed down for 10 seconds or so, he was verbally rewarded by his humans.

In a matter of weeks, Bigsby was fine! Now when they leave him in the car, they still respect him when they return!

Bigsby was the most unusual "stressful-situation" case I've ever seen. But remember, when dogs do sexually mount inappropriate objects, what you're seeing is strictly a frustration-release behavior. See the information in this chapter, under the heading "Inappropriate Sexual Mounting," about why this is not a sexual-release behavior.

A more typical stress-release story might be that of a small Schnauzer named Beany. But, again, Happy may be better suited to tell the story. After all, he's the one in the dog suit.

And I'm one well-dressed dog, if I do say so myself! Well-dressed and low stressed.

But you know, I may be the exception to the rule. It's a stressful world out there, this world of humans. Oh, sure it's exciting, too. Don't get me wrong. I wouldn't have it any other way. But sometimes we dogs aren't properly prepared for it. We never know quite what to expect.

That brings us to Beany. Actually, you'd think that no dog could be better prepared. Beany was quite well-to-do. He was a Miniature Schnauzer of unquestioned lineage. And he lived in the lap of luxury, or, at the very least, in the laps of a loving human family.

But for Beany, the ultimate stress was being left home alone.

In fact, in this situation he seemed to have a split personality. As soon as his humans left the house, his alter ego would appear. He'd head for his doggie door, and transform himself from mild-mannered mutt into a supercanine (of sorts).

Beany became "Denture Dog," destroyer of fine furniture.

Did he have super powers? His humans thought so. What other dog could sink his canines into every inch of fabric in an entire couch in one two-hour period?

But Beany could. And he did.

No matter where his humans left him, the results were the same. On their return, they'd find their meek little Mini cowering in the corner, and another chair chomped to bits.

It's too bad they didn't call The Master right then and there. Perhaps he could have prevented what happened next.

To keep him away from their furniture, these humans decided to leave Beany in the garage, instead of in the house. I guess they didn't understand the stress he was under.

Unfortunately, Beany wasn't alone in the garage. He was left there with the family's mint condition, antique Mercedes Benz with custom-made Italian leather seats.

Well, it didn't take long for "Denture Dog" to destroy the entire interior of the car, puncture-by-puncture.

"Why would you leave Beany alone with the most expensive car you own?" asked The Master when the humans finally called him in.

"It seemed like a good idea at the time," the shocked humans answered. "We just wanted to keep him out of the house!"

Happy and I solved Beany's problem faster than a speeding bullet, with standard destructive chewing techniques (the kryptonite of the canine home world). Please see Chapter 8, *Correcting Dog Chewing Problems,* under the heading "The Solution," for more information.

Oh, and one other thing, Beany's owners never left him alone in an antique car again!

Loss Of A Family Member Or Another Family Pet

It's unlikely that pets miss "loved ones" who have passed away in exactly the same way that we do. The same is true for dogs who lose a human friend from their household through divorce, or even normal life-cycle "attrition" (like when someone leaves for college).

We miss our friends and family members by thinking about them. Pets don't have the same logical thought capabilities.

Nonetheless, there's an abundance of information available suggesting that pets **do** miss lost loved ones – pets and people alike – in their own ways.

Happy has a quick example for us.

Another Schnauzer we knew, named Blue, showed signs of depression after his "family" divorced. As a dog, I can tell you that this diagnosis is typically human. But in this case, it happens to be correct, if for all the wrong reasons.

Blue wouldn't know a divorce from a hole in the ground (though he'd obviously prefer the hole). So he just couldn't understand it. But he did know that now there was a big hole in his life. One of the humans he loved so much was no longer around.

That's the whole thing about "divorce." From a pet's perspective, it means such a major split from our regular routines. Blue was left alone more frequently, and he didn't understand why. And as a dog, he was all alone with his anxieties.

Blue experienced some of the other changes that can often occur when a person departs. He received less attention, he was petted less often and he received fewer food rewards. Although Blue, like most pets, didn't dwell on what caused these changes, he missed the attention that no longer took place in daily life.

The same kind of stress can occur when a second pet dies. The change in the life of the remaining pet is significant. He loses his companion, there is considerably less play and not as much exercise.

7. CHASING CARS

These days, complaints about dogs chasing cars come most frequently from the countryside. This is where cars can still roar down rural roads well above posted speed limits.

The car chase is rarer today within the city limits. Dogs just don't have the same freedom to roam. Besides, in the city, dogs are surrounded by noisy, honking, intrusive automobiles from the time they're puppies. So by the time they're full-grown, the thrill is gone. And their owners are much more inclined to keep them on a leash, and to train them not to chase cars (or joggers).

So why do dogs chase cars? Especially out there in the country?

Because it's fun! Because it's a challenge! And because it's there! (Ooops, now it's gone!)

So what can you do about it? The easiest training technique is the use of a remote training collar. But most owners use them improperly for solving this particular problem.

What they do is to allow their pet to run after a car, and then they "zap" it. But what happens when you do this is that your dog will associate the correction with the passing car. She's already totally focused on this quarry, so when she receives a correction it only intensifies her chase. In fact, she'll act more aggressively than ever to catch the darned thing, and eliminate the stimulus that caused that correction.

That's certainly not what you want to teach her! Here's what you *should* do.

Let your dog know *why* she's being corrected. Set up circumstances that will tempt her to chase a car. Ask a friend to help by driving past your house several times. Then, when your dog begins to chase the car, use the "Come" command. Yell, "Come," only once. If your dog doesn't stop and begin its return within two seconds, correct it using the remote training collar.

Please refer to Chapter 6, *How Dogs Learn,* under the heading "Training Methods and Equipment," for a full description of how to teach this command to your pet.

Use the command to redirect your dog's attention from the automobile. That way, she won't associate the correction with the car, and you won't be sending her the wrong signal with your remote trainer. Once she'll come when you call her 10 to 15 consecutive times, those pesky cars will become just another passing fancy.

In our time on the road, we've dealt with our share of pets who enjoyed chasing down cars. One typical "track star" was an Airdale named Amelia, whom Happy has kept up with over the years:

Amelia lived in a slow "country" suburb in central Ohio. But for her, it was the fast-track.

Homes there were typically spaced 500 feet apart. Most of them had front yards at least 100 yards deep. So Amelia had plenty of room to roam. Still, she seemed to prefer hanging out with her human, hovering over the flower beds around the house.

That is, until one of her rival roadsters roared by. It didn't matter what make. It didn't matter what model. It didn't matter what horsepower. Nothing mattered but the power of

337

pounding pistons, and the lure of that asphalt strip. It really revved Amelia's engine. And she was off to the races.

Amelia accepted any challenge. She was a real speed demon. And once the chase was on, there was little her human could do about it. We're talking wide-open spaces here. So he had to catch her before she ever got the green flag.

About all he could use was an electronic training collar. But because it had a limited range, he could only use the remote device under precise circumstances. Usually, Amelia would beat him to the street as he raced to reach the remote. And by the time he got to the button, she was already too far down the track to bring her back.

When this was the case, the harried human would have to hop into his "pace" car, and drive down the road after her. Eventually, when he did catch up, he'd open the door and ask, "Does Amelia want a car ride?" to bring her home.

How did the story end? After a number of years on the circuit, consistent training collar corrections cured Amelia of her need to chase cars.

Besides, she's got a trophy room full of hardware to remind her of her glory days!

One complicating factor for this retraining regimen is the availability of the owner. If your dog can still chase cars when you aren't around, all of your hard work will be in vain. So contain your pet whenever you can't be there to supervise this situation during training. Do not give them access to an automobile chase.

Remember that if your dog can get away with this behavior even five percent of the time, you'll never be able to resolve your problem. You must be consistently present to correct the dog.

8. UNIQUE PROBLEMS

Technically, a problem is unique only if there's a single example of it. You may come across a unique "misbehavior" at some time during the relationship you have with your dog. (I'll always remember the German Shepherd with the fear of blimps mentioned in the next section.) But I hope that the *Behaviorist* perspective in *Tricks I Taught My Master* will stand you in good stead should you ever come across such a situation: a truly unique problem.

But most of the problems presented here as "Unique" might perhaps be better classified as "Unusual," or, better still, as "Disgusting." The key here is that they may be disgusting **to humans** – not necessarily to dogs, for whom they may be quite natural.

Fortunately, what I've found is that the stranger the circumstances are, the more traditional the retraining technique called for.

So here we go, from the most fantastic to the most basic of animal urges. From the unique to the unusual to the disgusting.

Fear Of Blimps

Yes, fear of blimps! Bridgett was a two-year-old Mix-Breed – mostly German Shepherd – whose owner called one day with an absolutely fantastic story. Here's how Happy tells it.

339

*One day, Bridgett looked out the window of her apartment and got the fright of her life. There, as **big** as life, was the Fuji Blimp. It didn't hurt that the Shepherd lived in a Chicago high-rise, basically right at blimp-level.*

After several weeks of fearful frenzy every time Bridgett went near the window, her roommate, a human named "Woof" (Bridgett's pet name for her) got The Master on the line.

At first, he thought she was probably full of hot air with the blimp story, but once he actually monitored Bridgett's behavior he became a believer.

Myself, I asked her point blank about it.

"Blimp," she answered, seriously. "Scared the heck out of me."

What are the symptoms of this phobia? Well, for weeks afterward, whenever she'd walk by the window, she'd look furtively over her shoulder, followed by a mad scramble for a hiding spot.

She was even afraid outside. When she reached a specific spot on the sidewalk, ostensibly below where the blimp had hovered, she would whimper and try to hide.

Bridgett's roommate responded instinctively. She wanted to comfort Bridgett. To coax her out and cuddle her. But The Master took the human aside and told her how she could really help her dog overcome this fear of the now-departed dirigible.

"When you're outside," he said, "try to redirect her attention. Command her to perform some on-leash tasks. Take her mind off it."

The human used the "Heel" command quite a lot thereafter. Sometimes she supplemented this with the "Come" command. And every time Bridgett carried out a request, she was praised and given food rewards.

Inside the condominium, whenever Bridgett showed signs of fear, her human used the "Sit" and "Stay" commands, for the same reason. And with the same effect.

And do you know what? It took only four days to beat the blimp!

Technically, Bridgett's owner eliminated this unique behavior by a combination of redirection, reassurance and reward. But if she'd given her pet the loving comfort she'd wanted to while Bridgett was acting fearful, she would only have reinforced the misbehavior and worsened it.

Dogs Eating Feces

Although listed here under "Unique Problems," this behavior isn't nearly as rare as you'd expect. In fact, many, many dogs actually **do** eat feces; and they may do so for a number of reasons.

In most cases, this doesn't occur because they're missing something from their diet. If so, why would their bodies eliminate it? Nor is it an attempt to control territory or to show dominance.

When dogs eat feces, they do so for one of two reasons:

1. they enjoy them, or

2. they are trying to hide them.

Are you finished blanching? Yes, I'm serious. Some dogs eat feces because they taste good to them! After all, they originate as the tasty, nutritious food they ingest. Apparently, to some dogs, everything is better the second time around!

Other dogs will eat feces only as a last resort. Usually they'll do so to eliminate any evidence of a housebreaking mistake. In such cases, they're so fearful of the repercussions of their behavior, that they're willing to hide the evidence by ingesting it.

For more information on this misbehavior, consult Chapter 9, *Correcting Dog Housebreaking Problems,* under the heading "Real Solutions."

A dog who feels forced to hide a mistake may find eating the evidence more palatable than the alternative. But many dogs find feces palatable enough to eat anyway; even to enjoy! Why? How?

When it comes to cooking, *people* react very positively to intense smells and tastes. Just look at the popularity of Cajun or Szechwan cooking. Well, dogs react to the same kind of intensity, it's just that their tastes are different. And, perhaps because their sense of smell is so well-developed, it takes something especially strong to tempt their tastebuds.

Some dogs will eat only their own feces. Nonetheless, the idea of a dog eating **any** feces is a problem for most owners. It gives new meaning to the term "dog breath," for example.

If your dog does this, first speak with your veterinarian. There are simple solutions that she can prescribe in powder form. Or try sprinkling about a half-teaspoon of Adolph's Meat Tenderizer on your dog's food for three consecutive days. This will stop the problem about 70% of the time. The working theory is that this makes the feces taste bad (to your dog, we already know your opinion).

Some people claim that feeding your dog a strip of black licorice after each meal will have the same result.

There are other solutions, but most of them aren't very convenient. One is to pick up the feces immediately, and discard them every time your dog has a bowel movement. Again, it is very hard to monitor every time your dog has to go.

Other dogs even enjoy eating the feces of other animals! Many masters are surprised to find their canines foraging for feline feces. The fact is, it's fine dining for many dogs. It's like "catviar" to them!

Correction is difficult in cases like this, because dogs seldom consume cat droppings in front of their owners. The simplest solution is to make the litter box inaccessible to the dog. This isn't difficult, and the cat will probably appreciate it, too.

When Happy was a young puppy, he had a pal named Hal who loved eating the feces of his housemate, a Siamese cat named Horatio. Horatio would dutifully use his litter box. Then we'd see Hal leave the room two minutes later, only to return shortly, burping happily. (By the way, Hal was short for "Halitosis.")

Another of Hal's favorites was fuzzy goose poop, which he always seemed to track down at any park or corporate office grounds with a lake.

Warning, the following section is even more disgusting than anything you've ever read before...not just in this book, but anywhere. It is not for the squeamish. Something stronger than parental guidance is suggested, if there is such a rating.

In fact, what follows is so nauseating that I'm happy to turn tail on it, turning the tale over to Happy, who may not find it so offensive.

In an effort not to seriously offend your human sensibilities, I'll try to keep this short and sweet.

The Master and I once worked with a Scottish Terrier named Albert, who enjoyed eating excrement. He couldn't get enough of it. Every sidewalk was a smorgasboard for Albert, and every curb a cafe.

His humans, the poor wretches, were caught retching on a number of occasions – until Albert gave that a try, too.

*We were called in when he developed the **really** bad habit. The habit he'll be known for the rest of his life.*

You see, there were two other Scotties living in this household, too. And when the three dogs were allowed outside after dinner, Albert would stand in a corner of the yard anxiously awaiting.

He watched for one of the other two dogs to do their thing. But they could never serve it up fast enough for his taste. So when he first saw them squat down, this determined dog would run over and eat it as it emerged! Every time out!

(We probably should have included a sick bag with each book.)

You'll be relieved to know that Albert no longer "eats on the run." But not as relieved as his humans.

How did we do it? With a remote electronic training collar. Now whenever his roomates get ready to go, Albert runs in the other direction!

For more information on how to correct your dog with this useful training tool, see Chapter 6, *How Dogs Learn,* under the heading "Remote Training Collars."

Inappropriate Sexual Mounting

Sexual mounting is used by many a dog to express dominance over another dog. This act is solely one of control.

But some couples become concerned when their dogs mount the bed. Many are embarrassed even to call, because this often occurs after they've used it for their own purposes of loving, sexual expression!

Dogs are perceptive. They know when there's something other than sleeping going on in that bedroom. They understand the unique odor. And many times they will even mount a bed immediately afterwards.

If your dog mounts the bed, you can bet it's probably just a release of frustration.

Dogs will actually mount just about anything – from a stuffed animal to a television to your Uncle Phil – in order to release a broad array of emotions.

Happy has a friend named Jimmy; a somewhat overweight, very friendly male Dalmation. In the middle of a tug-of-war game, he'll release his "play excitement" by mounting the toy being tugged on.

What's the solution for inappropriate sexual mounting? After all, it's embarrassing enough on its own, let alone in mixed company!

The best way to eliminate such behavior is with a simple "Sit" command. Use the training collar to pull your dog off his mount. Concurrently this serves as a correction, too.

If your dog is determined to return to its revelry, add the "Stay" command to your regimen. Follow the procedures outlined in Chapter 6, *How Dogs Learn*, under the heading "Training Your Dog."

UNCHANGEABLE BEHAVIORS

Some behaviors are unchangeable. Whether they're normal behaviors, ingrained misbehaviors or abnormal behaviors, there's nothing much that you can do about them.

Ingrained misbehaviors and abnormal behaviors are discussed in detail in Chapter 15, *Getting Started*, under the heading of "Accepting Final Responsibility."

But many misbehaviors, or behaviors classified as such by owners, are nothing more than common canine conduct.

Remember Duke, the one-year-old, 220-pound English Mastiff with the eating "disorder?" Well, he had his other "problems," too. His owner was constantly calling us in with countless complaints. I've outlined a number of these unchangeable behaviors below, along with some examples of the external changes that were possible to placate Duke's owner.

- Problem: Duke drops his rawhide in her lap. She doesn't want to touch it, so she calls for her husband to come and remove it. If he doesn't arrive in time, the rawhide stains her clothes.

  Solution: Give Duke his rawhide only in the kitchen behind a pet gate.

- Problem: Duke drools on people.

  Solution: Have guests get up and walk away from Duke when he's about to drool on them.

- Problem: Duke leans against the furniture, leaving it covered with dog hair.

  Solution: Have Duke groomed or brushed more frequently.

- Problem: Duke won't sleep in the kitchen when the weather warms, insisting on the cooler living room (where his owner doesn't want him). But when he whines about his sleeping arrangements, only she can hear his whining.

  Solution: Buy a fan to cool the kitchen.

Like most dogs, Duke is **perfect** in every way. He's your every day, typical, All-American dog. He walks like a dog. He talks like a dog. So he must be...a dog!

Owners must learn that their pets are animals, exhibiting normal animal behaviors most of the time. We can either accept those behaviors or learn how to change them.

In every relationship between dog and owner, the owner must ask himself, "Do I want to adapt to my dog, or do I want my dog to adapt to me?"

Ultimately, the decision is yours.

14

Handling The Occasional Relapse

Marriage is something we dogs will never understand. We just don't go for that sort of thing. We're already tied down as it is, with ropes and chains and leashes. So why would we want to tie another knot?

But as bewildering as marriage is to us, divorce is absolutely beyond our comprehension. Maybe that's because we have an instinct for understanding each other's needs.

Well, needless to say, it's different for humans. There're all those emotions to get in the way. And sometimes two humans – who vowed to be together until death do they – grow apart.

It's what we dogs call an occasional relapse. But whether it's back to bachelorhood or to maidenship, the course is never steady.

When two humans do get divorced, the first thing I think is, "Gee, it'll be so hard on the children." But we also know how hard it can be for us canines.

Take Jerry, for example. He's a Beagle that runs in my circle. And at four years old, he's been around the block a few times.

Still, he was really shaken when his old man and old lady split. In fact, after the break-up, Jerry just broke down.

The situation was far too complicated. His female had custody of him. They'd moved into a very nice new home. But Jerry started "leaking" like a sieve.

His human couldn't understand why; he'd been housebroken since he was a pup. So she called in The Master. I tagged along to see if there was anything I could do for Jerry.

The Master was quick to discover the nature of the problem. (And it wasn't because nature was calling!)

"You're dog is no longer housebroken," he told the human, "because he's heartbroken."

She was incredulous. "What do you mean?"

"The stress of your divorce is really affecting Jerry," The Master answered. "It's not uncommon. He misses the day-to-day routines. He misses your other house. And you may find it hard to believe, but he misses that louse you used to live with, too."

(The Master knew that louse pretty well, so he could say something human like that.)

She just laughed. "So what do we do?"

The Master was all business. He put Jerry on a program that included a consistent routine, similar to what he enjoyed before the break-up, plus some confinement until his housebreaking was repaired.

Jerry was back to "business" as usual in 45 days.

But just six months later, Jerry's human had us return. The Beagle was back at it again, and she didn't know why.

When we returned to Jerry's house, we were surprised to learn that the woman had remarried. I figured that was enough right there to release the floodgates. But there was more!

The female's new mate had an eight-year-old son, and his name was Jerry, too! Talk about confusing. Jerry – the dog – didn't know whether he was coming or going.

He was going, all right! And going, and going, and going!

I knew what to tell this woman, but The Master had the answer even faster. (He's such a whiz!) He told her to return to the consistent schedule that broke the dog's hydrant of a habit the first time around.

She agreed. But there was still the problem of the eight-year-old son. With the boy around, the furry Jerry kept hearing his name. But he never knew who was getting the talking to.

So The Master suggested that the human rename the dog; perhaps as something else she'd called him since he was a pup: "Squirt."

That makes Jerry the only dog I've ever known who reverted to his "maiden" name after a divorce!

To "grrr" is canine. But to "err" is human. That's why we, as humans, should be understanding when it becomes obvious that this is, perhaps, the one characteristic that our dogs **do** share with us.

No matter how well-trained your dog; no matter how sophisticated the regimen is for your puppy; no matter how successful your pet's retraining seemed to go...expect an occasional relapse. Because in this one area, I'll grant you that dogs are only human!

But that doesn't mean you can't have a strategy set in advance for dealing with such mistakes. In fact, that's what this chapter is all about.

You can expect to see some serious misbehavior during any traditional training process...especially during the second or third week. And it is important that you know this will be so before you start to implement the plan that you've developed. That way, you won't incorrectly assume:

- your dog has already forgotten its training;
- the techniques you've learned have stopped working;
- the methodologies have ruined your dog; or,
- your dog is an idiot!

It is vital for you to know in advance that at some point your dog's misbehavior will get worse before it gets better. Unfortunately, this paradox is never satisfactorily explained to pet owners, nor is it ever really described in terms of concrete experience. This void may provide the greatest challenge of all to the continuity – and even the very continuation – of any individual dog's training program.

THE ANDRYSCO ABERRATION

Because I have worked extensively with the phenomenon, this increase in misbehavior has been termed the Andrysco Aberration. This term describes the definite increase in misbehavior – both in intensity and frequency – before a pet will bend to an owner's will. **This increase is something that you will see and that you must cope with on the way to achieving your desired end result.**

This rebellious period can occur while you're trying to eliminate just about any type of misbehavior.

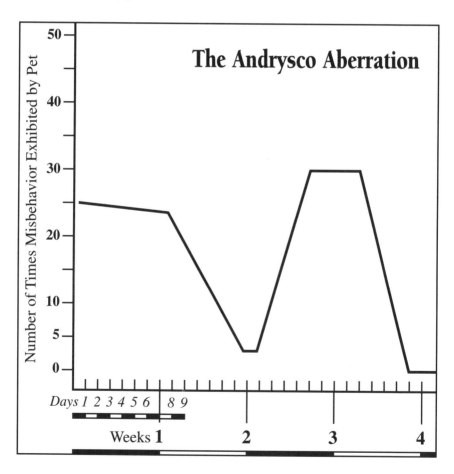

This chart tracks the trends of normal dog behavior during the Andrysco Aberration; it is a composite of the behaviors exhibited by the pets I treated over a 13-year period. This chart represents the learning curve that you can expect while training your dog.

Here's how this normal learning curve may affect your progress over the course of your dog's training period:

First Week
This is the average time it takes most owners to become consistent with the new techniques or interventions.

Second Week
The dog begins to respond to your consistency and shows improvement. This is due to the novelty of your new behavior. Because you're acting differently, your dog will take a wait-and-see attitude, "going with the flow" to see what this new behavior is all about. The result is that by the end of this week, your consistent technique will bring about the intended behavioral change, and your dog will perform better.

Third Week
This is the time that you need to be on your guard, because, in most instances, this is when a dog will become rebellious. As you continue to insist that your pet respond to your commands, the novelty starts to wear off. Your dog will begin to realize that the new situation isn't just temporary. And it will react as if it were saying, "Hey! I don't want you doing this to me *all* the time. Back off!" But by continuing to force the issue, and to demand obedience, your actions will tell your dog, "I'm not backing down. Do what I tell you to do."

What follows is a battle of wills. But you **must** persist until your pet finally gives in. Then you need to give the appropriate command, and demand compliance until your dog is calm and under control. Only then should you back off.

During this period, your dog has finally decided that enough is enough. Unhappy with your attempts at control, it decides to see what you're really made of. For the next week, your dog may seem like the biggest troublemaker in the world.

Stick with it. Essentially, your dog is testing you. And trying to train you back to your accomodating old ways. If you execute your new techniques inconsistently, your dog will win.

If you can get through this difficult period – which averages three to seven days – without panic and with unwavering consistency, your efforts will result in a well-trained dog.

But if you assume that the techniques you're using are ineffective, and change them, you'll play directly into your pet's paws. This will only reinforce its obstinance and make your job harder.

THE FOUR STAGES OF THE LEARNING CURVE

Some owners see a continuous pattern of Week 1 behavior through Week 3 behavior, reverting to Week 1 behavior. And, unfortunately, a common mistake made by many trainers when they receive owner complaints is to instruct them to try something new – spike collars, remote collars, food rewards, drugs.

This is the worst possible advice. Continuity is what your dog needs at this critical time. If you make a change, your dog is learning that **you** are easily controlled – **not** what you are trying to teach it. And you will be doomed to repeat that portion of the learning process.

The learning curve has four distinct stages:

1. you learn to become consistent with new techniques;

2. your dog has an initial positive response to Stage 1;

3. the rebellious or testing period occurs (the Andrysco Aberration); you must remain consistent;

4. a lifetime in which dog and owner live together compatibly.

The Andrysco Aberration occurs during training in over 90% of all pets. The occurrence of this natural phenomenon shows that the training is "taking" (not the opposite). When you hold your own and remain consistent, the final result is that you'll be happy with the training outcome.

DEVIATIONS FROM THE CURVE

Deviations from the normal learning curve occur in approximately 13% of all animal behavior modifications, causing an unsuccessful outcome. Here are the most common deviations for each of the four stages:

Stage 1

- The owner does not use a technique consistently.

  Why does this occur? The most common reasons are a weak-willed owner, a closed-minded owner, or an owner who believes she knows more than the consultant she's hired to help her. Some owners shouldn't have a pet, simply because they don't have time for it. Others don't even try the techniques suggested because they're too "difficult" or "time consuming."

  Occasionally, dogs and owners are mismatched; a dog may be too large, too aggressive or too strong.

- The owner is confusing the dog by trying more than one technique during training.

- An advisor (even a "professional") may be suggesting the wrong techniques to use.

- The dog has been misbehaving for so many years that it will never change.

- Something might be physiologically or neurologically wrong with the dog.

Stage 2

- The owner discontinues or reduces contact with an outside advisor, then frantically reinitiates contact as the dog enters into the rebelliousness of the next stage.

It is rare to encounter a pet that does not get through Stage 2, unless something is physically or neurologically wrong with the animal; or if the owner isn't following directions well.

Stage 3

•   The owner becomes inconsistent in the execution of the training techniques.

•   The owner makes changes as the dog continues to test the resolve of the owner.

If the owner acquiesces, the dog has won. If the dog reverts to its old behavior, the owner relinquishes control. Then it is *the owner* whom becomes the dominated animal, easily controlled.

Stage 4

•   Once a pet – and pet owner – successfully complete Stage 3, the dog's behavior has been modified according to the tastes of the owner. But this is not the final step. Nor is there one. Stage 4 is an ongoing process during which both dog and owner must maintain their new behaviors.

How long must this vigilance last? For the life of the dog, of course!

Every pet-owner relationship is a learning experience. And the learning lasts a lifetime, whether you're a novice "trainer" or an expert.

Before we finish up here, I thought it might be fun to tell you how Happy and I met, and when we decided we might make a good team. We sure didn't start out that way!

But perhaps Happy ought to tell you how it all happened.

The Master and I really didn't get off on the right paw. We met at the local Canine Society, where we dogs meet to place human families with loving dogs. I was just a pup at five months old, visiting friends who worked there.

I was pretty skeptical of the whole prospect of placing humans. I'd already tried to work with two different families, and they were the most irrational, inconsistent animals I'd ever come across.

In my youth, I was unruly and impatient, so I'd just given up on them after a few weeks.

So there I was, hanging out at the Canine Society, just biding my time, and in walks The Master. Oh, I didn't know him as The Master yet — or even as a master — but when our eyes met, something just clicked, like claws on the pavement in the summertime.

So I decided to give the human race one more run for its money. I adopted this one right on the spot.

When we got home, I realized that I'd probably made the the biggest mistake of my young life. This guy seemed just as flighty as the rest. I found his demeanor quite human, and very obnoxious. But I figured I'd give him the chance that every human deserves. Still, I had to put him to the test.

So for three weeks, I put him through his paces. And for three weeks he stayed right on my tail. Then, finally, my big break came. He had company in the house, so there was a lot of confusion, and somebody's child left the front door open.

I was outside in a flash. I knew he was behind me, but I kept going, as fast as my four legs would carry me. That's when I got carried away. I high-tailed it across the street, (ah, the reck-lessness of youth) and into a neighbor's yard.

This new "master" called out to me to "Come," but I kept going. In fact, I ignored him completely. But I came to a stop under a ladder. Perhaps it was superstitious of me, but it did turn out to be a bad omen.

The neighbor happened to be up on this ladder, cleaning the gutters. He looked down, saw me, and yelled something unin-telligible (and perhaps unprintable).

He was probably telling me to get out of his yard, but I was a brash young Beagle Mix, so I calmly walked over to the ladder and lifted my leg.

The neighbor was furious. That's when he dumped the "gutter goo" on me.

This made me very un-Happy, but I figured I'd make the best of the situation by giving the worst of it to my new human.

He wanted me to "Come," did he? Well, sure I would. I bolted back across the street, bearing down on him as he backed away. But as fate would have it, one of the visitors opened the front door, and I changed my course of action, flying past this would-be master and back into the house.

I have to admit, my mind was in the gutter that day when I did the old "rub and roll" on the living room carpet. Little did I know that this human would be the best friend I'd ever have. He passed the test that day. And he's passed it every day since. He's been as consistent a companion as a canine could ever ask for.

Over the years, I've grown to understand his true Mastery of the meaningful pet-owner relationship. And today we're a team, passing on tried-and-true training techniques for the betterment of both species.

SUCCESSFUL CURE STATISTICS

Just what *is* a "cured" dog? The definition varies widely by owner. Just as you decide what constitutes a misbehavior, so do you determine what behaviors are acceptable. In other words, your dog is cured if you are happy with the training outcome. But every owner has a different idea of success.

For example, when a *Pet Behavior Specialist* works to housebreak a pet, one owner might define success as a dog which never urinates in the house. Another owner – one who has suffered through months of having his dog urinate in the house several times a day – may be deliriously happy with a dog who makes "only" six mistakes a year.

With this floating definition of success in mind, let's take a look at some more concrete statistics. They're probably going to be much better than you were ever led to expect by other pet professionals – trainers, veterinarians and behaviorists alike. But the following percentages have been gathered from actual cases over a period of thirteen years.

To achieve such a high success rate, I maintained contact with the owners for one, or sometimes two, months; in the most severe cases, for as long as six months. This is because owners must first be educated and then guided to retain consistency, subtly adjusting techniques as necessary along the way.

My own success over this period of time increased steadily, and then leveled out over the last four to five years. Obviously, I experienced lower rates of success at the beginning of my practice, while I was learning the stages...and also what broke the learning curve. Incredibly, these statistics include dogs trained even in those early years:

Overall Success 87%

Housebreaking 87%
Destructive Chewing............................... 84%
Aggressive Behavior 71%
Obedience Response 97%
Excessive Noise Making 97%
Dog/Child Relationship Improvement 85%

I've seen - and resolved - many other misbehaviors in my career to-date, but I have not included them because the number of cases doesn't provide numbers that are statistically significant. These include true hyperkinesis in dogs (three cases seen, one improved), improper behavior riding in cars, fear of loud noises, sexual mounting behaviors and fence jumping.

GUARANTEES

What kind of guarantees can a *Pet Behavior Specialist* offer? None! Why not? There are too many variables outside of our control.

1. The owner might not carry out the advice offered, although in 87% of the cases, an owner will do so.

2. The dog may indeed be untrainable. These cases are rare, but they do occur. This doesn't necessarily mean that a pet is untrainable in **all** areas; it may only be untrainable in the area in which the owner has requested assistance.

3. A *Pet Behavior Specialist* cannot read a dog's mind! Therefore, the advisor may occasionally not suggest the right technique to try. But chances are 99.9% certain that the *Specialist* **will** be correct.

15

Getting Started

So now we've come full circle. The end of this book signals the start of something new. Hopefully, **Tricks I Taught My Master** will help you to revitalize the relationship that you have with your pet.

The techniques outlined in the first 14 chapters will enable you to teach your new dog – or to retrain your old friend – according to your needs and wishes. These "Tricks" were taught to me by thousands of dogs from all across the country. They represent a wealth of field experience (of the four-legged kind). These methodologies may just be the best way you can help your dog to adapt behaviorally. And that will help you give your dog the happier home life he deserves.

The pet-owner relationship is symbiotic. It offers many happy returns to both parties. But if you're ready to give your love to a new and deserving dog, be careful. You're about to invest in a friendship that will last a lifetime. And decisions like these must be made with great care and attention.

Picking A Pet

Whether you're picking your very first pet, or you're a long-time dog lover looking for yet another, you need to do your homework. The library is as good a place to start as any. There, you'll have access to all the breed information you'll ever need. There are literally thousands of dog varieties available, and with the library's vast resources, you'll be able to research the characteristics of the canine species you're most interested in.

Try to get a full understanding. Look for the breed's flaws as well as its positive attributes. Learn about its life span.

The trick is to select a breed that matches the needs of your family. That means you must be mindful of what those needs are. What will you expect of your dog? Do you have children? Of what age? Do you expect your dog to be a child's pet? Are you on the lookout for a watchdog? Will your new friend be an adult companion? Or will it fill still another function?

Once you know what your parameters are, perhaps the easiest way to proceed is to pick up the phone and talk to a *Pet Behavior Specialist.* Your local veterinarian is another good venue. Or a breeder. Any one of these pet professionals would be happy to help you out; especially in advance of your decision. That's because at this stage they still have time to head off many of the mistakes that people make.

Yet most people do not take this step.

Sure, it's more logical to consult with someone who understands breed characteristics. But picking pets has always been largely an emotional experience.

Most people make their purchase at a pet store; or they visit their local animal shelter. For them, it's almost an impulse decision, like the candy on the countertop in the convenience store.

It's hard to imagine anything much cuter than a puppy. They can be irresistible, no matter what you have on your list. So if you haven't thoughtfully considered all the possibilities beforehand, it's easy to choose an inappropriate pet. This will only cause heartache later.

No matter where you go to get your pet, it seems the sellers will tell you whatever it takes to make the sale. And sometimes it seems like the smaller the puppy, the taller the tale.

They make it seem like every dog out there is effortlessly housebroken, excellent with the kids, quite mild-mannered and easily trained.

Nothing could be further from the truth!

Every breed has its idiosyncracies. Black Labradors, for instance, are more prone to dominating behavior. Chocolate and Yellow Labradors may also be domineering, but to a much lesser degree.

You'll usually find the best example of a Black Lab's bad behavior beneath a table. That's where these dogs seem to settle when they've stolen something valuable. It's their refuge. And oftentimes, if you attempt to retrieve the object, the Labrador becomes aggressive.

(This behavior is not the retrieving instinct surfacing. More likely, it's an innate need to hoard something in a hard-to-reach place.)

The best example may be among the cutest of them all: the Blonde Cocker Spaniel. These little dogs often come as a big surprise to their owners.

In the pet store, parents are influenced by their enraptured children, who have the tiny puppies cradled in their arms.

"Oooh, Mommy, can I have him?" they'll squeal.

And the appeal of these precocious little puppies is hard to miss.

This is usually when the pet store employee will chime in, saying "This puppy's easily housebroken; she's great with the kids! And we accept VISA!"

Then when the family gets the Cocker Spaniel home, they can't believe it when it starts to act aggressively.

"How can this cute little dog act so aggressively?" they'll say. "Cute dogs don't act that way!"

But they do, especially little Blonde Cocker Spaniels. And they are often seriously aggressive. But apparently not nearly as aggressive as some of the people selling them to naive buyers.

See Chapter 10, *Correcting Dog Aggressiveness Behavior,* under the heading "Timetable For Correction (Breed - Cocker Spaniel)," for more details on what is now known as Cocker Spaniel Syndrome. This aggressiveness resulted from the inbreeding of these dogs when demand for them rose after the release of Walt Disney's "*Lady and the Tramp.*"

Once pet people were made aware of this problem, the affected dogs were humanely put to sleep, and breeders modified their breeding practices. The results were positive. There have been no reported cases of Cocker Spaniel Syndrome since the late 1970's.

Nonetheless, today almost every dog professional will tell you that the Cocker Spaniel has more aggressive tendencies than any other breed. They can become intense very suddenly, springing at someone with the intent to do harm.

Nowadays, though, there is usually a legitimate reason for such attacks. And there are ways to correct these behaviors. Try the techniques for correcting aggressive behavior described in Chapter 11, *Modifying A Biting Dog,* in the section titled, "The Solution."

These are just two examples. But the Black Labrador Retriever and the Blonde Cocker Spaniel serve to illustrate your need to know the characteristics of the canines you're considering. Only then can you make an informed decision on the best fit for your family.

__The Next Step__

Once you've purchased your pet, you'll want to train it.

Actually, new owners have a number of alternatives when it comes to training. Again, you can consult with a *Pet Behavior Specialist*. These professionals offer a valuable perspective, very different from most traditional training sources.

You could also hire a dog trainer or attend standard obedience classes with your pet. Or you can educate yourself with one of the many books or videotapes available on the subject, and train your dog yourself.

I hope that you'll find **Tricks I Taught My Master** useful in this regard. But whichever you choose, I'd recommend sticking with it. Because, as I've noted many times in this book, consistency is the key to canine conditioning.

Your best solution may depend on your pet herself. Actually, each of these are legitimate choices under normal circumstances.

But if your pet is exhibiting some truly serious misbehaviors, such as biting children, you must make an equally serious choice. And only three are available:

1. keep your animal and do nothing,

2. keep your dog and do something,

3. put your pet to sleep.

Most loving owners try to get by with choice number two. But to give yourself the best chance of saving your pet, it's imperative that you seek the assistance of a qualified *Pet Behavior Specialist* under such circumstances.

Accepting Final Responsibility

On rare occasions, even a *Pet Behavior Specialist* can't help you with your pet's problem. I introduced this situation in Chapter 13, *Other Dog Misbehaviors,* under the heading "Unchangeable Behaviors." If you'll remember, in the instances presented, most of these behaviors were actually normal canine conduct.

But there are two other types of unchangeable behavior that you need to be aware of: ingrained misbehaviors, which are virtually impossible to intercede; and abnormal behaviors, which result from imbalances inside a dog's brain. In either case, euthanization may be an alternative.

Here's Happy with one final example for you.

I'm never happy to discuss euthanasia. But I sure have seen some cases where it was necessary. One was Spence. He was a large Rottweiler. And basically he was a good egg. Almost all the time, in fact.

But every once in a great while, he picked on the wrong person. This person was very young. An infant, in fact. Not only did Spence draw blood, but the wounds often required stitches.

True, from Spence's point of view, his "fits" happened quite rarely...only once every seven months or so from the time the child was a year old.

But hey, we dogs know better than that! We can tell a defenseless baby, no matter what species it is. And our general rule of no-opposable-thumb is this: Paws off!

*Talk about scary! If anyone ever did something like that to one of **my** pups, I know how **I'd** react.*

Spence's humans did react, swiftly and surely. They recognized the threat to their child. And even though Spence showed no signs of aggression between attacks, they knew what they had to do.

The chances were that nothing would ever cure Spence. Paradoxically, this was due to the infrequency – and total unpredictability – of his attacks.

But euthanization was the only safe solution. Ultimately, it may even have saved their child's life. So today, they have a lot to be thankful for.

Taking your pet to a veterinarian to be euthanized can be an extremely difficult step to take. But, in the end, it's the most humane way for your pet.

Yes, there are always alternatives. Many people will try to give their problem pet to someone else. Others will take it to their local Humane Society. The ultimate fantasy for the problem dog owner is to find a farm for him; to put him out to pasture, so to speak.

But just **how** humane are these alternatives?

If your pet is getting old, and you do find a new home for her, it still doesn't cure her ailments. If your dog has behavioral problems, is it fair to foist these problems off on someone else? A change of scenery won't change the problem itself. In fact, it may even exacerbate the misbehavior.

Further, there is no way to know how a new owner will accept this behavior. Will your pet be abused in her new home? Will her new owner abandon her?

Even the fantasy of the kindly old farmer will probably fail you. There are fewer and fewer farms, these days. And less space to roam. Besides, any pet that has been a member of your household for several years would be totally bewildered in his new situation. He probably wouldn't adapt very well, and, ultimately, this too could contribute to his demise.

What it comes down to is this. The final responsibility of ownership is to see that your pet is lovingly taken care of at the end of his life.

Whether your dog is dying of old age, or he has major, incurable behavioral problems, you have to be strong enough to take him to a veterinarian and have him humanely put to sleep.

The Future Of Pet Ownership

So what does the future hold for you and your dog?

The rules and guidelines of ownership are constantly changing. This is because dogs themselves continue to evolve as they learn to make their home in the human household.

They adapt to their daily living environment. They adjust to the amount of space they're given. They change to meet the dangers of life in city, suburb, or rural area. They conform to the wishes of their individual owners.

Animal behavior changes due to the endless alteration of their environment.

How marked are these changes? One strange measure of this phenomenon is that today, on occasion, you'll see a female dog mark its territory! Their mannerism is more subtle – they don't hike their legs like the males do. But females aren't supposed to exhibit this behavior at all! They don't in the wild.

But dogs have been domesticated for a very long time now. Perhaps these females are *adapting* – acquiring the need to mark their own space – because of the decreasing size of their *adopted* world.

Yet owners can control just about any canine calling if they're willing to accept the responsibility. If not, we have to resign ourselves to the fact that we may be molding dogs with all kinds of behavioral problems, litter by litter.

People have brought dogs a long, long way from their lifestyle in the wild. Or is it the other way around?

But dogs still possess many of their primitive instincts, though many of them are obsolete. No longer must a dog protect, shelter or feed itself. No longer must they stalk prey, or mark and defend territory.

Today, humans do all this for them.

But these behaviors are **still integral** to the animal. They're part of what a dog is. If you remember only this, you'll have furthered your relationship with your dog.

If you understand that animals will be animals, and accept a great variety of behaviors on your dog's behalf as they are – as normal animal behaviors which cannot, and should not, be changed – you'll both be better off.

After all, a little animal was what you wanted when you brought that dog into your life!

Index To Tricks I Taught My Master

Dr. Robert M. Andrysco

Acknowledgements

ACKNOWLEDGEMENTS

Very special thanks to all of the pets and people that appear in this book. Yes, their names have been changed for purposes of privacy, but nothing will ever change the special relationships that we've developed with these many friends we've made over the years.

About the Artist - Dave Odell

Dave founded Odell Illustration in 1983. His specialty is creating humorous illustration for the advertising market. He and his family make their home in Columbus, Ohio, where they live in servitude to their Peke-a-poo "Cubbie."

ABOUT THE AUTHORS

Dr. Robert M. Andrysco is a graduate of Ashland University, with degrees in biology and chemistry. He has a Master's degree in Veterinary Physiology and Pharmacology from The Ohio State University. But it is his unique doctoral degree, also from Ohio State, that sets him apart. It combines veterinary medicine, animal behavior and human behavior. Widely known as a pioneer in the field of Pet Behavior Management, Dr. Andrysco has served much of the midwest. For five years he had his own TV show on NBC in Chicago, called "Talking Pets." He is the Pet Behavior Specialist for the Radio Systems Corporation, which is dedicated to improving relationships between pets and their owners.

Happy is a Beagle/German Short-Hair Pointer, Mixed Breed. Dr. Andrysco rescued him from the Capital Area Humane Society when he was just a pup. Although he doesn't have the bloodline, he does have the instincts. And what he lacks in formal education, he more than makes up for in street smarts. He's been Dr. Andrysco's partner since 1981. They've learned all of the tricks of the trade together.